Theory and Reality in Foreign Policy Making

Theory and Reality in Foreign Policy Making

Nigeria After the Second Republic

Ibrahim A. Gambari

HUMANITIES PRESS INTERNATIONAL, INC.
Atlantic Highlands, NJ

First published in 1989 by
Humanities Press International, Inc.,
Atlantic Highlands, NJ 07716

Library of Congress Cataloging-in-Publication Data

Gambari, I. A. (Ibrahim A.)
Theory and reality in foreign policy making : Nigeria after the Second Republic / by Ibrahim A. Gambari.
p. cm.
ISBN 0-391-03603-3
1. Nigeria—Foreign relations—1960– 2. Buhari, M. 3. Gambari, I. A. (Ibrahim A.) I. Title.
DT515.84.G36 1989
327.669—dc 19 88–15884
CIP

Printed in the United States of America

Dedicated
to
Fatimah, Mobolaji, and Olaitan
and to
General Buhari's famous proposition
that "this generation of Nigerians and indeed future generations have no other country than Nigeria. We shall remain here and salvage it together."

Contents

Preface

On a slightly drizzling Saturday, 14 September 1985, I put my books, papers, and other personal belongings inside a vehicle loaned by my former neighbor and then Chief of Naval Staff, Rear-Admiral Augustus Aikhomu. I was leaving the official residence in Lagos for my small personal house in Ilorin, Kwara state. My tenure of office as Minister of External Affairs of the Federal Republic of Nigeria had come to an end as it began—with a military coup d'état.

I had been appointed minister following the fourth successful coup in post-independent Nigeria, which overthrew the civilian regime under President Shehu Shagari on the eve of the New Year, 1984. And it was on 27 August 1985 that the news of another coup d'état came on the air at my home town, Ilorin, where we were celebrating the *Idel-Kabir* (Muslim New Year). In that change from one military administration to another, the Federal Executive Council (Cabinet) of which I was a member as Minister of External Affairs, was dissolved.

The coming into power of General Muhammadu Buhari in January 1984 was an important crossroad for Nigeria at home and abroad. Within that context, my personal journey as Foreign Minister was one of constant and intense movements, activities, and challenges. For instance, during the 19 months of my tenure of office, I met or interacted with the head of state (president) or foreign minister, or both, of the following countries: United States, Soviet Union, Peoples' Republic of China, Great Britain, France, Federal Republic of Germany, Saudi Arabia, India, Indonesia, Singapore, Australia, New Zealand, Cuba, and all the 50 members of the Organization of African Unity (OAU).

Also, during my time in office, we received in Lagos on official visits such distinguished world leaders as the Secretary General of the United Nations, Javier Peres de Cuellar, the former Saudi Arabian minister, Sheik Yamani, former President Nimeiry of Sudan, the late President Sekou Toure of Guinea, the Libyan number-two man to Col. Gaddafi, Major Abdulsalam Jalloud, as well as Col. Mengistu Haile Mariam, head of state of Ethiopia, President dos Santos of Angola, Captain Sankara of Burkina Faso (now deceased), President Diouf of Senegal, Lieutenant Rawlings of Ghana; President Dauda Jawara of Gambia, and presidents Eyadema and Kerekou of Togo and Benin. President Kountche of Niger Republic, the former President of Sierra Leone, Siaka Stevens (now deceased), and a vice-president of the Democratic Peoples' Republic of Korea, Pak Song Chol, also visited us.

Several foreign ministers also came to confer with us in Lagos, including Claude Cheysson of France, those of Zambia, Angola, Togo, and Benin, and Boutros Ghali, Minister of State for Foreign Affairs of Egypt.

In addition, Nigeria hosted crucial multilateral meetings, such as the Quadripartite summit involving the heads of state of Ghana, Togo, Benin, and Nigeria; the United Nations Special Committee Against Apartheid's International Conference on the Legal Status of Apartheid; and the International Military Monitoring Group involving Libya, France, and Nigeria, operating from Baguada (Kano) and aimed at implementing an agreement whereby Libya and France would withdraw their armed forces from Chad.

Of course, a foreign minister does not and cannot operate in a political vacuum. He has to relate to the economic, political, and institutional environment both inside and outside the government which he serves. Nonetheless he soon realizes that the primary focus of his support must be the confidence generated and sustained from the head of state and the highest levels of government. I was very fortunate that my activities and principles soon earned me the support and confidence of General Buhari and his number-two man, General Tunde Idiagbon. That high-level support enabled me to transcend or effectively manage the usual kind of opposition or subtle obstruction to be expected from some individuals within the ministry and inside the government as a whole.

Notwithstanding the personal dimension of this study, its main purpose is to reflect on the tension between theory and practice in Nigeria's foreign policy and the formulation and execution of foreign policy at a particularly difficult time for our country's domestic political and economic development. After about one-quarter of a century of independence, we may indeed have come to the end of the age of innocence in the management of our domestic and external affairs. Yet the current era is beset with serious internal and external economic difficulties at a time when the national question is far from being resolved. Worse still, the affairs of Nigeria are in the hands of a national elite that, for the most part, is neither truly national nor known for selfless service, patience, justice, and clearly defined common goals—the prerequisites of true liberation and sustained development for a Third World country.

Reflection on my tenure of office was encouraged by the fact that I was privileged to be the first Nigerian with relevant academic qualifications, training, and experience to be appointed Foreign Minister. And, as I said at a public lecture in China (full text in Appendix 3), a scholar in government at that level has a special responsibility to explain the policy-making process and relations with the bureaucracy, other power centers, and pressure groups in the formulation, articulation, and execution of the foreign policy in a developing country such as Nigeria. The special experience of the author, when applied to the analysis of the foreign policy issues discussed in subsequent chapters, will make this study particularly useful to students of public administration and foreign policy, as well as to professional diplomats and practitioners of public affairs.

Grateful mention must be made of the institutions and individuals without whose support and encouragement this would not have been possible. General Muhammadu Buhari and the Supreme Military Council gave me the opportunity to serve as our country's ninth Foreign Minister. It was, of course, during my tenure of office at the Ministry of External Affairs that I gained invaluable experience and collected the materials for this study. My gratitude goes to all the senior and junior officers in that ministry for their assistance to me, which made my work and this book possible. Ahmadu Bello University gave me a one-year sabbatical leave, which I spent at the School of Advanced International Studies, Johns Hopkins University, Washington, D.C., campus, where I completed this study.

My sincere thanks also go to President I.B. Babangida for his kindness and for raising no objections to this effort on my part to put on record the activities of the immediate predecessor regime in the foreign-policy area. Several colleagues and friends read all or part of the manuscript prior to publication and their comments and advice were of great help: Dr. Oga Ajene, Wilberforce Hinjari, and Umaru Birai, all of the Political Science Department, Ahmadu Bello University, and Ambassador I.C. Olisemeka, then Ambassador of Nigeria to the United States, Professor I. William Zartman, Dr. Gary Sick, Ms. Carolyn Benbow, Ambassador (Professor) S. Suleiman, Dr. O. Fasehun, S. Adekanye, General O. Obasanjo, and my wife, Fatimah, patiently read most of the chapters in draft form.

I am greatly indebted to Ms. Janet Craswell and Ms. Theresa Taylor Simmons of the School of Advanced International Studies, Johns Hopkins University, for typing several drafts of the manuscript.

Finally, for any errors of fact or interpretation, I am alone responsible.

Ibrahim A. Gambari,
Ahmadu Bello University,
Zaria

PART 1

Background to Policy

1

From Theory to Practice

As a student of international relations for over two decades, this author has been intrigued by the nature of power, in particular the interplay of domestic forces and the external environment which informs the foreign policy of a developing country. On the one hand, we have an international system which is hierarchical in its political and economic dimensions. The political domination of the international system by the two superpowers and their major military allies is clearly illustrated by the permanent seats which they occupy and the veto power they exercise at the United Nations Security Council. Concomitantly, great-power dominance of the international system is registered in the economic sphere by the post-World War II Bretton Woods arrangements. These arrangements are like a global stool with three legs—the International Monetary Fund, the World Bank, and the General Agreements on Trade and Tariffs (GATT)—upon which the Big Powers sit so comfortably and so conspicuously while Third World countries hang uncomfortably around its edges.

On the other hand, however, the forces of the status quo in the international system confront forces demanding change in the distribution of power and resources. This is the source of the dynamics of contemporary international politics, within which the relatively small or weak states are able to exercise considerable influence if not power. This influence is made possible by two major developments. First, the military and economic preponderance of the superpowers and their major allies does not automatically translate into preponderance of influence or wisdom:

> The mass armies and navies, the wielding of huge explosive might, most of the factors that once permitted only the big and powerful to be great are no longer directly related to political influence. On the contrary, essential international political resources today are such factors as astute, highly competent and highly sensitive and perceptive statesmanship; capabilities for world awareness both physical and intellectual . . . if it is true that mind rather than muscle is the key to contemporary

international political influence, then even very small states may have potential for greatness.[1]

Of course one must not push this view too far because there are serious limitations to the emergence of the countries of the Third World as centers of power at the international level. There is still some significant correlation between muscle and mind in the behavior and impact of states in the international system. Nonetheless, the potential exists for the exercise of significant power and influence by relatively small and weaker states through the manipulation of the system either to their advantage or to frustrate the realization of certain aims and goals of the great powers.[2] The roles of Cuba, North Vietnam, Singapore, Saudi Arabia, Algeria, and Tanzania are examples of this possibility—in varying degrees.

The second potential source for the exercise of power and influence by the relatively small states is the interdependence that exists in the international system. Certain problems have arisen that transcend exclusive national solutions, including population movements, developments in health and ecology, the arms race, and exploitation of the ocean bed and other physical resources. A global approach is needed to address problems that have assumed global dimensions. The corollary of globalization is the emergence of forms of interdependence between nations, communities, and groups.[3] The forms taken by this growing interdependence are not only economic, technological, and military, but also political, social, and cultural. It should be noted, however, that "interdependence exists side by side with imbalances, disparities and forms of tension, if not antagonism, which, from time to time become more acute between societies and internally."[4]

No country, big or small, poor or rich, can exist in isolation from the other states within the international system. Therefore, a systematic study of the forces at play in the international arena is necessary for the development of national policies toward other members of the global system. It is within this context of both interdependence and the potentialities for the exercise of power and influence by countries of the Third World that this book was written, to examine Nigeria's search for a coherent voice that is taken seriously abroad and projects interests clearly defined at home.

Nigeria has the human and physical resources necessary to manipulate the international system for its national interest in an interdependent world. By the end of the first decade and a half of the country's independence, Nigeria was showing clear signs of a growing political stability and wealth at home and influence abroad, at least in the West African sub-region and the African continent.[5] Two major elements of potential power have been responsible for this: population and oil resources. With the end of the country's Civil War and a successful policy of national reconciliation, Nigeria as one people of over 80 million constitutes the largest concentration of

African population in one country. Probably one out of every five Africans is a Nigerian, and the next most populous state in the continent, Egypt, has less than half as many inhabitants as Nigeria. Secondly, as a member of the Organization of Petroleum Exporting Countries (OPEC), Nigeria through its oil production quotas has earned unparalleled wealth, especially in much valued foreign exchange.

These major strengths have also served as sources of weakness. The national unity question has eluded resolution, largely because of the intense competition for a share of the growing wealth among the segments of the national elite. To paraphrase a leading Nigerian author, it is often easy for things to fall apart since the center often cannot hold. The management of the petroleum resources has been so inept and often corrupt that the country's oil "boom" has almost become its economic and social "doom." All along, Nigeria's vast human and physical resources have very rarely been matched with the entrepreneurship, unity, integrity, and vision on the part of the country's highest political leadership. We shall return to this point several times again.

Suffice it to say now that in Nigeria there is a direct link between domestic politics and the making of foreign policy.[6] The domestic political arrangement and the manner of conducting political business invariably affect the conduct of external relations. The question must be asked: Whose foreign policy are we talking about anyway? Nigeria's foreign policy has never been directly related to the needs of the masses of the people; rather it is formulated, articulated, and implemented in highly elitist circles. Hence, the country's foreign relations have reflected the needs and aspirations of a national super elite of business, bureaucratic, military, and traditional ruling groups (not necessarily in that order). Never very cohesive, this national elite is deeply divided along ethnic, regional, religious, and ideological lines. Hence, the history of Nigerian foreign policy has been to some extent related to a search for national consensus behind the major outlines of the country's externally projectable goals and objectives.[7]

The absence of a sustained unity of purpose abroad has resulted in the conflict between those who represent what one may call the radical impulse on the one hand and those who reflect a conservative weight on the other. From this enduring conflict comes foreign policy positions which are often tentative and uneasy compromises. Alternatively, successive post-independence governments have often adopted the loud rhetoric of the radical elements in the country, while quietly pursuing essentially conservative policies abroad.

The logic of this asymmetry between radical rhetoric and essentially conservative external policies can be found in Nigeria's economic structure and external economic relations. Other than the energies and resources put into building a wider sub-regional market for future manufactures, which culminated in the establishment of the Economic Community of West African States (ECOWAS), no serious efforts have been made to change the direction and pattern of Nigeria's external trade. The national elite has not been known to accept the high level of sacrifice that accompanies a real change toward a self-reliant economy. On the contrary, their penchant for the conspicuous consumption of goods imported mostly from Western countries is well documented. The pattern of production, consumption, and export ties the country's economy ever closer to the West. Moreover, as the economic situation deteriorates, attempts to find solutions are anchored in the expectations of Western aid, investment, or the prescriptions of the international financial institutions dominated by the West. The net result is what Douglas Anglin correctly identifies as the policy of political nonalignment and economic alignment.[8] This is, of course, a contradiction in terms but it is a contradiction which almost all Nigerian post-independence governments have felt they must live with. And this is really why there has been far more continuity than change in Nigeria's foreign policy since independence.

Nonetheless, the history of Nigerian foreign policy is not simply an activity whereby, as the French would put it, *plus ça change, plus c'est la même chose*. There have been important shifts of emphasis and use, by the leadership, of the room that a state with a dependent economy has to manoeuver in the external realm. Nigeria's foreign policy had moved through a number of major phases since independence before the administration of General Muhammadu Buhari, whose foreign policy is the main subject of this book.

The first phase, one of uncertainty and timidity, coincided with the period of the First Republic (1960–65). The major issues were the Official Foreign Policy Declaration itself: the Anglo-Nigerian Defence Pact; the Congo crisis and African unity; negotiations for associate status with the European Economic Community (EEC); the Rhodesian crisis and Commonwealth relations; and the Arab-Israeli antagonism and the search for a cohesive policy toward the Middle East. On all these issues, Nigeria did not speak with one voice, and when she spoke she leaned toward the West.[9] The reasons for the uncertainties of Nigeria's foreign policy, which reflected the defective nature of the process and substance of the country's domestic politics from independence to the Civil War, are well known and require only a brief review.

Foreign policy was made and conducted by a government which reflected the country's disunity in that it was a weak coalition of regional and ethnic-based political parties. Faced with powerful regions and religious and ideological groups, Prime Minister Sir Abubakar Tafawa Balewa had a constitutional authority which was not always matched by the political power needed to override these divergent groups' encroachments upon Nigeria's foreign policy. Western countries were deliberately courted in the economic sphere, whereas the Soviet Union and other socialist countries were repelled and mistrusted.[10] There was no national ideology or even nationwide political consciousness to aid the formulation of foreign policy. The Prime Minister was himself not averse to the pragmatic, nonideological, and compromise approach to policy-making at home and abroad.

Largely as a result of these disabilities in policy-making, Nigeria opted for a nonaligned policy that was in reality pro-West; ratified then abrogated but later retained the basic elements of a defense pact with Britain; sent troops to the Congo under the United Nations umbrella without fully supporting Patrice Lumumba, who requested the troops; opted for a weak Organization of African Unity; negotiated and signed but did not ratify an agreement with the European Economic Community, and professed a "neutral" federal policy toward the Arabs and Israelis in the Middle East that was actually inoperative in northern Nigeria.

A number of factors caused Nigeria's movement away from the "moderate" and timid foreign policy approach and orientation to a relatively more activist, positive, and influential role during the 1970s. First, the military government succeeded in dramatically and effectively redressing the balance of power in favor of the central government in relation to the regions and states. The centralized and hierarchical nature of military command structure and the military government's decision to divide Nigeria into twelve, and later nineteen, states and the swelling of the federal financial purse helped to end regional challenges to a federally controlled foreign policy. Second, the Civil War was fought and won by the federal authorities, but the bitter taste left in the government's mouth by the recognition of secessionist "Biafra" by some African states required a post-Civil War reassessment of Nigeria's African policy. The previous low-keyed, hesitant, and often apologetic approach to African affairs had to be changed. Third, and perhaps most prominent, was the increasing wealth from oil revenues and OPEC membership, which strengthened Nigeria's capability to pursue a new, active, and effective policy toward Africa and the world in the 1970s.

The next identifiable phase of Nigerian foreign policy followed the end of the Civil War and several initiatives abroad made by General Gowon. He took tentative but positive steps of reconciliation with those African states that recognized "Biafra." His government recognized the People's Republic of China and showed a warmer attitude toward the Soviet Union. Nigeria also stepped up its condemnation of the policies and activities of Western powers toward Southern Africa, while increasing financial and other contributions to the liberation movements there. General Gowon was made chairman of the OAU in recognition of his role in African affairs. He made several friendly visits to neighboring and other African states. On the Middle East, Nigeria moved sharply against Israel and broke diplomatic relations with her, although Nigeria once joined a group of OAU leaders in the futile search for a peace formula in the Middle Eastern conflict.

Nigeria also helped lead the collective African approach to negotiations with the EEC. The African states were joined by Caribbean and Pacific countries in the negotiations which led to the signing of the Lome Convention, trading Pan-African membership for an abandonment of association and reverse preferences. Along with Togo, Nigeria provided the diplomatic impetus and financial backing which made possible the creation of the regionwide Economic Community of West African States (ECOWAS).

As the domestic political situation deteriorated by 1974–75, however, General Gowon's foreign policy suffered a corresponding loss of momentum. Indeed, the highly publicized state visit to Britain by Gowon in July 1973 created a suspicion in Nigeria that, once more, Nigeria was being lured back to the pro-West fold. General Gowon was overthrown in a bloodless coup in July 1975.

The third phase of Nigeria's foreign policy came under the brief but exciting administration of General Murtala Mohammed. He strove to move the country's foreign policy to a more truly nonaligned position. The most significant act of his government in external policy was to recognize the MPLA as the sole legitimate representative of the people and government of Angola, a decision that split the OAU but later gained majority support in the organization. Nigeria's diplomatic, financial, and material support to the liberation movements in Southern Africa also increased significantly.

General Mohammed was not afraid to confront the Western powers when necessary. In a memorable speech to the OAU extraordinary summit conference at Addis Ababa in January 1976, he boldly stated that Africa had "come of age" and did not need foreign counsellors to warn Africans against Communism and the alleged Soviet-Cuban threat.[11] The continent, he said, would henceforth choose its friends and foes in an independent manner. A private letter from U.S. President Gerald Ford to all African leaders, warning them against the Soviet-Cuban role in Angola and calling for support of the U.S. position in Southern Africa, and the Nigerian government's rejection of this request, were published to the loud applause of informed Nigerian opinion.

There was an apparent soft-pedalling in the pursuit of an activist foreign policy in the next phase (1977–78), when General Obasanjo assumed power, after General Mohammed was assassinated in an unsuccessful coup. In February 1978, there was an exchange of state visits between General Obasanjo and U.S. President Jimmy Carter. Nigeria also showed initial support for the Anglo-American peace proposals for Zimbabwe. The country's decision to establish diplomatic relations with Iran under Shah Mohammed Reza Pahlevi and the government's decision again to resort to heavy borrowing from the Western money market came under sharp public criticism and put the government on the defensive. Moreover, ECOWAS—the showpiece of Nigeria's diplomatic and financial endeavor—could have received greater attention from the Obasanjo regime. It should be noted that these acts of apparent soft-pedalling from the activism of Murtala Mohammed coincided with the beginning of an economy increasingly dependent on oil revenues, which were fluctuating, generally downward.

It is to the credit of General Obasanjo and owing to a temporary increase in oil revenues that in the last years of his administration he returned to the activism of his predecessor. He terminated Nigeria's support for the Anglo-American peace proposals for Zimbabwe and he increased diplomatic, financial, and other support for the Patriotic Front. Nigeria rejected the results of the elections in Zimbabwe which produced Bishop Muzorewa as the first black Prime Minister of that country. British Petroleum's assets in Nigeria were nationalized and a 10 percent cut in oil supply to that company was ordered by the Nigerian authorities.[12] These actions doubtless helped convince British Prime Minister Margaret Thatcher to suspend her earlier intention to recognize Muzorewa's regime and lift economic sanctions. Nigeria carried the Commonwealth leaders with her on this matter, much to the satisfaction of the Patriotic Front, but to the chagrin of Britain.

On the wider front, the OAU commended Nigeria's attempt to reconcile the warring factions in Chad—a costly and frustrating involvement. Nigeria also stepped up her mediation efforts in the Tanzania-Uganda schism (which later developed into open warfare), the Western Saharan conflict, and the Ethiopia-Somalia dispute.

However grudging, some recognition of Nigeria's growing diplomatic, economic, and political status in Africa and perhaps the world was being given by the West. For example, Nigeria's veiled threat to reduce its oil supply to the United States, if that country lifted economic sanctions against Muzorewa's Zimbabwe-Rhodesia, led an American official to declare that it was "incredible that a superpower should feel these foreign policy constraints from Nigeria."[13] The *Economist* of London admitted that "a world outside the old Euro-American heartland has developed its own centres of power: its Arabias, Brazils, and Nigerias."[14] These illustrate how astute statesmanship in developing countries could exercise leverage made possible by the possession of a desired export commodity whose price can be defended by a non-Western organization. The West has understood this point more than the Third World countries that can exercise such power and influence; hence it has moved to tilt the international economic and financial scales against them.

The next phase in the development of Nigerian foreign policy came with the return to civilian rule (1979–83). The civilian administration under First Executive President Alhaji Shehu Shagari came into power in a system of government closely patterned after that of the United States, in an election that involved no significant debate on foreign-policy issues. The presidential candidates were well aware that the overwhelming majority of supporters and the electorate as a whole had little interest in foreign policy—except in a few cases of external crises. Therefore, it was through the actions or inactions of the government of the Second Republic that the pattern of foreign policy must be discerned. Two points were already becoming clear. First, Nigeria was operating a presidential system with a parliamentary-system mentality. The President and his government appeared to be comfortable with "coalition politics"—reminiscent of the First Republic—with the attendant compromises, however unsatisfactory they might be to the parties involved and to coherent national policies.

Second, the new decade of the 1980s was going to be more complex for Nigeria, which faced difficult choices, especially in foreign policy, as the country adjusted to the rapidly changing internal and international environments. In a real sense, the 1970s were a decade of transition. Nigeria had moved from the first decade of independence, characterized by political and ideological naivete and the teething problems of a newly attained sovereignty. The next decade witnessed relative political stability following the end of the Civil War, a higher rate of growth, and increased governmental spending made possible by the billions of *naira* accruing annually to the national treasury from oil exports. The second decade closed with a return to civilian rule.

Several challenges faced the new regime as it ushered in the decade of the 1980s. Internally, it had to keep its electoral promises to revolutionize agriculture, improve and expand social services, provide employment to the rapidly growing population especially in the urban areas, and maintain political stability. All these were in the face of sharply declining prices for oil, the mainstay of the economy. On the foreign policy front, the main challenge was to maintain the momentum of those activist or progressive actions taken since Murtala Mohammed came to power that continued to enjoy the support of the informed elite. There was an even more problematic question. In view of the fact that the source of Nigeria's oil-based national wealth is the West, her national power is anchored in Africa, yet the greatest threat to the country's African policies, particularly regarding ECOWAS and the liberation of Southern Africa, emanates from the West. How then does the civilian regime, or indeed any regime in Nigeria, interact economically with the West in a dependent manner, while looking vaguely and without deep conviction or sustained effort to the Eastern bloc for models of social justice and national liberation, yet walk in the ideological "nonalignment" middle?

In the end, after three years, the leaders of the Second Republic generally failed to meet the challenges they faced. The economy deteriorated, weighed down with huge internal and external debts accumulated amidst charges of mismanagement and large-scale fraud. The nation's social services were in a shambles. There were serious threats to domestic peace and stability, especially after the 1983 elections which were accompanied by much dispute and widespread violence. Nigeria's leadership in African affairs eroded seriously as the country vacillated on issues such as Western Sahara and Namibia. The government's intervention in the Chad conflict and participation in the ill-fated OAU peace-keeping force led to the probably unintended and possibly disgraceful consequence of installing in power a regime in Ndjamena opposed to Waddeye, the Chadian leader who had invited the force in the first place. Nigeria's neighbors had scant respect for the country, and some of them even crossed into its territory and attacked and killed civilians and soldiers with impunity. ECOWAS was in a state of disrepair. In general, it was as if Nigeria had rapidly slipped back into the policies of subservience to the West and hesitancy in African affairs, closer to the situation in the 1960s.

The perceived failure of the Second Republic to deal with the nation's domestic problems and external relations was used to justify the second coming of the soldiers. The military coup which overthrew President Shehu Shagari and installed General Muhammadu Buhari enjoyed widespread popular support as the new year of 1984 began.

Before the coup of January 1984, I had served briefly as the Chief Executive and Chief Research Officer of the Nigerian Institute of International Affairs in Lagos—the leading think tank in foreign affairs—modelled after Chattam House of the Royal Institute of International Affairs in London. This was a useful though short-lived halfway house in my personal transition from theoretical preoccupations in the academic world to full immersion in the practical world of diplomacy as Foreign Minister.

The Nigerian Institute of International Affairs has no formalized way of making direct contributions to foreign-policy formulation and its implementation by the administration. However influential the views expressed within its walls, the institute does not have foreign-policy positions. It simply conducts research on foreign-policy issues, provides the forum for the articulation of various views on foreign policy, and through the publications that come out of these intellectual and research activities the government is made aware of various options available to it. Sometimes the government would directly commission the institute to undertake special studies on foreign policy and national security issues.

Nonetheless, over the years, the director-general of the Institute has acquired stature in the internal debate on important foreign-policy issues, and his views are often taken seriously by the general public, among the diplomatic community, and in government circles. He also has to walk a tightrope between the independent status of the institute and the government's attempts and sometime success in making it part of the executive office of the head of government.

In view of the short time spent at the institute as its director-general, I was able to achieve only two main objectives. First, a document titled "The Mission of the Nigerian Institute of International Affairs"[15] was prepared that established three priority areas of research. One was to focus the attention of the institute on a closer study of domestic politics and the making of foreign policy in Nigeria: What country are we really and what and whose concerns are we talking about when we attempt to define the "national interest"? Another area of priority was the economy, especially the interplay of internal economic power centers, governmental economic policies, and the international economic system. How feasible was the demand by the countries of the southern hemisphere for a New International Economic Order and how could it be achieved under the so-called North-South dialogue? Finally, the document attempted to establish as a new area of priority the role of science and technology in foreign policy and international affairs in general.

Several developments in science and technology are rapidly affecting the concept of national security and the nature of diplomacy and international relations. While the debate on the nuclear arms race continues, we seem to be mere onlookers, yet, should a nuclear war ever be fought, Nigeria along with other countries would not escape from the holocaust. We may not be able to affect the strategic balance of forces, but we ought to understand it. With South Africa having acquired the capability to produce nuclear bombs, the issue is coming closer to home in a real way.

On a more positive side of the issue, how do we harness the forces of science and technology to develop the ocean bed beyond our continental shelf? How do we use the multinational corporations to harness science and technology to exploit, yet still control, our natural and mineral resources?

The second major activity as the institute's director-general was my personal engagement in public debate on the general orientation of the country's foreign policy at the onset of the second term of President Shagari's administration. While expressing some sympathy with the administration's difficulties in reconciling declining national income from oil exports and competing domestic and foreign policy demands, I pointed out that the government could have better implemented its African policies. On Southern Africa, for example, the administration's support for the liberation movements and the pursuit of Namibian independence were relatively lukewarm. A hesitant and timid official policy toward Chad, Cameroon, and almost all of Nigeria's neighbors inspired little or no respect for the country. The administration's commitment to the Organization of African Unity did not appear particularly strong, and President Shagari's failure to attend the organization's summit, scheduled to take place in Tripoli, was clearly a minus, as was vacillation over the Western Saharan issue.

Under the Shagari administration, Nigeria appeared to be a demographic and economic giant on the continent, but a political and diplomatic dwarf in African affairs. This was sadly reminiscent of the early 1960s, when Ghana contemptuously referred to Nigeria as "big for nothing" (i.e. failing to use economic strength for bold action) when African issues were concerned. Of course, a country may have relatively huge resources without playing a role commensurate with its status or potential. The example of the United States between the two world wars is a clear illustration of such an undesirable possibility. The challenge for Nigeria's diplomacy was, in my view, how to translate the country's real and potential resources and its power position in Africa into reality by bringing our weight to bear creatively and constructively in solving African problems.

On the whole, I felt that Nigeria's foreign policy under President Shagari was bureaucratic, vague, and possibly out of tune with the aspirations for our country held by the informed public.[16] The concept of Africa as a centerpiece of Nigeria's foreign policy coined earlier in the Adedeji Report on Foreign Policy was imprecise and weak in its implementation. Several questions were raised which were not adequately addressed, let alone resolved by the administration. Should we, for example, be a fire-fighting brigade, available at any time and place on the continent, to put out conflagrations? Alternatively, should we respond selectively to crisis areas on the continent that are closer to home or closer to our fundamental security and national interests and objectives? Or should we do both? These issues were raised publicly, and represented the author's subtle criticisms of the foreign-policy orientation of Shagari's administration.[17]

From having operated as an outside critic, this author assumed a position of relative strength by using the institutional platform to become a critic from inside. Of course, this newly acquired influence had its cost, and that was the modification of theoretical and critical approaches as a result of closer proximity to the realities and constraints of government. My personal progression from theory to practice was made complete with the appointment as Foreign Minister.

NOTES

1. Donald Puchala, *International Politics Today* (New York: Dodd, Mead & Co., 1971), p. 196.
2. See expositions of this idea in Ibrahim A. Gambari, "The Third World as a Centre of Influence or Power," in *Ibadan Journal of Humanistic Studies* 2 (1981), pp. 60–72, and "Power in the Third World," *Journal of International Affairs* 29, no. 2 (1975), pp. 155–169.
3. Ahmadou Muhtar M'Bow, Director-General of UNESCO, "UNESCO and the Major Problems of Today's World" (Cannes, UNESCO, 11 March 1983—DG/83/6), p. 1.
4. Ibid.
5. See I.A. Gambari, "Nigeria and the World: A Growing Internal Stability, Wealth and External Influence," in *Journal of International Affairs* 29, no. 2 (1975), pp. 155–169.
6. See I.A. Gambari, *Party Politics and Foreign Policy: Nigeria under the First Republic* (Zaria, Nigeria: Ahmadu Bello University Press, 1981).
7. I.A. Gambari, "Nigeria's Foreign Policy: the Search for Consensus on Major Issues," paper presented at the "National Conference on Nigerian History since Independence" (Ahmadu Bello University, Zaria, 31 March 1983).
8. Douglas Anglin, "Nigeria: Political Non-Alignment and Economic Alignment," *Journal of Modern African Studies* 2, no. 2 (1964), p. 26.
9. For details, see Gambari, *Party Politics*.
10. See Anglin, "Nigeria."
11. Speech by General Murtala Mohammed at extraordinary summit conference of the OAU (Addis Ababa, 11 January 1976).
12. See "Nigeria Flexes Her Muscles," *West Africa*, 6 August 1979, p. 1399.
13. *Newsweek*, 25 June 1979, p. 37.
14. *The Economist*, 4 August 1979, p. 11.
15. See "The Mission of the Nigerian Institute of International Affairs: Research Dimension" (Lagos: NIIA, January 1984).
16. Statements by I.A. Gambari in *New Nigerian*, 31 October 1983, p. 1.
17. Ibid.

2

Ministry of External Affairs as Primary Foreign-Policy Instrument

An analysis of the organizational structure and the senior personnel of the Ministry of External Affairs that I inherited in January 1984 will provide a useful background to the changes made later. My objective while in office was to enhance the capability of the ministry to become the primary instrument of the country's foreign policy under the new military administration. This ministry differed from the home ministries in at least four ways.

First, it had no Permanent Secretary (the nomenclature for the civil-service head). Under the organizational chart available at that time, there was a Coordinating Director-General with responsibilities for Special Missions, Lateral Liaison Outside the Ministry, Policy Planning, Internal Audit, Inspectorate, and Protocol, as well as the Public Relations and Cultural Department.

Second, there were, in addition to the Coordinating Director-General, five other directors-general in charge of directorates dealing with substantive matters. One directorate dealt with service matters—i.e. Administration and Management, Staff and Establishment, Finance and Budget, and the Foreign Service Academy, including the training of other Foreign Service officers and responsibility for overseas communications. In view of the centrality of African affairs in foreign policy, there was a Directorate of African Affairs separate from the directorate that dealt with all other geographic regions of the world. Other directorates were International Organisation; International Economic Cooperation, and Consular Affairs.

Third, the ministry had 14 top management officers on Grade Level 17 (salary grade level equivalent to the rank of Federal Permanent Secretary) and below them there were about 60 Grade Level 16 officers, which adds up to more than all the officers in the home ministries in Lagos on that grade put together. Fourth, only the Ministry of External Affairs had overseas missions, the number of which grew from 11 at the time of independence in 1960 to about 92 in 1981 and, after some reduction, to 86 by the middle of 1984. The total staff strength also grew from about 20 indigenous employees in 1957 to about 4,500 in the early 1980s (this figure included staff locally recruited to serve in the ministry's overseas missions).

The organizational structure of the directors-general and their directorates was relatively new. It was designed to give more effective management to the large number of departments within the ministry. There was also the need to give leadership positions and enhanced status to very senior ambassadors who, following their recall home, had to serve at headquarters. The arrangement had much to commend it but there were also several operational problems.

On the one hand, the directorates helped to reduce the work load of the professional head of the ministry and hence the bottleneck there. On the other hand, the directors-general saw the Permanent Secretary as little more than the *primus inter pares*, since they too were appointed and sworn in by the head of state in the same way as the Permanent Secretary was. The coordinating lines through the Permanent Secretary to the minister were often deliberately ignored. On his part, the Permanent Secretary often excluded his senior colleagues in the ministry from important administrative, financial, and budgetary matters. Worst of all, the directors-general and the Permanent Secretary spent much time and energy subverting one another and, on occasions when they agreed, subverting their minister as well.

There was much debate within the government in early 1984 as to whether or not to retain the directorates-general. I favored retention of the organizational arrangement for a number of reasons. The innovation was indeed sound management theory, since the ministry was really too big to be effectively administered otherwise. Also, there was an unfortunate national tendency to scrap innovations even before they had been given adequate chance to prove their worth, and a start had to be made somewhere to try to change this. Moreover, it was observed that the major obstacle to the smooth operation of the directorate system came largely from personality conflicts rather than the organizational structure itself. Hence the appointment of new directors-general and a new Permanent Secretary could improve the operations of the system. As things turned out, however, the new directors-general appointed by me after consultations with the head of state did not behave much differently than their predecessors, largely because their perceptions and personal interests did not really change.

Two major personnel changes also occurred, one of which created a state of flux and a sense of job insecurity in the ministry. First was the rather extensive retirement exercise involving all cadres of the service. In that exercise, the ministry compulsorily retired officers who had disciplinary actions pending against them, unproductive staff, or those whose continued stay in the ministry was not considered to be in the best interest of the organization. Unfortunately, some very good officers were also forced to leave for reasons that were not publicly disclosed, and this damaged morale in the service. It was also alleged that, in some of these cases, malice and prejudice were involved. Actually, I was only a few weeks in office when the exercise took place. On a more pleasant note, however, several new heads of missions were appointed and the balance of representation was deliberately tilted in favor of career officers. Several important missions, such as those to the U.S., France, Spain, U.S.S.R., China, Australia, Egypt, Angola, and Kenya were headed by career ambassadors.

The key personnel decisions in which I had a relatively free hand were in the recommendations to the head of state that led to the appointment of the Permanent Secretary, Ambassador George Dove-Edwin, and the new directors-general. The Permanent Secretary was later asked by me to take over the duties previously performed by the Directorate of Service Matters. The new men at the ministry's senior level of directors-general were Ambassador Hamzat Ahmadu (African Affairs), Ambassador B.T. Balewa (Regions), and Ambassador Peter Afolabi (International Economic Cooperation). The substantive area of international economic cooperation was elevated to a separate directorate in line with the new administration's priority. Ambassador Nuhu Mohammed took charge of the Consular Affairs Directorate, while Ambassador Olu Adeniji became Director-General of International Organisations.

What were these senior men like and how did they relate to me while in office? First, Ambassador George Dove-Edwin. I recommended him for the post of Permanent Secretary largely because he was the most senior of his Grade Level 17 colleagues. He joined the foreign service even before there was a Ministry of Foreign Affairs. He was part of the small office of the Prime Minister established in 1957 as the nucleus of a future Foreign Office after independence. Ambassador Dove-Edwin had a long civil service career but did not attain the pinnacle of that career until he was appointed Permanent Secretary in 1984, only a few years from retirement age.

His father was a Sierra Leonean citizen until his death, although he had served as a respected High Court judge in Calabar (Cross River state of Nigeria) and married a Calabar woman (Ambassador (George's mother). Ambassador Dove-Edwin married a Canadian woman of West-Indian origin. This personal background may be responsible for Ambassador Dove-Edwin's sensitivity about his lack of full Nigerian nationality. He may also have been sensitive about his rather limited academic training, since, prior to joining the foreign service in 1957, the highest academic qualifications which he had earned was a Diploma in Social Welfare.

However, he was good at details and bureaucratic arrangements and his command of the English language was excellent both in oral and, especially, written forms. Relations between the Permanent Secretary and me soon soured, as I discovered that he lacked the capacity or willingness to give imaginative leadership to the ministry. Indeed, under his administration, favoritism and double standards ran rampant. It was unfortunate that as minister I was served by a Permanent Secretary who turned out to be less than committed to the ministry.

Next in order of seniority at headquarters was Ambassador Ahmadu. He served for many years at Dodan Barracks (seat of military administration) and for about ten years as principal private secretary to two heads of state (generals Ironsi and Gowon). He also served in sensitive overseas missions such as the Soviet Union, the Netherlands, and Cameroon. Ambassador Ahmadu attained the rank of Special Grade Ambassador (Grade level 17) on 1 September 1977. Liked by his colleagues and in official and unofficial circles, he had excellent public relations. Although a traditional titleholder in Sokoto, he devoted considerable time and energy in cultivating and maintaining valuable social and political contacts at state and national levels.

Ambassador Ahmadu had a tremendous capacity to recall historical events and the particular roles of actors in major national decisions which took place around him several years before. In general, he cooperated well with me and made effective use of some outstanding officers in his directorate to produce positive policy recommendations and outcomes.

They sometimes called Ambassador Nuhu Mohammed the "Ayatollah" within the ministry and behind his back. It was a title which was neither greatly inaccurate nor one which he would have found particularly objectionable. His deep religious convictions tended to color his views on the Middle East and policy matters affecting Muslims and Christians. He was a fearless person and his opinions about individuals in the ministry and on policy matters could be too blunt. One gained the impression that colleagues who may have had something to hide tended to be genuinely afraid of him. One always knew where Ambassador Mohammed stood. He was also a hard worker and, if encouraged, would serve with honesty and dedication.

Ambassador Peter Afolabi demonstrated considerable intelligence. He was capable of producing work and ideas of high quality at short notice if he put his mind to it. He was an officer well known to me years before holding office in the ministry, and I had much regard for him. Nonetheless, he often believed he must get whatever he wanted and therefore would go to great, but not always dignifying, lengths in obtaining it. A man of considerable experience and versatile talent with a background as varied as colonial administrative service, law and, to an extent, economics, Ambassador Afolabi could also be a formidable personal and policy ally if one succeeded in enlisting him. I found him to be quite good in his work and generally supportive.

A clever, rather quiet, and somewhat aristocratic officer, Ambassador Balewa was capable of producing superior work if he applied himself. Unfortunately, some people inside and outside the ministry thought of him as a man with extensive business interests capable of adversely affecting the devotion of full attention to official duties. As an individual, he was very pleasant and possessed demonstrable organizational and administrative abilities. Ambassador Balewa worked well with me as minister and I saw him as a shrewd and intelligent man with considerable talents which could be an asset to any organization.

Last, but far from least, was Ambassador Olu Adeniji. Intellectually he was, along with Ambassador I.C. Olisemeka (who also served briefly under me as a director-general before going to Washington), among the brightest if not the best within his grade in the ministry. An officer whose humility concealed a sharp intellect, Ambassador Adeniji was a pleasure to work with on policy matters. His grasp of complex issues (for example disarmament, arms control, and security issues, of which he is a respected expert in international circles) and analyses of international political situations were clearly superior. He articulated and wrote superbly and with much substance. However, Ambassador's Adeniji's critics said that although sound in political subjects, he was weak in administrative matters. My own assessment was that he was a superb foreign service officer of limitless potential.

These senior people were all highly experienced men who were also for the most part nearing retirement age. The challenge was how to establish and sustain their respect for the political leadership of the ministry by a much younger man whose major strength was his academic background. What major instruments were used to motivate the professional leadership of this huge ministry to accept changes and initiatives which had major administrative and policy consequences?

First, there was the exploitation of one's newness in office. During the early period in office, change is often expected and that is the time to manipulate the fleeting disposition to change by the bureaucratic leaders. Using persuasion and occasional cajoling, the Permanent Secretary and the directors-general were encouraged to accept and support administrative and policy changes.

Secondly, I made a deliberate effort to identify with the "Young Turks" in the ministry by seeking them out and encouraging them to present their ideas directly to me while recruiting them to assist in collating and analyzing important materials. They also drafted some important documents which were later presented to the head of state and the Federal Cabinet. There was a fairly wide pool of highly talented and sometimes highly experienced External Affairs officers immediately below the level of directors-general. These relatively young and energetic officers were generally eager to make policy inputs and demonstrate their capabilities.

Finally, there was the crucial need to consolidate and lean heavily upon support from the top leadership of the government. Once the professional diplomats realized that their minister enjoyed solid support and confidence from his political bosses, they would generally fall in line with proposed changes in the ministry. The converse would also have been true, of course.

The first major organizational change, other than insisting upon and getting a Permanent Secretary appointed for the ministry, was the creation of the Office of Minister. Prior to this initiative, the minister was served by only one special assistant and one personal assistant. Such an arrangement was clearly inadequate for a minister who wanted to exercise greater supervision of the bureaucracy, get on top of the paperwork, and undertake creative projects and important initiatives in foreign policy. The new Office of Minister was created, headed by a director (Grade Level 16) with two special assistants in middle level grades and three personal assistants drawn from the junior ranks of External Affairs officer grade. The office soon developed a soul and mind of its own, which any subsequent minister would find useful.

Fortunately, this new office had as the very first director Remi Esan, who was brought back from Nigeria's Permanent Mission to the United Nations in New York where he handled economic matters. He worked extremely hard and provided loyal and dedicated service to me. It came as no surprise that my successor retained him as director of the minister's office. He was subsequently appointed as ambassador to Togo. Ably assisting the director were two fine officers, Kehinde Olisemeka and Abdul Rasaq Yunusa. The personal assistants were bright young men who served with great enthusiasm and worked for long hours on the official and personal needs of the minister without any complaint: Abdullahi Omaki, Sani Bako, and Shola Adeeyo.

On substantive policy matters, I appointed several special task forces to examine, review, and make recommendations on almost all aspects of Nigeria's external relations. These task forces were invariably headed by or strongly represented the input of, the Young Turks.[1] Their reports were extremely useful in the urgent task of producing a comprehensive policy paper for the Federal Executive Council which presented the conceptual framework to guide the new administration's foreign policy.

The paper was considered by the Federal Executive Council in June 1984.

It was then decided that in view of its importance, the paper incorporating the views expressed in the council should be referred to the highest ruling body, the Supreme Military Council, for consideration and approval. The highlight of the conceptual framework for the country's foreign policy, as approved by the Supreme Military Council, was the "concentric circles" principle which was to guide Nigeria's behavior on the African and world scene. Although Africa was to remain the primary focus of foreign policy endeavors, we were going to operate, henceforth, within a series of concentric circles—i.e., priorities within the broad priority.[2]

The innermost of these "circles of national interests" involved Nigeria's own security, independence, and prosperity, which are inextricably tied to those of our immediate neighbors. The second circle involved our relations with the ECOWAS sub-region. The third circle related to general African continental issues (African unity and cooperation, peaceful settlement of disputes, and development). The fourth circle concerned Nigeria's relations with organizations, institutions, and states outside the African continent. Nigeria did not consider this circle as unimportant, but not being a global power and constrained by limited and declining resources, she could nonetheless achieve much in this area by collaborating more actively with others in the Non-Aligned Movement, in the Group of 77, in the Commonwealth, and in the United Nations.

An issue which did not fit into these geographic and substantive circles of interests related to support for self-determination and opposition to apartheid. To the administration, self-determination was indivisible and we had to support the independence of Namibia under the leadership of SWAPO (South West Africa People's Organization), just as we supported Polisario in Western Sahara and the PLO (Palestine Liberation Organization) in the Middle East. These concerns related to our own definition of "self" in terms of inalienable rights to freedom, human dignity, national security, and world peace.

Another major intellectual effort, involving at first the input of the able and younger External Affairs officers and later the directors-general and the Permanent Secretary, was the preparation of an annual foreign policy agenda for the head of state's consideration and approval.[3] This had never been done before, yet we considered it necessary to set out the major issues of concern, rationalize Nigeria's exertions in the external realm, and identify priorities and options before the head of state and government on an annual basis and in advance of the year of operation. Ambassadors Z.M. Kazaure, A.D. Blankson, and 'Deinde George, and S.O. Ogundele, A.O. Esan, and Brownson N. Dede worked on several drafts of the document, which was later adopted by the Policy Planning Committee in the ministry and subsequently approved by the head of state.

The next major initiative concerned the development of a comprehensive training program for External Affairs officers. As far as I knew, the only institutionalized training effort by the ministry was concentrated on the Foreign Service Institute established under Professor Ishaya Audu's leadership. Designed for the training of newly recruited officers, the institute did not address the needs of the officers at middle and upper levels of service, who lacked clear guidelines and criteria for the selection of who would go where for what courses and for how long. This unsatisfactory situation had to be changed. Armed with strong backing from above and a special budgetary allocation, I embarked upon a new training program for all categories of External Affairs officers.

On 25 July 1984, I inaugurated a nine-man committee chaired by a distinguished jurist, former High Court judge and scholar Dr. Akinola Aguda, Director-General of the Nigerian Institute of Advanced Legal Studies, to review the training needs of External Affairs officers and make appropriate recommendations. Other members of the committee were Ambassador Aminu Sanusi, former Permanent Secretary of the Ministry of External Affairs; Professor G.O. Olusanya, Director-General, Nigerian Institute of International Affairs (NIIA); Professor Justin Tseayo, Director-General, National Institute of Policy and Strategic Studies (NIPSS); ambassadors B.A.T. Balewa and Olu Adeniji, directors-general (Regions and International Organizations, respectively) in the Ministry of External Affairs; Dr. I.B. Mnobuosi, Acting Director-General Administrative Staff College of Nigeria (ASCON), and Ambassador E. Martins, Director of Protocol, External Affairs Ministry. J.A. Sodipe served as secretary to the committee.

The committee submitted its report to me on 26 September 1984. The highlights of the recommendations were, first, that the recruitment of External Affairs officers should be based on passing a prescribed examination followed by an intensive oral interview, although the resulting recruitment could still be spread throughout the states of the federation. Second, the Foreign Service Academy was a good idea and officers who failed the final examination after two attempts should leave the Foreign Service. Third, a training program of at least six months' duration in different areas of diplomacy, international affairs, and foreign languages should be established for mid-career officers. Fourth, senior officers (Grade Level 14 and above) including ambassadors should also be made to undergo short courses in collaboration with the Nigerian Institute of International Affairs, Nigerian Institute for Policy and Strategic Studies, and ASCON. Finally, the committee recommended that senior ambassadors should be released to attend the senior executive courses at NIPSS and similar institutions abroad.

These laudable recommendations were immediately put into operation. For example, about 74 mid-career officers were sent to various Nigerian universities, where they pursued courses at post-graduate level in subjects related to international affairs and advanced public administration. At the senior officers' level, two ambassadors (Balewa and Ekong) went to the senior executive course at NIPSS, while another ambassador, E.A. Oba, was sent to a similar institution in Pakistan. Some of the committee's recommendations, however, required policy decisions by the Federal Executive Council (e.g., recruitment, probation, and confirmation of new External Affairs officers and even the idea of a separate Foreign Service). The processes for taking action on such decisions were initiated during my tenure of office.

Related to the emphasis on training at all levels of the Foreign Service were the preparations for renewing the annual seminars for Nigerian ambassadors. The last was in various world regions in 1982. When the seminar finally took place at the National Institute for Policy and Strategic Studies in Kuru (Jos, Plateau state of Nigeria) from 29 July to 10 August 1985, it proved to be more than a long briefing session for the country's principal representatives abroad. It was the second time that the seminar was held in Nigeria and the first time that it took place outside Lagos. The venue made it possible and perhaps even pleasant for several senior officials and ministers from the home ministries to participate in the proceedings. The exchange of ideas and the conclusions and recommendations which emanated from the seminar were extremely sound and thoughtful. They would, in my view, stand the test of time in our country's medium- and long-term foreign policy planning and implementation.

Finally, serious efforts were made to de-bureaucratize the process of making foreign policy. This took two main forms, both of which were new to the experience of the ministry. First, as minister, I gave several public lectures in the universities, made many television appearances, and granted several personal interviews to newspapers and weekly or monthly journals. The objective was to promote interaction between foreign-policy practitioners and members of the informed public who had a special interest in Nigeria's external relations. By encouraging the public's right to know, we could also create the opportunities for better understanding of and wider support for our Administration's foreign policy.

For the same reason, as a sounding board, an informal consultative committee on foreign policy was established, whose membership varied with the issues to be discussed at different sittings. Members generally included senior lecturers from the universities, senior research officers from NIIA and NIPSS, leaders of the Nigerian Labour Congress, representatives of the business community, and senior External Affairs officers. An unintended but positive consequence of the recommendations from this committee was to bolster the minister's political position in dealing with the bureaucracy in the External Affairs Ministry and with the highest levels of government. The case of Nigeria's recognition of the Saharawi Arab Democratic Republic (SADR), to be discussed later, is a clear illustration of this point.

The Ministry of External Affairs did not and could not have a monopoly of advice to the head of government. However, we made constant efforts to be the primary source of advice and major instrument of foreign policy. This was not always easy, especially in dealings with other ministries, agencies of government, and national institutes whose subject matter impinged on foreign affairs.

The relationship with the Nigerian Institute of International Affairs (NIIA) and the National Institute for Policy and Strategic Studies (NIPSS) was much easier for the minister than the Ministry of External Affairs. This was largely because in both institutes I was dealing with fellow academic colleagues. Indeed, during the first few months of my tenure of office as minister, I enjoyed the unprecedented honor of continuing to serve as the Director-General of NIIA. The ministry and NIIA had long experienced institutional rivalry in foreign policy matters that centered more on personalities than substance. The change of leadership in both institutions gave an opportunity for creative and constructive interaction that was seized throughout my tenure of office.

Dealing with the Ministry of Internal Affairs was generally smooth. There were three major issues on which both ministries had to work in close collaboration: the posting of immigration officers to overseas missions; negotiating the Quadripartite Agreement involving cooperation on immigration, police, customs, and general security matters between Nigeria and her neighbors to the west; and the mass expulsion of illegal aliens, mostly from Ghana. I had excellent personal relationships with the Minister of Internal Affairs, Major-General Maman Magoro. This permeated to the senior officials in our respective ministries and made resolution of joint problems much easier. On the first issue, the head of state also sought and received my recommendations on the proposal sent to him by General Magoro. A compromise reduced the number of overseas missions to which immigration officers would be posted to five: New Delhi, Moscow, Bonn, London, and Washington.

The two ministries worked smoothly together on the negotiations that led to the eventual signing of the Quadripartite Agreement in Lagos (December 1984). However, on the mass expulsion of the illegal aliens, our ministry did not fully support the method of the expulsions but did all it could to manage the diplomatic fallout in the sub-region and the adverse international publicity. This will be discussed further in a later chapter.

The relationship between our ministry and the Ministry of National Planning was more testy. This had little or nothing to do with the personalities leading each ministry; on the contrary, I had good relations and communications with Chief Michael S. Adigun. However, for historical reasons, the subject of ECOWAS was placed under the control of the Ministry of National Planning, to the virtual exclusion of the External Affairs Ministry. My ministry felt that this arrangement was not satisfactory, because ECOWAS is both an economic and political grouping and diplomatic efforts were constantly required to give it impetus. I therefore encouraged the Ministry of External Affairs to extend its capability on economic matters and challenge the dominance of ECOWAS affairs by National Planning. A strong memorandum seeking the transfer of ECOWAS from National Planning to our ministry was prepared for the head of state, although the issue was not resolved before my tenure of office ended.

The most problematic relationship between the Ministry of External Affairs and another government agency was with the National Security Organisation (NSO). There were two main dimensions to the uneasy coexistence between the two bodies during my time. First, there was the organizational. By the Decree establishing the NSO, the Research Department of the Ministry of External Affairs was brought under the Organization as its external wing and renamed the Directorate of External Intelligence. The staff of that directorate were in the difficult position of being, in effect, responsible to two masters. (This arrangement was not unique to the Nigerian situation; almost all other diplomatic services work under a similar difficulty.) The Ministry of External Affairs faced the problem of having administrative supervision over this category of staff while operational control was with the mother agency. Moreover, the reports of the staff members went directly to their own headquarters where they were sifted and made available to the highest levels of government. The Minister of External Affairs had to make special and occasionally unsuccessful overtures to know the contents and individuals behind such reports.

The other sensitive aspect of the relationship between the ministry and the NSO was more personal. Ambassador Lawal Rafindadi, head of the NSO, was a member of the Supreme Military Council, and I was not. He had also served as a foreign-service officer for many years, culminating in his appointment as ambassador to West Germany prior to becoming head of the NSO. He knew the Ministry of External Affairs perhaps better than myself; indeed he appeared to have seen himself as the member of the Supreme Military Council with the supervisory role over this ministry—a view I did not accept.

His perception must have been enhanced by his deep involvement in major government decisions affecting our ministry (such as cut-backs of the total number of overseas missions, the retirement of senior officers, and the appointment of new heads of overseas missions) even before my own appointment as minister was made or when I was only weeks in office. Worse still, some senior officers in our ministry were fond of currying favor with the NSO boss and attempted to involve him in personnel or policy decisions.

With time, however, the personal relationship between Ambassador Rafindadi and myself improved, largely because I was able to show the head of state and the government that our ministry could deliver the goods. By the end of the first year of the Buhari administration, the Ministry of External Affairs was becoming better able to meet the challenge of operating as the primary although not the exclusive instrument for making and implementing foreign policy. This was accomplished by working for a better motivated, increasingly better trained, and better managed Ministry of External Affairs capable of producing well-thought-out, clearly articulated, and generally well-implemented foreign policy.

NOTES

1. Among several excellent reports were those submitted by Ambassador Fowora, Mr. (later Ambassador) Ajakaiye, Dr. O. Fasehun, Ambassador Ade Adekuoye, and Mr. (later Ambassador) A. Ayeni.
2. Address of I.A. Gambari, Princeton University (United States), as reported in *West Africa* (22 October 1984, pp. 2117–2118). Full text is given in Appendix 1. General Buhari later spoke more authoritatively on Nigeria's new focus of interests and concerns: "Annual Foreign Policy Address, Annual Patron's Dinner, Nigerian Institute of International Affairs" (3 December 1984).
3. I was at the University of Ife, Ile-Ife, two or three times. Lectures delivered by me in person or read on my behalf included:

    (a) "Nigeria's Defence Posture in Africa—My Views" (Command and Staff College, Jaji, 2 July 1984)

    (b) "Review of Nigeria's Foreign Policy and Prospects" (Ahmadu Bello University, University Public Lecture, 26 July 1984)

    (c) "The World-Wide Economic Recession since 1980/81: Lessons for Nigeria." Annual Conference of the Nigerian Society of International Affairs (University of Ilorin, 2 to 5 November 1984)

    (d) "Diplomacy and Reality in Nigeria's Foreign Policy" (University of Jos, 1 February 1985)

    (e) "Nigeria and the United Nations" (University of Nigeria, Nsukka, 18 March 1985)

I also gave hour-long television interviews on national network, made several national broadcasts on important international events and commemorations, and spoke without notes to editors of *Newswatch*, *Spectrum*, and *Foreign Report*.

3

Domestic Political and Economic Background

The predecessor regime to General Buhari's was the civilian one that administered Nigeria from October 1979 until 31 December 1983. It came amidst great hopes and widespread optimism, caused in part by the release of the "democratic" spirit deeply embedded in the psyche of most politically aware Nigerians. After almost thirteen years of unbroken military rule, the Nigerian populace was keenly awakened by the prospect and subsequent reality of civilian rule.

It can be argued, with some justification, that the dichotomization of Nigerian rulership between civilians on the one hand and the military on the other is a false one. There has never been a "pure" military rule in post-independence Nigeria; on the contrary, the military has often used civilians as political heads of the various state bureaucracies and organizations. The longer the military men stay in power, the more they tend to behave like civilians in order to retain office. And with respect to civilian administrations, the potential of military intervention in the political order of the country has never been far from the minds of the politicians. This is probably why former President Shehu Shagari was quoted as having said that, in reality, there were only two major parties during the Second Republic: all the five registered political parties on the one hand and the military on the other.

In any case, whether civilian or military, the governance of Nigeria has been conducted with the active involvement if not guidance of the enduring alliance of the bureaucratic, military, and business elites and some traditional rulers. These groups constitute the relatively permanent power base while those installed in public office change periodically.

What is difficult to dispute is that President Shehu Shagari and his administration, anchored by the tentative and uneasy cooperation agreement between his party, the National Party of Nigeria (NPN), and the

Nigerian Peoples' Party (NPP) enjoyed relatively widespread goodwill during the first two years of the regime. It should also be noted, however, that the years of the administration's relative popularity coincided with a relatively buoyant economy, the result largely of favorable oil export prices (average \$40 per barrel) and a relatively comfortable production level of two million barrels per day until the end of 1980 and beginning of 1981. We shall return later to the problems caused when oil prices fell and the economy took a downward turn.

A detailed analysis of the political parties and the dynamics of their interaction during the Second Republic will not be made here. Suffice it to note that in the breadth and sources of their membership and general support, almost all the registered political parties reflected the differing ethnic orientations of the national elites. The NPP was unable to obtain solid support outside of Anambra and Imo states in the East, except for areas dominated by Christian minority groups in Plateau. The Unity Party of Nigeria (UPN) came to register most of its support in the Ondo, Oyo, Ogun, and Lagos states in addition to Bendel—territories that almost exactly coincided with the old Western Region.

The Peoples' Redemption Party (PRP), at least in the first term of the presidential system, retained the revolutionary fervor of the "Talakawa" (Common People), the party represented by its old antecedent, the Northern Elements Progressive Union (NEPU). Nonetheless, under Mallam Aminu Kano's leadership, PRP did not gain control of more than two states (Kano and Kaduna) and its hold on Kaduna was particularly precarious given the control of the state assembly there by the NPN. The Great Nigerian Peoples' Party, led by Waziri Ibrahim, did rather well nationally in the spread of votes received during the first two elections to the National Assembly in 1979, but it ended up controlling only two states (Borno and Gongola). The eccentricity of the GNPP leader and the serious internal contradictions were later to prove disastrous for the survival of the party as a cohesive, disciplined, and national entity.

The NPN was the most "national" of the five registered parties in the spread of the electoral support obtained during the 1979 elections. One of the key attractions of the party was the "zoning" arrangement whereby different regions and ethnic groups were allocated leading party and governmental offices. In time, however, this potentially unifying arrangement was abandoned, and the office of president was not allowed to rotate among the zones of the party following the renomination of Alhaji Shehu Shagari to contest the presidential elections once more in 1983. The NPN also came to be seen by its opponents as a tool for Hausa-Fulani domination of Nigeria. As the party which controlled the central government but not a majority of the state governments, it began to experience stiff opposition from a united front of the state governments that the other political parties controlled.

The First Republic's pattern of ethnic and regionally based political parties and confrontational politics soon began to reappear in the Second Republic. Ethnic and regional loyalties seemed, once again, to be the really sure sources of political support. Governments, either at the center or in the states, still used all instruments at their control (largely the Electoral Commission, security forces whether official or private, intimidation, and large-scale purchase of votes) to stay in power. The situation was aided by the fact that most leaders of the political parties of the Second Republic were little more than the proverbial "old wine in new bottles." Worse still, several of the newer-breed politicians who teamed up with the "old brigade" were often abrasive, amateurish, and corrupted by newly found wealth, power, and influence.

By the time the second round of national and state elections took place in 1983, the political class in Nigeria had developed serious credibility problems. There were three main dimensions of this situation, which eventually led to heightened political instability in the country. First, there was the demonstrable inability or unwillingness to manage the economy properly. Second, the civilians proved incapable of conducting free and fair elections. Third, there was widespread corruption involving many party leaders, their followers, and the governments which they controlled. These will be discussed in reverse order.

The issue of large-scale corruption severely damaged the reputation of the operators of the political system. Although this was not a new issue in Nigeria, the nature of the new presidential system and the increase in oil-based revenue accruing to the federal and state governments, especially in the early 1980s, helped to elevate corruption to new heights. Corrupt practices became pervasive at local, state, and federal levels, especially in the award of contracts and the manipulation of the import-licensing system. When these practices continued without much regard to declining governmental revenue, they poisoned the social and political climate, since less and less funds were made available to maintain, not to mention develop, social services and related institutions. It was not long before essential medical services and the educational system degenerated and were on the verge of collapse. Social tensions were heightened and antisocial behavior of the underclass increased very rapidly.

The elections of 1983 were not conducted in an atmosphere of freedom or with fairness. On the contrary, they were accompanied by serious abuses, blatant malpractice, and communal violence. In view of the ethnic pattern of support and voting by the general public, the claims of "victory" by one party in the traditional strongholds of the others stretched credibility to the limit and led to outbreaks of violence. The resulting bloodshed and confusion damaged the reputation not only of the law enforcement agencies, which were often part of the problem, but also of the federal government and politicians in general.

However, it was the economic problems which the civilian regime failed adequately to address that exacerbated social tensions and domestic unrest. The economic problems pre-dated the civilian regime of 1979. The root of the emerging problem had been the rapid dependence of the country on a single export item—crude oil. As was observed in a government document,[1] the price of crude oil jumped more than threefold, from $11.70 per barrel (between 1973 and 1974) to $40 per barrel (in 1980). The increases in the posted price for oil and the increased production, which reached 2.05 million barrels per day by 1980, pushed Nigeria into the oil economy in the sense that the levels of oil production and price obtained from its export dictated the state and pace of the country's economy.[2]

The danger signal arising from dependence on oil revenue flashed toward the end of General Obasanjo's regime when, due to a drop in oil production and price, the federal government had to resort to heavy borrowing from the international money market to build up the reserves needed to finance mounting import bills and also sustain the exchange rate of the national currency, the *naira*. Between 1981 and 1982, the demand for Nigerian oil fell sharply, as did the posted price. The sharp drop in oil revenue upon which the country had become so dependent weakened the external payments position of the nation, and also the financial positions of the federal and state governments, from 1981 until the civilian regime was overthrown at the end of 1983. One simple illustration of this may be given here. In 1979/80, federally collected revenue was estimated at N12.272 billion, to which petroleum contributed N9.489 billion; whereas by 1982 the figures were N8.942 billion and N5.161 billion respectively.[3] The result was that Nigeria found it increasingly difficult to finance her import bills for consumer goods and food as well as raw materials and machinery for domestic manufactures. The various governments in Nigeria found it difficult and often impossible to pay salaries and fringe benefits to the workers under their direct employment.

In a later analysis of the dismal economic record of the civilian administration, the Nigerian Labour Congress highlighted the "inability [of that regime] to revamp the economy, which by its mismanagement it ruined" and "the malpractices which the civilian administration inflicted on the broad masses on the Nigerian people."[4] These included the incalculable hardships caused by the inability to pay workers' salaries promptly and regularly, the imposition of compulsory pensions on some employees by some state governments, mass retrenchments, and insecurity of employment, especially in the private sector.[5]

The document went on to recall the widespread "closure of factories and industrial undertakings prompted by indiscreet issuance of import licenses thereby denying genuine manufacturers of imported raw materials."[6] These unwelcome developments were taking place amidst what the NLC called "galloping inflation and excessive increases in the prices of basic food and other consumer items."[7] It is for these reasons that the NLC then declared its support for the termination of the life of the last civilian administration by the military intervention of January 1984.

The question could be asked as to why the NLC did not organize and fight the unjust economic system and the mismanagement of the nation's economy by the last civilian administration. The answer is simple. The NLC is a workers' organization with big potential but little actual unity or capacity for effective defense of the workers in the face of a government determined to pursue policies detrimental to the interests and well-being of the working populace. It may be instructive to note that the new military government's reaction to the NLC document referred to above was to circulate it to federal permanent secretaries, heads of extra-ministerial departments and secretaries to state military governments, along with a pro forma covering letter signed for the secretary to the Federal Military Government for "information and any action [they] may deem appropriate." It took several months for an appointment to be made for the NLC leaders to meet with the head of the Federal Military Government, General Buhari, in order to personally press their viewpoints on the government. Even then, the outcome of the eventual meeting was not satisfactory to either side.

Nonetheless, the NLC was probably correct in its assessment, shared quite widely in the country as a whole, that the mismanagement of the economy by the civilian administration and the conspicuous consumption exhibited by some of the corrupt politicians of the Second Republic had the combined effect of moving the country perilously close to "civil strife, rebellion and anarchy."[8] The intervention by the military and the overthrow of the civilian regime was therefore seen as a political act designed "essentially to prevent the country from imminent collapse, since all indications point to the fact that the former civilian regimes (at federal and state levels) have exhausted their capacity and legitimacy to withstand the reaction of the people."[9]

Another serious dimension to the economic problem was the enormous debt burden. On the domestic level, the last civilian administration converted the budget surplus of N1,461.6 million inherited from the predecessor military regime in 1979 into a deficit of N1,975.2 million by the following year.[10] Between 1980 and 1983, federal and state governments appeared to be competing with one another in recording huge budget deficits. While the federal budget deficit came to between N4,000 million and N6,000 million, the combined budget deficits of the states rose from N3,295.0 million in

1980 to about N6,000 million in 1983.[11] Huge expenditures continued to be made by the governments despite continual falls in income.

On the external front, the former civilian administration wiped out the credit balance of N2.5 billion inherited from the preceding military regime in October 1979. It also left the succeeding military regime with the task of having to refinance trade arrears on letters of credit of $1.88 billion and to refinance another accumulated short-term trade arrears on the open accounts of about $5 billion.[12]

In addressing these economic problems in their various dimensions, the Buhari regime decided to resume negotiations with the International Monetary Fund (IMF). It soon became clear, however, that the talks were going nowhere, because the IMF pressed upon the new regime the usual conditions regarding substantial devaluation of the national currency, reduction of state subsidies, especially on petroleum products, and liberalization of imports, while the Nigerian authorities argued that these would worsen the illness which the country's economy was undergoing.

For instance, because Nigeria depends on imported capital goods and raw materials which cannot be adjusted in the short run, outright devaluation of the magnitude suggested by the IMF would raise local costs of production and general price levels enough to vitiate the supposed benefits to exports which devaluation is expected to bring. Moreover, since Nigeria was operating an essentially monocultural economy, devaluation was unlikely to have any significant impact on her earnings of foreign exchange. In any case, the prices of most of the country's export commodities are fixed externally in foreign currencies under those organizations that protect producers' interests, such as OPEC, the Cocoa Alliance, and the Tin Council.

Furthermore, devaluation would increase the external debt-service burden in *naira* and thereby eliminate the supposed net gains to government revenue from exports, on which the IMF places much premium. Finally, the inflationary effects of devaluation would ultimately provoke workers' demands for wage increases in order to protect their real incomes.

The economies of those developing countries which accept IMF loans on the standard conditions have hardly ever recovered. On the contrary, the implementation of IMF conditions often exacerbates existing social tensions from inequalities in distribution of income and invariably inaugurates a new era of domestic political instability. This fact has prompted me to join other Third World colleagues in characterizing the IMF as a doctor who prescribes the same medicine for all his patients irrespective of the type or degree of illness.[13] This was, of course, a political statement but it was probably not too far from the economic target.

Before these arguments by the Nigerian authorities led to an impasse in the IMF negotiations, General Buhari looked actively for alternatives. First, he dispatched his number-two man, Brigadier (later General) Tunde Idiagbon, to Saudi Arabia in early February 1984 to renew Nigeria's request for the balance of a loan of $2 billion which the former civilian administration sought from the Saudis. General Buhari also communicated privately with Sheik Yamani, Oil Minister of Saudi Arabia and his former colleague at OPEC, to advance the Nigerian request.[14] Some friendly African countries which had good links with the Saudis were also contacted to help.

Furthermore, the new administration faced the herculean task of trying to bring aggregate demand in line with greatly reduced oil income. It was also understood that internal policies must be pursued to stimulate domestic production and non-oil exports and thus create a more positive external payments position at least in the medium term. Strict priorities were also established in allocating increasingly scarce foreign exchange earnings with emphasis placed on agricultural and allied industries that had the capability to help reduce inflation and increase levels of employment. Deficit budgeting at state and federal levels was discouraged.

This was the economic and political state of affairs when General Buhari and his military administration took over in 1984. Notwithstanding these problems, the expectations of the public and the goals set by the new administration were very high. These included better management of the economy and the establishment of greater discipline by the rulers and the ruled, which culminated in the War Against Indiscipline (WAI) campaign.

On the economic front, the expectations were that salaries of workers would be paid promptly and regularly, that retrenchments would end and that production levels in the manufacturing sector would be restored to full or near full capacity, thereby raising employment levels. The Nigerian Labour Congress expected the new administration to involve "mass organisations like the Trade Unions, students [NANS] and relevant professional bodies and economic groups [in] the present political set up at both the national and state levels."[15] The apparent rationale for this rather unusual plea for cooptation was that those in the social strata that suffered the most from the recklessness of the past civilian regime should receive a chance to contribute toward finding solutions to the nation's socioeconomic and political problems.

In a related and perhaps more profound observation, the NLC regretted the fact that while all previous military governments professed to serve the ordinary people, "they [often] cooperate [with] and incorporate the very group they have overthrown."[16] This often meant that the objectives of the military rulers were "diverted, moderated and at a stage hijacked for the benefit of the same class whose misrule invited and necessitated military intervention."[17] The exclusion of mass participation in government then exposed the military to the machinations of the previous civilian regime and paved the way to the civilians' return to power—a vicious circle.

Unfortunately for the trade unions and professional organizations, and perhaps even more for the nation as a whole, the plea for a "social contract" between them and the government was not accepted. The warning against coopting the ideas or sections of the national elite that had just failed the country could not really be followed in a systematic or complete manner. The alliance between top civil servants, leading businessmen, senior military officers, and traditional rulers still constituted the political environment of the new regime, if not the pillar upon which it leaned. These developments had serious consequences for the Buhari regime, which will be further discussed later in this study.

On the external front, the Buhari administration was poised to use foreign policy as an effective instrument for rebuilding the shattered economy and internal security. It would also appear from General Buhari's initial statements that where the national interests of Nigeria conflicted with those of our neighboring states in particular and African countries in general, there would not be an automatic yielding to the latter. Therefore, tough bargaining was on the horizon in the pursuit of the nation's external relations, as Nigeria attempted to regain her national pride and national prosperity at the sub-regional, continental, and international levels.

NOTES

1. "On the State of the Nigerian Economy" (Lagos: Federal Ministry of National Planning, February 1983).
2. Ibid.
3. Ibid.
4. See "Nigerian Workers' Socio-Political Viewpoint in the Situation of Military Take-Over of the Governments of the Federations—Presented to the Federal Military Government" (Lagos: Nigerian Labour Congress, 6 January 1984).
5. Ibid.
6. Ibid.
7. Ibid.
8. Ibid.
9. Ibid.
10. See, "Moment of Truth: Collected Speeches of Major General Muhammadu Buhari" (Lagos: Federal Government Press, 1984).
11. Ibid.
12. Ibid.
13. Speech by the head of the Nigerian delegation, general debate, United Nations General Assembly, 39th session, New York, 8 October 1984.
14. At General Buhari's invitation, Sheik Yamani visited Nigeria to discuss this and other matters relating to Nigeria's economic recovery.
15. "Nigerian Workers' Sociopolitical Viewpoint," 14(11).
16. Ibid.
17. Ibid.

PART 2

Regional Issues

4

Relations with Neighboring Countries

Nigeria shares colonially inherited international boundaries with the republics of Benin to the west, Niger to the north, and Cameroon in the east. Although Chad has no land border with Nigeria, both are neighbors since they share boundaries on Lake Chad. Equatorial Guinea lies to the southwest of Nigeria, with the major island Bioko, formerly known as Fernando Po, being situated off our Atlantic coast. As the immediate neighbor to the west, off Benin Republic, Togo shares with other countries the problems of neighborly relations with Nigeria. All these neighbors of Nigeria, with the exception of Equatorial Guinea, are former French colonies which maintain close economic, political, and security ties with France.

At a superficial level, none of these neighboring countries poses direct or serious military threats to Nigeria. That is why, at the time of independence, some analysts felt that Nigeria hardly needed an elaborate foreign policy, given the absence of military or security threats from these countries.[1] On her part, Nigeria showed no expansionist tendencies toward neighboring countries. Occasional voices urged Nigeria to annex Fernando Po, then under Spanish colonial rule, just as India had annexed Goa and ended Portuguese colonial rule in the Indian subcontinent. Such an imperialist impulse was, however, out of tune with the generally conservative policies of Sir Abubakar Tafawa Balewa's government under the First Republic. On the contrary, Sir Abubakar deliberately cultivated good relations with the country's neighbors.

Nigeria's strong commitment to the principles enshrined in the OAU charter also attracted her relatively weaker neighbors and allayed their fears and suspicions. The principles included sovereign equality of member states, non-interference in the internal affairs of other states, respect for the sovereignty and territorial integrity of each member, condemnation of international subversion, and promotion of African unity. The impact of

Nigeria's commitment to these principles was made greater by the suspicion that, under Nkrumah, Ghana had violated them.

In general, the policy of good-neighborliness was pursued throughout the First Republic, and received a reciprocal response from neighboring countries. The personal friendships which developed with the leaders of neighboring countries proved indispensable during Nigeria's Civil War. If Hamani Diori of Niger Republic and Ahmadu Ahidjo of Cameroon had succumbed to international pressures to allow their countries to be used against the territorial integrity of Nigeria, the history and outcome of the Civil War would have surely been different.

The neighboring countries recognized, sometimes grudgingly, the dominant position of Nigeria, and often attempted to use her economic and political weight to their own national advantage. It has sometimes appeared, also, that they used their relatively powerful neighbor as a trump card in dealing with their more powerful patron—France.

When the economy of Nigeria was buoyant, relations with her neighbors tended to be generally good. Nigeria served as a pole of growth, attracting traffic in goods, services, and people. Trade often increased significantly, although largely in contraband goods. There were also opportunities for greater financial and other aid from Nigeria, as well as investments in joint ventures in the neighboring countries, especially Benin Republic.

If, in general terms, Nigeria and her neighbors have had a love-hate relationship, periods of prosperity and economic growth in Nigeria have often accentuated the love aspect. However, when the Nigerian economy takes a downturn, the relationship with neighbors has tended to become correspondingly sour. This has often followed from the restrictive and purely nationalistic measures which Nigeria has taken to revamp her own economy. The Buhari regime's decision to close Nigeria's land borders and expel illegal aliens is a case in point.

Neighboring countries often felt that Nigeria had responsibilities to do more for them than she usually did, or at least to avoid taking measures capable of destroying their own economies, which are dependent on Nigerian markets. This expectation was not always shared by policymakers or those segments of the informed public in Nigeria that wanted more cost-benefit considerations applied in dealing with our neighbors, particularly during bad economic times, while at the same time expecting these countries to check negative activities such as smuggling and the molestation of Nigerian citizens in border areas.

The reality of this love-hate relationship is compounded by another reality, which derives from the limitations of Nigeria's power or influence on her neighbors. In the relationship with these neighboring countries, Nigeria has had to develop policies which take into account very powerful French,

American, and, to a lesser extent, Spanish interests in the sub-region. Hence, a policy of good-neighborliness in our geographic area must be supplemented with the avoidance of direct confrontation with the metropolitan friends or patrons of the neighboring countries. Clear examples are the history of Nigeria's multilateral diplomacy in ECOWAS, the difficulties of moving the francophone countries away from the competing, French-inspired CEAO, and the constraint which inhibited Nigeria from taking strong retaliatory action against Cameroon when she engaged in acts of aggression in 1982.

It is against this background that we may examine our relationship with our immediate neighbors. A credible foreign policy abroad must of necessity start with security and stability at home. One of the best means to guarantee this is a skilful cultivation of our neighbors in a manner that will ensure their continued friendship at affordable costs to Nigeria. In fact, nothing threatens and disturbs a nation's internal stability and sense of well-being more profoundly than the existence of hostile neighbors.

We must put to full use the lessons learnt from our occasional friction and armed clashes with some neighboring countries. We need to secure our main base of operations before our intervention in other places, such as southern Africa, the Horn, or Western Sahara, can be more credible. Admittedly, friction is virtually inevitable or even expected among the best of friends or neighbors. George Bernard Shaw once said that the British and Americans are two peoples separated by a common language. Similarly, Nigeria and her immediate neighbors sometime behave as countries separated by common borders, history, indigenous languages, and cultures.

Nigeria happens to be surrounded by neighboring countries with vast differences in ideology, wealth, national interests, and political and diplomatic styles. It is only sensible that we reach a new and lasting understanding with them. Our country's more recent experiences, first with Cameroon in 1982 and later with Chad in 1983, when border clashes almost degenerated into all-out conflict, remind us of possible neglect in perhaps the most vulnerable point in our foreign posture.

It was, therefore, highly commendable that one of the very first diplomatic activities of General Buhari's regime was to despatch a high-powered delegation to the neighboring countries. Led by Major-General Domkat Y. Bali, Minister of Defence and Senior Member of the Supreme Military Council, the special mission met with presidents Matthieu Kerekou (Benin), Seyni Kountche (Niger), and Paul Biya (Cameroon) as well as Vice-President Tahiru Ginaso (Chad), respectively on 11, 12, 16, and 17 January 1984. The objective of the special mission was to reassure these countries that the new administration was committed to the policy of good-neighborliness while seeking their cooperation in enhancing Nigeria's security and checking smuggling and hostile activities toward our citizens. The larger goal of this and subsequent diplomatic efforts was to create in the sub-region an atmosphere of friendship and mutual confidence conducive to the peaceful domicile, coexistence, and well-being of our many citizens spread throughout West Africa, while promoting greater economic integration and growth in the sub-region.

We may now examine these neighboring countries one by one to highlight their particular relationships with Nigeria, beginning with Benin Republic. In Benin, we are involved in a number of joint ventures, such as the Onigbolo Cement Works and the Save Sugar Project, with potential benefits to the economies of both countries. There are also links between institutions of higher learning, namely, the University of Ibadan and National University of Benin. A number of places for the training of Benin citizens were made available at the School of Aviation in Zaria, Nigeria. The two countries cooperate in road construction, salt development, energy, surveying, and mapping. Steps have also been made to promote cooperation in commercial banking. In some of the cooperative projects, Nigeria was almost the sole financier for security and strategic reasons, as in the building of the Semi-Podji-Cotonou, Bolico-Ijaro, and Nikki-Chikkenda roads.

There is also a joint commission between Benin and Nigeria, whose periodic meetings have been useful for discussing common issues, resolving problems, and facilitating cooperation in general. A military accord of 1979 enables the armed forces of the two countries to cooperate in military and security matters. These projects and instruments were designed to enhance cooperation and provide positive linkages between the two countries.

Yet, the two countries are not free from mutual irritants. In addition to the closing of our borders throughout Buhari's regime and occasional border clashes, political cooperation with Benin has not been very close. While Benin has turned out to be a generally reliable bilateral and ECOWAS partner, her posture at the OAU and the United Nations has often differed from our own, partly from a desire to exercise her sovereign and independent status in foreign policy issues. There was also the Marxist ideology adopted by the Beninois leadership, influenced no doubt by a greater concentration of extra-African powers there than is commensurate with that country's size and political importance. The challenge facing Nigeria is how to take advantage of our exceptionally close economic relations, in which we have invested so much, to forge stronger political relations.

The relationship between Niger Republic and Nigeria can be described as a "twin sister" one. Considerable interaction and cooperation in the areas of security, economy, and culture take place between the two countries which share an exceptionally long border. Nigeria considers the Republic of Niger as her most peaceful, friendly, and valued neighbor, a feeling almost always reciprocated by Niger. From Hamani Diori to Kountche, the leaders of Niger have worked hard to maintain close and fraternal relations with Nigeria that transcend diplomatic niceties. President Kountche was the first African leader to pay a formal visit to Nigeria during Buhari's tenure of office.

Unlike any other joint commissions in which Nigeria has been involved, the Niger-Nigerian Joint Commission for Economic Cooperation has a permanent secretariat in Niamey and a Nigerian secretary-general resident there on a permanent basis. Under the auspices of the joint commission the two countries have concluded a number of agreements on air, road, transport, health, trade, and cultural and technical cooperation. Nigeria has also negotiated with the Republic of Niger and her foreign partners from Britain, West Germany, Belgium, and France for a 16 percent participation in the exploitation of uranium deposits at Afasto East. An understanding was also reached regarding the supply of meat and livestock and the breeding of cattle. The protocols were signed on 10 May 1978 in Niamey. The trade in meat and cattle later commenced after protracted negotiations between the Nigerian Food Company Ltd and its Niger counterpart, SONARAN. Other areas of cooperation include management of water resources, mineral resources development, and the supply of electricity to the Republic of Niger.

There are no territorial disputes or controversies between the two countries, except for occasional border incidents, immigration problems, and religious riots involving citizens of Niger resident in Nigeria. These problems have been resolved in a brotherly and understanding manner. Cooperation between the security agencies of Niger and Nigeria has been as close as political consultations between the leadership of both neighboring countries. As with Benin, there has always been considerable trade, visible and invisible, across the largely porous border.

There is, however, a strategic problem in the extremely close relations between Niger and France. France and Nigeria are strategic rivals in West Africa. And it is believed, for example, that the French security agency (SEDEC) has its strongest African presence in Niger and Gabon. Nigeria would have to consider taking policy steps to build stronger political ties with Niger aimed at undercutting French influence there. The experience of Niger's contest with Nigeria for a United Nations Security Council seat in 1977 was a bitter one for both countries. However, the support given by Nigeria for the election of Niger's Foreign Minister, Idi Oumaru, as substantive Secretary-General of the OAU in July 1985, served to reduce if not eliminate that bitterness.

For security and geopolitical reasons, Chad has taken a priority spot in Nigeria's national concern. We have dealt with Chad both as our neighbor and as a continental trouble spot requiring our involvement. Whenever the level of violence increased among the various belligerents in the Chadian conflict, there were direct and indirect threats to peace and security in the Borno state, contiguous to that country. The flow of refugees into Nigeria increased as did the traffic in arms and ammunition. External interventions in Chadian problems escalated the fighting and created wider political and security problems, not only for Nigeria but for the African continent as a whole.

Nigeria's major objectives include support for a politically united Chad under an acceptable representative government; prevention of the emergence of a political leadership hostile to Nigeria, and the frustration of activities by extra-regional and extra-African powers whose intentions toward Nigeria and the sub-region may be questionable. Meanwhile, on bilateral matters, Nigeria has worked with Chad on the Chad Basin Commission and in delineating the boundary between the two countries that affects some islands in Lake Chad, disagreements over which have led to armed clashes between both countries. The involvement of Nigeria in the Chadian peace process will be discussed more fully in chapter 9.

Solutions to the bilateral problems with Chad and to the Chadian conflict will be difficult to find, but the closure of our land borders in 1984 demonstrated the strong economic card which we hold in dealing with that country. Without the relief supplies and other goods transiting from Nigeria to Chad, there would be serious threats to the socioeconomic and political structures and perhaps even the survival of the country. Our challenge is to use that card to promote peace in Chad and to induce cooperation with and positive behavior toward Nigeria.

Although the Cameroon-Nigerian border is probably our most sensitive security zone, Cameroon is the neighboring country with which we do not have strong economic ties. Yet that country has a strong economy and serves as a pole of attraction to other francophone countries in Central Africa. In addition, Nigeria shares an ethnic affinity in both the north and the southwest of Cameroon. Former President Ahidjo was very supportive of the federal government's efforts in ending the Civil War in Nigeria in favor of our country's national unity and territorial integrity.

Nonetheless, many forces cause discord in the relationship between the two neighboring countries. French influence has always been particularly strong in Cameroon—a fact which arouses suspicion and concern in Nigeria. The Cameroon leadership is extremely sensitive to latent separatism in the western Cameroon—which was administered as part of Nigeria until the United Nations plebiscite in 1959, when the people of that region opted to join the Republic of Cameroon. Finally, the unresolved border problem is potentially the most explosive factor of all.

The Military administration under General Buhari viewed with great seriousness the strategic and security consequences of the unresolved border dispute in the Bakasi Peninsula. An inter-ministerial committee on the Nigeria/Cameroon border was set up to make appropriate recommendations to the government for dealing with the issue. The National Institute of Policy and Strategic Studies, submitted a thoughtful report on the matter.

One of the major dimensions of the maritime border dispute related to the protection and welfare of the Nigerian citizens who live on the Bakasi Peninsula. The estimate most commonly referred to, on the Nigerian side at least, is that between 90 and 98 percent of the people who live on that peninsula are Nigerians. According to the NIPP's report there are wider strategic interests which Nigeria should defend in the disputed area. Access to Calabar port on the southeastern coast of Nigeria is controlled by the Bakasi Peninsula. This port is used for both merchant and naval shipping, which makes it important for security purposes. Plans by Nigeria to set up a naval base at James Town will require changes in the present arrangement whereby the Cross River estuary is shared with Cameroon. In addition, Cameroon is exploring and exploiting oil in the neutral corridor marked out in the earlier tentative accord at Maroua between former heads of state Gowon and Ahidjo. The Cameroonian oil rigs constitute navigational hazards to Nigerian vessels because they obstruct the passage on the estuary.

Finally, the Cameroonians have neither settled on the island nor allowed Nigerian fishermen to operate without hindrance in the Bakasi Peninsula. Cameroon refuses to recognize the extension of Nigerian territorial waters and thereby limits Nigeria's economic exploitation of the region. Moreover, any broadening of Nigeria's defense interests in the zone from Equatorial Guinea to Angola would be inhibited by the failure to secure the Bakasi Peninsula. Extra-regional or even extra-African powers with hostile intentions toward Nigeria could establish bases there or sign defense agreements with the countries in the peninsula.

The urgency and importance attached to these and related issues caused the Federal Military Government to expand the Task Force on Chad and extend its mandate to include Cameroon. The new task force remained under my chairmanship as Minister of External Affairs. Although two other groups were working on the border issue with Cameroon (the Inter-Ministerial Committee on the Cameroon/Nigeria Border Dispute and the Ministry of Defence Contingency Committee on Border Defence) our task force had the advantage of making recommendations that went directly to the head of state and the National Defence and Security Council, which functioned as a standing committee of the Supreme Military Council.

The Cameroon task force also included the Permanent Secretary and the director-general of African Affairs in my Ministry. Actually, Ambassador Hamzat Ahmadu, the African Affairs director-general, served as our ambassador to

Cameroon just before his new position at headquarters. We also had the input of a Permanent Secretary from the cabinet office of the Cross River state government. Representatives of Supreme Headquarters, Naval Headquarters, Police, Immigration, Nigerian National Petroleum Company, Ministry of Justice, Customs and Excise, Nigerian Ports Authority, National Electric Power Authority, and the Director of Military Intelligence were active participants. Our current ambassador in Yaounde, A. Yusufari, and an External Affairs Officer in the Nigerian Consulate-General at Buea (Cameroon) were invited to attend some task force meetings.

The task force wrote periodic reports and recommendations which were considered by the highest levels of government. Several options were presented to solve the border problems with Cameroon in particular and improve neighborly relations, including actions that could be taken unilaterally, bilaterally, through a multilateral body, such as the Chad Basin Authority, and international arbitration through the International Court of Justice at The Hague.

While our bilateral relations with Cameroon suffered setbacks in the past, the Biya administration demonstrated a greater willingness to improve relations with Nigeria and win our support. Nigeria was one of the first countries President Biya visited after becoming head of state of Cameroon. As noted earlier, within days of the change of government in Nigeria in January 1984, General Buhari sent a special mission to Yaounde. There now appears to be enough goodwill to set bilateral affairs on an even keel. Since the attempted coup in Cameroon and attendant political difficulties there, Nigeria has been in close contact with the authorities in the country. The former head of state of Nigeria, General Obasanjo, was sent on a special mission to Cameroon by General Buhari. The one-day mission, which took place on 12 May 1984, was very successful in the quiet but effective counselling of the leadership there to temper justice with fairness and caution in view of the ethnic and religious heterogeneity of that country. This delicate and secret assignment was carried out with flying colors by General Obasanjo without his appearing to interfere in the internal affairs of Cameroon. President Biya was very appreciative of our concern and support at those critical times for his presidency and his country.

Equatorial Guinea is a country situated off our coastal territory and containing large numbers of Nigerians who live and work there. This dimension of our relationship goes back to several years before the independence of the two countries. It has had its ups and downs, mostly downs. Apart from the apparently intractable problems of immigration and labor relations, Equatorial Guinea is important strategically, politically, and economically for the execution of our foreign policy. The country is only thirty minutes' flight time from Lagos and only ten minutes from some of our oil rigs. Whichever power controls Equatorial Guinea can easily destabilize Nigeria or, at least, sabotage our economic interests.

Furthermore, the country's sensitive and strategic location at a point connecting Africa, Europe, and the Americas makes it an attractive candidate for military occupation by a strong foreign power. The same result could also be obtained through military pacts with Equatorial Guinea. Reports indicate that the Soviet Union, China, France, Brazil, and the United States use the island of Bioko (Fernando Po), Equatorial Guinea, for one type of military activity or another. Perhaps most ominous of all is the reported use of the island by Israel and South Africa.

For these reasons Nigeria has to pursue a more activist and forward looking policy toward Equatorial Guinea. The idea of evacuating large numbers of our citizens who live and work there whenever they face hostility needs to be reexamined. If they are so vital to the plantations and general economic survival of Bioko Island, should we not help consolidate and expand their hold on the socioeconomic and political life of Equatorial Guinea? We should honor the request made by President Obiang Nguema Mbasogo for the extension of Nigeria's naval surveillance to cover his country's territorial waters. The Ministry of External Affairs recommended that a military officer be appointed as our resident ambassador in Malabo and that President Mbasogo be invited for friendly but frank discussions with our head of state in Lagos. These recommendations were accepted, but the visit did not take place until after General Buhari left office.

Togo and Ghana are not immediate neighbors, but they occupy an area of very close concern for the security and economic interests of Nigeria. Both countries were actively involved in the negotiations which culminated in the Quadripartite Agreement signed in Lagos on 10 December 1984. Togo was a prime mover, along with Nigeria, in bringing about the realization of the efforts to have the four West African countries agree to cooperate on immigration, customs, police, and security matters. Togo saw advantages in having Ghana involved in the discussions and eventual agreements which were to govern interstate behavior in those crucial areas. Nigeria also recognized the importance of having Benin Republic participate, so as to formalize relations with that neighboring country, especially in the areas of trade and the general movement of goods and people. The aim was to eliminate or at least greatly minimize the illegal traffic in goods and services.

The process leading to the Quadripartite Agreement began with the arrival in Lagos of a special envoy from President Eyadema of Togo in 1984 seeking a meeting at the highest levels of government between his country and ours as well as with Ghana and Benin. Apart from getting acquainted with the new head of state of Nigeria, President Eyadema wanted to discuss ways and means to deal with "security" problems in the sub-region. His primary concern was with the activities of Togolese dissidents, who in his view were operating freely in Ghana, perhaps with support from the Ghanaian authorities, and who should be extradited to Togo to face criminal charges.

General Buhari, in replying to President Eyadema's message, suggested a less restrictive focus to such a meeting of the four heads of state. He proposed a wider agenda to include cooperation agreements to deal with all illegal trafficking in the sub-region: arms and ammunition, currency, goods, and services. Nigeria's objective was to formalize the trade relationship, reduce smuggling, and check illegal immigration. Cooperation in security matters could also cover extradition of criminals from one country to the other, or to others where they might be wanted to face charges and prosecution. It was clearly unsatisfactory that Nigeria and Ghana had extradition treaties with Britain but none with one another or with their neighboring countries.

The expanded agenda appeared to satisfy Ghana, which would probably not have shown interest in the earlier, restrictive concerns of Togo. Benin Republic was initially cool to the idea of a new and comprehensive system designed to check illegal movements of goods, currency, and peoples. However, her economy was suffering badly from the continued closure of Nigerian border. A very shrewd man, President Kerekou probably endorsed the negotiations for the agreements on the assumption that that was what Nigeria wanted before agreeing to reopen her land borders.

The negotiations began at the ministerial level. The ministers of External Affairs and Internal Affairs (Interior) of each of the four countries and their officials held the first meeting in Lome, Togo, in June 1984. Our Togolese counterparts and hosts were Dr. Anani Kuma Akakpo-Ahiano (External Affairs) and Kpotivi Lacle (Interior). Lacle was believed to be very powerful and influential in the Togolese government and was also very close to his president. Although Dr. Akakpo-Ahiano presided over the first meetings, it was clear that Lacle was the man to watch. On the Ghanaian side was Kofi Djin (Minister of Interior) and his team; the Ghanaian Foreign Minister was not in Accra at the time and could not attend the meeting. Mr. Djin was a fellow student of mine at London University in the 1960s, although we had not been in contact since we both completed our studies; indeed, I was not aware that he was holding high political office in Ghana. Our personal relation was an asset, since the Nigerian delegation performed a strong mediatory role between the Togolese and Ghanaian delegations, which interacted rather uneasily throughout the deliberations.

The Nigerian delegation was very well prepared for the negotiations and tasks ahead. Although we came with a fairly large team, all the members were experts in different aspects of the business at hand. As Minister of External Affairs, I led the Nigerian delegation, although in the delegation was Major-General Maman Magoro (Minister of Internal Affairs), who should have taken precedence over me as a member of the Supreme Military Council. However, we are close personal friends and this protocol point caused no rift between us. In any case, the four ministers of foreign affairs later constituted the bureau of the meeting, which enabled Major-General Maman Magoro to head the Nigerian delegation at the plenary sessions.

By the end of the meeting, the four countries had agreed on the format and principles to guide the drafting of an eventual agreement. There were several follow-up meetings at the level of officials and two more meetings at the ministerial level before the Quadripartite Agreements were finally ready for signature by the four heads of state. The last meeting for the ministers took place in Lagos on the very morning of 10 December 1984, preparatory to the formal signing that evening. Assisted by my friend and colleage Kofi Djin and the strongman of the PNDC military regime under Rawlings in Ghana, Captain Tsikata, who stood in for the foreign minister of Ghana, I was able to move the meeting to a swift and positive conclusion, having removed the remaining obstacles.

The Quadripartite Agreements were in three parts. In the first, an extradition treaty, the four parties agreed to extradite to each other, on the basis of reciprocity and according to the rules and conditions stated therein, those persons accused or convicted of specific crimes or offenses committed in one country and found in another. Political offenses were excluded from extradition requests. The second agreement concerned criminal investigation cooperation between the four signatory countries. Recognizing the need to mount a multinational fight against the upsurge of crimes that posed serious threats to the security, peace, stability, and development of the West African sub-region, the four countries agreed to cooperate in searching for persons involved in criminal activities.

The third and very crucial part dealt with mutual administrative assistance in customs, trade, and immigration matters. The objective was to combat smuggling and other activities prejudical to the economic, fiscal, and commercial interests of the four countries. Care was taken, however, to place this particular agreement within the framework of ECOWAS. Emphasis was also placed on respect for the equality of signatory countries in the operations of the agreement,which was aimed at promoting the mutual interests of the peoples of the four countries. Smuggling and how to combat it were particularly sensitive issues to Benin and Togo, while Nigeria and Ghana sought strong measures to combat the menace in the sub-region.

The visiting heads of state of Benin Republic, Togo, and Ghana were received by their host, General Buhari, at the Nigerian Institute of International Affairs—venue for the ceremony to sign the agreements, scheduled for 5:00 p.m. on 10 December 1984. All the ministers, senior officials and other dignitaries and invitees and the world press were already seated waiting for the ceremony to commence. Meanwhile, the four heads of state, having all arrived and gone to the reception room, were then to appear collectively for the signing. But thirty minutes passed and they did not show up to sign the agreements. One hour went by. I sensed trouble. This was confirmed when General Buhari sent for me to join the heads of state in the little reception room. There I found out that the heads of state of Togo and Benin, in a move which must have been carefully prearranged, questioned the whole rationale for the Quadripartite Summit meeting. Lieutenant Jerry Rawlings sat speechless, almost motionless, barely concealing his disgust for what he considered unbecoming and obstructionist antics. General Buhari and his number-two man, General Tunde Idiagbon, sitting by him, were perplexed by the fact that, after six months of negotiations by the ministers and officials, the two heads of state were asking why they were in Lagos. Generals Buhari and Idiagbon were trying hard not to let their exasperation show, since they could not afford a spectacular failure.

My immediate hunch was that presidents Eyadema and Kerekou, sensing that Nigeria could not afford to let the meeting collapse, were trying to pressure General Buhari to consider reopening the Nigerian border, which had remained closed since January 1984. This was the prize they apparently wanted to extract from the meeting so that, on return to their respective countries, they could announce this achievement and their triumph. Anyone who knew General Buhari would know that such a tactic would not work. In his view, the decision to close the borders was based on the national interest and could be rescinded only after careful consideration.

As the only minister in attendance at this high-stakes, unscheduled parley of the heads of state, I suggested a compromise. If the heads of state wanted to raise important but extraneous issues with General Buhari, this could be arranged for the next day and could last the whole day if necessary. Meanwhile, the heads of state could proceed to sign the Quadripartite Agreements as scheduled, since all issues directly relating to the agreements had been resolved by the ministers, who must have fully briefed their respective heads of state. Fortunately, this carried.

Interestingly, the two heads of state who most vigorously questioned the signing ceremony were later comfortably seated at the conference venue, carefully reading their prepared statements with the usual fluency one expects from them while facing television cameras. The ceremony went very well; an important milestone in the history of the relationship between Nigeria and her western neighbors was reached. When implemented, the treaty had great possibilities for cooperation while minimizing illegal activities in the sub-region.[2] It was also capable of giving political push to the spirit of ECOWAS and bridging the gap between the anglophone and francophone countries within the organization. One other positive outcome was the fact that not for a long time had the heads of state of Ghana and Togo sat together in one hall. A small step was thus taken toward improving the bilateral relationship between the two feuding states whose leaders appeared to genuinely mistrust and dislike one another.

For Nigeria, this was a diplomatic triumph. Without giving in to a precipitate reopening of the country's borders, it somehow laid the foundation for making border closures unnecessary. Nigeria was so satisfied with the Quadripartite Agreements that the Federal Military Government directed that negotiations be commenced immediately to extend their spirit and substance to Niger and Chad. This was, however, not accomplished before the termination of the Buhari administration.

NOTES

1. See Claude Phillips Jr., *Development of Nigerian Foreign Policy* (Evanston: Northwestern University Press, 1964).
2. A full text of the Quadripartite Agreements is in Appendix 2.

5

Irritants in Relations with Neighboring Countries

Two major decisions taken by the Buhari administration developed into serious irritants in Nigeria's relationship with countries in the sub-region: the closure of the land borders and the expulsion of illegal aliens. Neither the legality of these measures nor the purely national considerations behind them were seriously questioned by most analysts and commentators. Nonetheless, these decisions did not promote good-neighborliness. On the contrary, they may have undermined the spirit of ECOWAS and our leadership pretensions, not only in the sub-region but on the continent as a whole.

It is ironic, however, that notwithstanding these two decisions taken to promote Nigeria's national interests, our country was asked to host the first Quadripartite Summit meeting, attended by Nigeria and her immediate neighbors to the west. As noted earlier, the meeting was successful. Far-reaching agreements were signed in Lagos and General Buhari was installed as chairman of the follow-up arrangements to implement the provisions of the agreements. In the same vein, the Nigerian head of state was to assume the chairmanship of ECOWAS at the end of the community's summit meeting in Lome, Togo, in November 1984. General Buhari declined the honor at that time due to a pressing domestic schedule (he was to begin extensive visits to the nineteen states of Nigeria). However, he agreed to be the next chairman of ECOWAS when this nomination was renewed at the summit meeting in Lome in July 1985—just a few months after the mass expulsion of illegal aliens from Nigeria.

Perhaps it was a testimony to the collective wisdom of the leaders of our sub-region that General Buhari was made chairman of the Quadripartite Agreements and later of ECOWAS, precisely to encourage Nigeria to reopen her land borders and to induce more community-mindedness. In any case, the pursuit of firm nationalist policies toward other countries in the sub-region did not lead to Nigeria's isolation. It may well be, of course, that these countries and the multilateral organizations in the sub-region could not afford the isolation of Nigeria. They worked hard to coax the Buhari administration out of pursuing restrictive nationalist policies which adversely affected them.

Benin Republic, which felt the impact of the border closure most strongly, made passionate pleas to the Nigerian authorities to reopen the border as early as 11 January 1984. The occasion was the visit to Cotonou by General Bali, Minister of Defence, to explain the reasons for the change of government in Nigeria and to sketch the external politics of the new military regime. Recognizing Nigeria's concern about illegal activities, which dominated bilateral trade and other interactions between his country and ours, President Kerekou assured General Bali that Benin's security agencies would actively assist in apprehending smugglers and currency traffickers. The host president, however, argued that only with the reopening of the border could normal activities be resumed between Benin and Nigeria, especially in the border areas.

Similarly, President Kountche of Niger made strong representations, through the visiting defense minister, to the highest leadership of the new regime in Nigeria on the border issue. The closure of the land border was adversely affecting Niger's economy, which depended almost entirely on Nigeria for supplies of petrol and petroleum products. Severe shortages of these essential items were already manifest in Niger. In a parting message sent through the visiting defense minister, the host president made the passionate declaration that "Nigeria will continue to find her proper place in Africa and the world [as a whole] economically and politically. Don't let Nigeria down. If you do, the whole of Africa is down." His point was that the destiny of Nigeria remains inextricably linked to the destiny of other African countries. Sometimes, however, this point seems to be more clearly understood outside Nigeria than inside it.

The closure of the Nigerian border also affected Chad in direct and urgent ways. The French were particularly concerned and so were the Americans. President Reagan sent General Vernon Walters, then roving ambassador and later United States Permanent Representative to the United Nations, to Lagos twice with the special mission of persuading the new administration to reopen the borders or at least allow urgent supplies and relief materials to pass through Nigeria to Chad.

General Walters had an unenviable reputation as a special envoy, usually sent by the United States to twist the arms of recalcitrant foreign governments or to convey unpleasant news. Even when bearing ominous messages, General Walters always remained pleasant. He was to recall several times later a particularly amusing anecdote which took place during one of his visits to Lagos as President Reagan's special envoy. During the initial meeting with General Buhari, General Walters recalled the very first visit he had made to Nigeria during World War II in 1942. In his reply, General Buhari recalled that he too visited Nigeria for the first time in 1942! And looking across the room to where I was sitting, General Buhari added that his foreign minister had not even visited Nigeria by then!

By the time General Walters came to Nigeria for the second time, we had agreed that the United States could use the facilities in Port Harcourt as well as Calabar to convey supplies, petroleum, and relief materials through our country to their destination in Chad. However, for security and other reasons, we did not agree to the United States' request to allow the use of Lagos as the main port for the off-loading and transit of these materials to Chad. Our land borders remained closed as a general principle. One lesson of these U.S. interventions was that our nationalism could not prevent a powerful state on which Nigeria had come to be economically dependent from achieving its strongly pursued aims. This has wide implications for the future of our country's foreign policy, especially in dealing with the West.

What, then, were the main reasons for the decision to close the Nigerian border and for keeping it closed in spite of external pressures? Security considerations were almost certainly paramount, especially at the initial period of the military administration's assumption of power. It was strongly believed by the new regime and some other Nigerians that some of the politicians of the Second Republic, who were on the list of most wanted persons, had gone into hiding with the intention to flee Nigeria by land through the neighboring countries. However, the economic dimension was the more important consideration. The activities of smugglers and currency traffickers were very damaging to the Nigerian economy. Severe loss of revenue took place whenever goods of Nigerian origin were illegally exported through neighboring countries—especially Benin, Niger, and Chad. There was also large-scale but unrecorded flight of Nigerian currency into these neighboring countries which made it virtually impossible to know the exact volume of our currency in circulation at any one time. Under such circumstances, it would be futile for the government in Nigeria to adopt new monetary policies for revamping the country's battered economy. That might well have been why the new government also decided to change the color of the currency, so that old notes could be recalled and effective public policies could then be adopted based on the data relating to the exact volume of new currency to be released for circulation.

Furthermore, there was an uneasy feeling in high government circles that our neighbors were cheating Nigeria twice over. Initially, their citizens effectively devalued our currency through extensive currency trafficking. Then, with the heavily devalued *naira*, they purchased legal as well as contraband goods from Nigeria, especially those goods which our country imported with increasingly scarce foreign exchange earnings. The Nigerian government therefore felt that the land borders should be opened only after establishing a new system of trade between our neighbors and checking the abuses.

Finally, the new administration reasoned that its predecessor regime had collapsed in large part from the leadership's inability or unwillingness to take tough decisions to manage the economy, especially in the face of declining oil revenues. Hence, one of the first duties of the new rulers was to adopt measures to put the economy back on track, and the closure of the border was one such corrective measure. In that context we explained to our neighbors that much as the border closure was a regrettable inconvenience to them, the collapse of the Nigerian economy would be even more catastrophic for their economies. Incidentally, France, which appeared to understand this logic very clearly and took several steps to aid the recovery of the battered Nigerian economy, had the strategic objective of protecting the economies of our francophone neighbors. These steps included increasing the purchase of Nigerian petroleum and assisting in our negotiations with the IMF.

Still, the continued closure of the land border was reaching a point of diminishing returns to Nigeria's diplomatic standing, especially in the West African sub-region. After the first few months of the closure, it was difficult to demonstrate that smuggling and other illegal activities were on the decrease in the border areas. Indeed, the closure of the border for an indefinite period was clearly enriching the perpetrators of illegal activities while also corrupting the military and other security officers posted for patrol duties.

The heads of state of the neighboring countries, careful not to challenge Nigeria's sovereign right to close the land border, seized every opportunity available to register their displeasure. Mention has already been made of the attempt by presidents Eyadema of Togo and Kerekou of Benin Republic to link the reopening of the border with their consent to sign the Quadripartite Agreements in Lagos. Although the impasse that developed on that occasion was broken and the agreements were then signed by the four heads of state, the two visiting presidents remained sour about the issue. President Eyadema's point was not lost on General Buhari when he said that delegates to the next ministerial meeting of the Quadripartite Agreements, scheduled for June 1985 in Lagos, should be able to travel by road!

President Kerekou was even more vigorous in his appeal for the reopening of the land border during the private talks he held in Lagos with General Buhari on 9 and 10 December 1984. The visiting president reiterated assurances that his country had not and would never allow anyone to operate against the security of Nigeria. He felt, however, that Nigeria did not fully appreciate the hardships which Benin was experiencing as a result of the border closure but promised that, on his part, the Quadripartite Agreements just signed in Lagos would be put into immediate operation in Benin Republic.

It must have been particularly irritating to Benin Republic that despite the assurances made by their president, the border with Nigeria remained closed throughout the tenure of the Buhari administration. Nonetheless, Benin and other neighboring countries knew that they probably needed Nigeria more than the other way around. They accepted but never liked the situation whereby the borders would be opened only on Nigeria's terms. This bad situation was made worse in the eyes of our ECOWAS neighbours as a result of the purely national decision made in 1985 to expel aliens illegally residing in Nigeria.

These aliens were largely citizens of Ghana and, to a lesser extent, Benin Republic, Togo, and Niger. The mass expulsion order and the chaos and confusion that characterized the tail end of the exercise deepened the strain in Nigeria's relationship with her neighbors. Moreover, the experience of an earlier mass expulsion of Ghanaian and other citizens of ECOWAS, which took place during the civilian regime in 1983, was neither pleasant nor positive. Apart from the international media coverage of the event, which was quite damaging to our external image, the reality was that many of the aliens involved had returned and new ones came from the same countries to work in Nigeria.

The reactions of the neighboring countries and the international community to the latest expulsion order by Nigeria were swift, instructive, and generally uncomplimentary. Although Ghana's official position on Nigeria's closure of the border was sympathetic, the same was not so with respect to the expulsion of their citizens. The Ghanaian leader, Lieutenant Jerry Rawlings, remained suspicious of President Eyadema in particular and also President Kerekou. He considered the leaders of both francophone countries as partners in their endeavors to undermine the security and prosperity of their respective neighbors, Ghana and Nigeria. As far as he was concerned, Nigeria could keep her borders closed as long as possible if considerations of national security and economic recovery demanded it. Perhaps Ghana's only moderation on the border issue concerned the long-term damage which closures of international borders might cause for ECOWAS—especially regarding the provisions for the eventual free movement of goods and peoples.

However, on the aliens expulsion issues, Ghanaian opinion toward Nigeria was far less benign. In the government-owned *Ghanaian Times*, an editorial captioned "Give Them More Time" commented that Nigeria's failure to extend the deadline for completion of the expulsion exercise created conditions which were intentionally punitive to the immigrants.[1]

The small amounts of money which the expelled immigrants were allowed to take out of Nigeria and the dehumanizing conditions under which they lived prior to the expulsions across the border were also criticized.[2] A much tougher editorial captioned "PNDC Must Protest" asked, "For how long and how many times [will] Nigerian governments resort to this quit order?"[3] The paper further reminded Nigerian authorities that Ghana was also capable of retaliating but was restrained by her deep commitment to the spirit of ECOWAS.[4]

In Niger, official and unofficial opinion did not appear unduly disturbed by the expulsion order. There was no public word of criticism levelled against Nigeria in the country's main newspaper, *Le Sahel*. Reactions in Ivory Coast were also generally muted. Guinea apparently did not object to the Nigerian decision, which was based on the claim of sovereignty and the right to take certain economic measures, but feared that "Lagos never perceived the impact of [this] policy on the future of OAU."[5] The comments in the Senegalese government-owned *Le Soleil*, however, were highly critical of the way Nigeria handled the expulsion of aliens.[6]

The reports in the Togo daily *Nouvelle Marche* were generally balanced. The newspaper carried both the Benin and Nigerian accounts of the border incidents surrounding the exit of the illegal aliens. For example, quoting foreign wire services, the newspaper reported that four aliens were killed at the border and that about 25,000 aliens camped at a pilgrim (Hajj) camp at Ikeja Airport, preparatory to their exit, went on a wild rampage there and destroyed telephone exchanges and electric equipment while pillaging stores.[7] However, quoting *Ehuzu* newspaper in Benin, the Togolese paper also reported that 40 persons including children were killed when Nigerian law-enforcement agents opened fire on immigrants trying to cross the border at Seme post—an allegation vigorously denied by Nigeria.[8]

Benin Republic initially closed its border with Nigeria during the expulsion exercise for fear of being saddled with illegal aliens. Speaking through the government paper *Ehuzu*, the authorities said that their country lacked the capability to handle the immigrants even on a transit basis.[9] Foreign Minister Frederick Affo made urgent appeals to international organizations to assist Benin in handling the immigrants.[10] These appeals were accompanied by deliberately self-serving and probably highly exaggerated accounts of the misery and deaths of immigrants at the border. According to one such account by Benin officials, 40 people including children died when exasperated immigrants drove their vehicles into Benin territory and the Nigerian security officers opened fire on them. When the credibility of the Benin officials was challenged, their government invited all ambassadors and representatives of international organizations resident in Cotonou to visit the border posts of Krate/Seme and Idiroko/Igolo on 11 May 1985, to see things for themselves.

Benin was attempting to portray Nigeria negatively and publicize the unfortunate conditions of aliens in distress as they were trying to leave Nigeria before the expiration of the deadline. Benin already had a grudge against Nigeria arising from the border closure. Some observers in Benin's capital believed that the accounts of the immigrants' sufferings were deliberately exaggerated to appeal to the conscience of international relief agencies to render assistance to Benin.

The Western press also covered the issue extensively, as they are disposed to do whenever unfortunate or tragic events occur in Africa. The major Western newspapers attributed Nigerian action against the aliens to falling oil prices which slowed the economy, and hence foreigners were seen as depriving citizens of jobs while also contributing to the increase in the crime rate in Nigeria. Surprisingly, however, the *New York Times* praised the Nigerian government for serious efforts to avoid the violence which marked the 1983 expulsions.[11] The *Washington Post* went further to state that "instead of the harassments and violence of 1983, Nigerian officials, this time, were providing tents, water and medical assistance to the immigrants."[12]

In Britain, the *Guardian* observed that "the Administration of General Buhari, already seen by its critics as vindictive and oppressive in some areas, is actually sensitive to world opinion."[13] The reporting by the *Times* of London was generally factual and fair,[14] while *Le Monde* of France carried exaggerated reports concerning the incident between the police in Nigeria and aliens who were trying to escape from the transit camp in Ikeja.[15] In Canada, the *Globe and Mail* wrote a very scathing editorial titled "Leaving Nigeria" in which Nigeria's action was contrasted with her championing of the cause of Pan-African solidarity.[16] The Italian newspaper *Il Giornale* reported that policemen on the Nigerian border stripped the departing immigrants of all their possessions and savings, but agreed that "the scenes of chaos and physical violence that transformed the exodus in 1983 into a march of death were not repeated this time."[17] Finally, in this sample of opinion from the Western press, the Dutch newspaper *Nieuwe Rotterdamse Courant* reported that the causes of crime and religious disturbances in Nigeria could not be linked exclusively to the aliens but argued that the government's expulsion order was completely within the law and regulations of ECOWAS.[18] In general, the external reporting of the expulsion was not complimentary.

Nonetheless, the expulsion and the closure of the border often provided relief for the Nigerian government if not the populace as a whole, although the relief turned out to be more psychological than real. The expulsion, like the prolonged closure of the national borders, never really solved the underlying problems of the unequal distribution of wealth and economic opportunities among countries. As long as there are poles of relatively high economic growth in one or more countries, these will attract people and goods, especially from the less well-to-do countries. Only through common commitment to change and the tackling of problems in a spirit of give and take can the negative aspects of the relationship between economically unequal neighbors be minimized.

The United States will need to realize this point in dealing with the problems of immigrants from Mexico and other Latin American countries and the Caribbean. France and Germany will have to do the same in respect to immigrants from Southern European and North African countries. And this lesson has to be learnt by Nigeria in dealing with her neighbors in the West African sub-region. To accomplish this, there is need for foresight and community-mindedness by the leaders and people of Nigeria. It is possible to balance the pursuit of national interests with tolerance of aliens, especially through the development of a more diversified and high-growth economy in Nigeria.

Unfortunately, the Ministry of External Affairs was not really consulted in the decision to close the border and it was also not fully involved in the decision to expel illegal aliens on a mass scale. The decision to close the border, made by the Supreme Military Council, took effect concurrently with the coming into power of the new military government under Buhari. That was understandable. However, in the expulsion of illegal aliens, the Ministry of External Affairs' involvement was peripheral and its input was made as a less than enthusiastic junior partner to the Ministry of Internal Affairs. For example, out of the 21 or so participants in the two meetings between Nigerian officials and the ambassadors of some of the neighboring countries convened to discuss the expulsion issue, which took place on 2 and 15 May 1985, presided over by the Minister of Internal Affairs, only one was from the External Affairs Ministry.

External Affairs did its best to minimize the damage to Nigeria by using our principal representatives abroad and the ambassadors of foreign countries who were resident in Lagos. Particular efforts were directed at the countries in the ECOWAS sub-region, for obvious reasons.

The neighboring countries have exercised considerable tolerance of Nigerian decisions that have often brought enormous difficulties to them. This may be because they have little or no real choice except to continue to deal with their relatively bigger and more affluent neighbor, or because they have not always been completely blameless in dealing with Nigeria. However, there are limits, which may well relate, for example, to the duration of the closure of the border and the number of times we engage in the mass expulsion of citizens of other countries of the sub-region. There are growing possibilities of retaliatory actions by some of these countries.[19] Prolonged closure of our border and repeated mass expulsions could hurt Nigeria's long-run national interests at ECOWAS and OAU as much as, if not more than, they hurt our neighbors.

These major irritants in the relationship between Nigeria and her neighbors do not necessarily invalidate the new conceptual framework for our country's foreign policy with the approved emphasis on concentric circles of national interests. However, they clearly illustrate the problems of bringing diplomatic practice in line with new policy concepts. The challenge is not to abandon a sound conceptual framework but to work for an enduring symmetry between such concepts and the implementation of policies that follow from them.

NOTES

1. *Ghanaian Times*, 9 May 1985.
2. Ibid.
3. *Free Press*, 26 April 1985.
4. Ibid.
5. *Horoya*, 14 May 1985.
6. *Le Soleil*, 10 May 1985.
7. *Nouvelle Marche*, 14 May 1985.
8. Ibid., 17 May 1985.
9. *Ehuzu*, 6 May 1985.
10. Ibid.
11. *New York Times*, 4 May 1985.
12. *Washington Post*, 19 May 1985.
13. The *Guardian*, 25 April 1985.
14. The *Times*, 15 May 1985.
15. *Le Monde*, 15 May 1985.
16. *Globe and Mail*, 17 May 1985.
17. *Il Giornale*, 10 May 1985.
18. *Nieuwe Rotterdamse Courant*, 8 May 1985.
19. Burkina Faso made an attempt to give Nigeria a taste of her own medicine by rounding up our citizens resident in Ouagadougou, with the apparent intention of expelling them in sympathy with Ghana. However, Buhari's government protested that at no time did Nigeria ever round up or expel all aliens working in Nigeria. We expelled only those aliens illegally residing in our country. In response to this protest and the announcement of our readiness to receive all Nigerians that may be rightly or wrongly expelled by Burkina Faso, the authorities in Ouagadougou relented and left our citizens alone—at least for the time being.

6

ECOWAS: Theory, Practice, and Prospects

The perceived gains made by the European Economic Community since its establishment in 1957, have attracted Third World nations wishing to pursue economic integration in their respective regions. As a consequence, traditional Western theories of integration have often been applied in justifying or evaluating integration efforts being made in the developing regions of the world.[1] Such traditional theories of integration, however, with concomitant emphases on the customs union and its impact on trade creation or trade diversion, are usually of limited relevance to regional integration in developing countries.[2] For these countries, the major rationale for regional integration lies less in the potential benefits to be derived from changes in existing patterns of trade or production than in the impact of proposed regional markets on fundamental socioeconomic and even political problems.

Put simply, integration efforts in developing countries represent the triumph of hope for a better economic future over their experiences of a generally grim economic present. The possibilities of economies of scale, investment opportunities from internal and external sources, and the consequent mobilization of unemployed or underemployed human and physical resources through regional integration point to brighter futures in industrial development. However, the fact that agriculture remains the primary economic activity in most of the developing regions of the world means that a system of agricultural rationalization and development should also be emphasized in integration arrangements.

The political factors need to be considered as well in analyzing the major motivations for economic integration in the Third World. Collective self-reliance is as much a political clarion call as an economic rationale in the pursuit of regional integration schemes. In reality, the degree of commitment to the political dimension of integration varies in different parts of the Third World.

It is from the totality of these motivations and objectives that one can usefully evaluate integration efforts in developing regions of the world. Such a holistic viewpoint provides a more adequate analytical tool than conventional customs-union theory, derived from classical comparative cost considerations based on the experience of West European economies.

In the West African sub-region, the benefits from economic integration appear obvious. There is the clear potential for creating a strong industrial base through a structured program of regional industrial development, based on region-wide investment policies and a common policy on the location of industries. The immediate benefits of such a regional industrial program could be greater output and a reduction in the high rate of unemployment and underemployment, especially in the urban centers of West Africa. Furthermore, a serious program for rationalization of commercial and cash-crop production in the sub-region could raise the income of farmers engaged in the production of the wide range of crops there (cocoa, groundnuts, cotton, coffee, and rubber, to name just a few).

Cooperative exploitation, consumption, and the export of mineral resources could also expand production and wealth while reducing costs. Similarly, cooperation in transport and communication as well as other infrastructure facilities in may reduce costs, avoid unnecessary duplications, facilitate higher levels of trading activities, and perhaps even generate a new pattern or direction of trade. Furthermore, the land-locked states of West Africa, which are among the world's poorest countries, would be able to reduce their transportation and general developmental problems by being part of a functioning regional economic community.

In spite of these potential advantages of integration, the journey toward establishing the Economic Community of West African States (ECOWAS) and the eventual signing of the treaty which gave birth to it in Lagos on 27 May 1975 was tortuous. Several objections, reservations, obstacles, and foot-draggings involving member states prevented a smooth delivery of ECOWAS. After almost ten years of existence, whose anniversary coincided with the Buhari administration in Nigeria, the progress made by ECOWAS remains rather slow.

Indeed, the two main pillars upon which ECOWAS was built appear to be shaking rather badly. These are trade liberalization (Article 2 [2] of the treaty) and free movement of people (Article 27). The agreed schedule for the implementation of trade liberation has been seriously delayed. Originally proposed to be in place within 15 years, taking effect from May 1975, the various phases of trade liberalization were to culminate in the elimination of all tariff and non-tariff barriers for unprocessed products and industrial goods.

There are a number of reasons for the delay in implementing the trade liberalization. First, new objections were raised by CEAO—the competing sub-regional integration arrangement exclusive to the francophone states in West Africa—and the Mano River Union. Both organizations repeatedly called for preferential treatment in the trade relations between them, outside of the ECOWAS arrangements, and timetables for liberalization. Second, there were considerable difficulties in agreeing to a Common External Tariff (CET), which is essential for any meaningful liberalization. Third, tariffs have always made significant revenue contributions to the national treasuries of member states, hence their reduction and elimination do not appeal to many members. In 1973 the United Nations estimated that in West Africa custom duties constituted a share of total governmental revenue ranging from 35 percent in the Ivory Coast to 50 percent in Gambia.[3] This proportion has not really changed since then. Fourth, the generally poor performance of the economies of member states has not encouraged an active commitment on their part toward trade liberalization.

Another casualty of the low level of economic activity in West Africa, especially in the late 1970s and early 1980s, was the implementation of Article 27 and the free movement of peoples. When the economies of the West African countries picked up, there were few obstacles to the movement of people, but during downturns ECOWAS members tended to adopt restrictive national policies which frustrated movement and retarded the momentum toward integration in the sub-region. For example, Nigeria and Ghana have at different times closed their respective national borders. In addition, Nigeria and some other countries in the sub-region engage in mass or sporadic expulsions of ECOWAS citizens living or working in their countries. Unfortunately, the poor performance of the economies of member states of ECOWAS since the mid-1970s has been compounded by repeated or prolonged incidences of natural disasters—flood, and desertification—all of which require external assistance to ameliorate and thus perpetuate the dependence which ECOWAS was designed to remove or minimize.

Notwithstanding these adverse conditions, ECOWAS has made progress in some important areas. Several commissions have been working deligently on transport and communications, energy and industry, trade and agriculture.[4] With respect to agriculture, for instance, the interesting concept emerged of pursuing ecological complementarity of production in the sub-region. Parallel to the Equator are four major ecological zones in West Africa: equatorial, tropical and humid, tropical dry or Sudan, and Sahelian. Each zone reflects different production activities which could form the basis for potential agricultural and economic complementarity in ECOWAS. For example, the northern zone, specializing in animal and cereal production, provides opportunities for cooperation between producers of these commodities within and outside that zone, just as the southern humid zone specializes in root and other crops and provides a basis for intra- and inter-zonal exchanges.[5]

The prerequisites for a common agricultural policy were spelled out. Emphases were to be placed by member states on food production aimed at reducing or eliminating the importation of food from outside the sub-region; the multiplication of seeds through the efforts of the research institutes in West Africa; a strategic food-products storage system; the joint financing of agricultural projects; a redirection of trade from export orientation to internal market; a coordinated policy for external market while taking advantage of high added value through processing into semi-finished or even finished products wherever possible; and an emergency and support fund for agriculture and a permanent framework for the coordination of efforts by ECOWAS ministers of agriculture.

The Energy Sub-Commission also had the very bright idea of a Common Energy Policy (CEP) and an ECOWAS Energy Development Program for short-, medium-, and long-term purposes. Such new ideas are needed, because the situations of oil-importing ECOWAS members are reaching alarming proportions. Some countries in the sub-region spend more than 70 percent of their export earnings on oil importation. Under such circumstances, which restrict development and threaten economic survival, some ECOWAS members are tempted to resort to wood and charcoal for fuel, an alternative that has led to the disappearance of forests, higher prices for such energy sources, and severe damage to the already delicate ecological balance, especially in the Sahel. The Energy Sub-Commission suggested to member states the adoption of several phases for the execution of short-, medium- and long-term programs for energy conservation, the reduction of oil imports from outside the region, and the development of alternative sources of energy from methanol, solar power, and ocean thermal conversion.

Another area in which important efforts were made by the ECOWAS Council of Ministers relates to the definition of community enterprises. The main objective was to enable such enterprises in member states to enjoy most-favored-nation treatment regarding industrial, financial, and other incentives. There would also be guarantees of the right of such enterprises to operate in sectors previously reserved for national enterprises.

The negotiations leading to the acceptance of the definition of community enterprises have been difficult, owing to attempts by members of ECOWAS to protect their national advantages. Nonetheless, it was agreed in principle that qualification as a community enterprise would occur if: (a) not less than 51 percent of the equity holding of the capital of the enterprise is vested in citizens, entities, governments, or agencies of two or more of members states; (b) a majority of the board of directors or an equivalent body are citizens of member states; (c) its operations affect two or more member states; (d) its capital in local currency is not less than 200,000 units of account and, where the investment is to be made in an industrially less developed region of the community, not less than 150,000 units of account, and (e) its purposes would promote the development policies and programs of the community.

On a different matter, for which the ECOWAS treaty made no provisions, steps were taken to strengthen the common defense of member states. The leaders of the community sought special arrangements to enhance internal security as well as collective regional security. A Special ministerial commission was constituted with the mandate to produce a draft protocol on mutual assistance on Defense. The commission produced the protocol, which was later adopted by the Authority of Heads of State of ECOWAS in May 1980. The mutual defense arrangements arose out of a feeling of insecurity largely domestic in nature but sometimes induced or aggravated by external military or paramilitary interventions. Togo, Benin Republic, Sierra Leone, and Liberia showed particular concern.

Provisions were made in the Protocol on Mutual Defence for institutions such as the Authority of Heads of State (the supreme decision-making body), which could delegate power to a defense council made up of ministers of foreign affairs, Defense or any other ministers as the case may be. The defense council, acting in times of crisis, was to be served by a defense commission, basically a technical body, as well as a management body to be headed by a deputy executive secretary of ECOWAS.

In addition, Community Armed Forces (CAF), consisting of units earmarked in each national army, would be placed at the disposal of the commander-in-chief, who would function as in a national army and be appointed by the Authority of Heads of State. The conditions for intervention by CAF were also clearly spelt out. An act of aggression by a third country against a community member must occur before intervention by CAF. With regards to conflict between two members sates, intervention by CAF could only take place at the request of a belligerent state, or, failing that, the defense council could decide to request intervention if the conflict affected the security of the sub-region. CAF would not intervene in purely internal conflicts unless such conflicts were being sustained from outside the sub-region.

The protocols have not yet been put to the practical test. There would probably be considerable difficulties in implementing the provisions of the mutual defense protocol. Meanwhile, member states prefer to rely on traditional allies inside and outside the sub-region to deal with threats to their national security and defense. Nonetheless, by adopting this protocol, ECOWAS was responding to the changing needs of its members. There are, however, several dangers arising from this particular focus on defense. First,

CAF may, when operational, cause discord among members; second, the key purpose of ECOWAS, which is the eventual establishment of a Common Market, may be pushed to the background; third, the problems of African continental defense and security (especially colonialism and apartheid in Southern Africa) may take back seats while organizations such as ECOWAS engage in their own arrangements for sub-regional defense.

We may now ask what role Nigeria should continue to play in moving ECOWAS toward the attainment of its principal and long-term objectives. Nigeria is expected to play a role in the community commensurate with its size and population. This is for the benefit of ECOWAS as a whole and also for the long-term economic, political, and security interests of Nigeria. The assessment made by the Buhari administration regarding ECOWAS was that several obstacles still remained in the community's efforts to promote regional economic integration and development. These were the results of years of division in the sub-region between anglophone and francophone countries. Unfortunately, these divisions also tended to be perpetrated by former colonial powers, most especially France, even after the establishment of ECOWAS.

The ministers concerned with ECOWAS matters under General Buhari also felt that another obstacle in the community's efforts toward accelerated integration was the continuing reluctance of some member states to give up the known for the unknown. Several members were unwilling to leave the benefits of bilateral relations with countries outside our sub-region or membership in an exclusive economic community like CEAO for an ECOWAS that represents a promise for the future.

The Buhari administration believed, however, that ECOWAS could move forward much faster if member states would implement the protocols and agreements which had been signed during several summit meetings of the heads of state and government of ECOWAS. We used every available opportunity to press the argument that members of the community should view their national interests in a wider perspective and that a more prosperous ECOWAS, an ECOWAS that promoted greater trade between member states and also tried to modify the direction of existing trade from intercontinental to intra-regional, would bring more lasting benefits to our respective countries.

Although Nigeria's relationship with her immediate neighboring countries was soured by the closure of our land borders in 1984–85, efforts were made to repair the relationship by putting them on more formalized and mutually beneficial bases. Meanwhile, Nigeria worked hard to develop friendly ties with Togo, Ghana, Sierra Leone, Senegal, Gambia, Cape Verde, Liberia, and Burkina Faso. Through extensive consultations and dialogue, as well as concessionary terms for the export of our crude oil, General Buhari's administration developed close ties with the leadership of these countries. All the heads of state of the above-named members of ECOWAS made official or states visits to Nigeria. These high-level contacts and the understanding which grew from them helped to promote the holding of two successful summit meetings of ECOWAS during Buhari's tenure of office. Furthermore, the visits to Nigeria and the official discussions induced positive attitudes toward Nigeria which softened the negative impact of our border closing and mass expulsion of aliens.

Still, the seventh summit of ECOWAS, which took place in November 1984 in Lome, Togo, was characterized by tensions. First of all, the community had no chairman and the summit should have met several months earlier according to its statutory provisions. The death of President Sekou Toure of Guinea was responsible for both of these situations. Second, there were several important statutory positions in ECOWAS which were to become vacant by the end of 1984. These included the top positions in the community, such as the Executive Secretary and Managing Director of the Fund. There was keen competition by member states to fill these posts—especially the post of Managing Director of the Fund in view of important capital projects soon to be embarked upon by ECOWAS. Third, resentment of Nigeria appeared to be growing within the community, especially from some members of CEAO, owing to the perception that Nigeria was trying to move the community too far and too fast. There was also a controversy over the high cost of rent for secretariat staff in Lagos and allegations of unfavorable living conditions in the Nigerian capital. Those who pushed these concerns even threatened that, unless conditions improved in Lagos, the headquarters of ECOWAS might be removed to Togo where the Fund was located.

However, the reality was that Nigeria faithfully contributed one-third of both the ECOWAS annual budget and the paid-up capital of the community fund. Successive Nigerian governments also subsidized the operations of the secretariat in Lagos and provided loan funds to assist ECOWAS pay the rent of several of its staff members in the Nigerian capital. Nonetheless, General Buhari complemented a hard-hitting opening speech with a low-profile appearance and contributions to the 1984 summit meeting. This helped to reduce tensions. Indeed, at the end of the summit meeting, Nigeria was proposed for the chairmanship of the community for the following year.

We discussed several major issues at the summit. One of the most touchy was the review of the Protocol on Free Movement of Persons. The implementation of this protocol would have caused severe problems for Nigeria. Therefore, the first phase of the protocol was, at the instance of Nigeria, extended for another two years. Although Nigeria was current in the payment of her contributions to the two main organs of the community, most other member states continued to default in the payment of theirs. Liberia and Burkina Faso were among the worst offenders. Nonetheless, the summit approved a budget of U.A.5,070,929 for the secretariat and U.A.4,870,797 for the Fund.

Another divisive issue was the derogation from the Single Trade Liberalization Scheme for Industrial Products. Members of CEAO and the Mano River Union—two sub-groupings in the ECOWAS region—asked for exemptions until a later date when they would be better able to implement the scheme. This was turned down because it was felt that the Single Trade Liberalization Scheme for Industrial Products need not threaten the existence of CEAO and MRU, as the experience of Benelux within the EEC framework proved. However, a concession was made to CEAO and MRU members to the effect that a working group was to be constituted with chairmen of the Councils of Ministers of the three organizations as members and serviced by experts from member states as well as the three respective secretariats to monitor the progress of the trade liberalization scheme.

On the matter of the community enterprises, Nigeria took active part in the preparation of the protocol. In view of Nigeria's Public investments in some ECOWAS member states (Benin, Senegal, Guinea, Niger) and interest in preventing unfair competition from other countries against her own private industries, efforts were made to limit the application of the protocol to joint ventures with government participation, however minimal these might be. The door was left open to extend the provisions of the protocol to wholly privately owned enterprises under special conditions. The lingering fear was that the interests of foreign multinational corporations might be enhanced at the expense of indigenous enterprises in the community, unless a careful watch was made when the protocol became fully operational.

The proposals for the summit to adopt a Lome Declaration on Economic Recovery in West Africa were non-controversial and the declaration was so adopted. The declaration enjoined member states to implement all previous decisions taken by the community, called for pursuit of realistic national economic policies, and suggested the establishment of a ministerial consultative committee to coordinate national development efforts and to monitor the implementation of the declaration. One more declaration would not hurt but another committee could well become a costly duplication for the community.

Finally, the summit examined the report prepared by the Economic Commission for Africa (ECA), at the instance of a previous meeting of ECOWAS heads of state, concerning the rationalization of economic integration in West Africa. There are about 40 inter-governmental organizations in our sub-region and the task was to find a suitable system to rationalize them in the overall interest of West Africa. Nigeria's position was that ECOWAS should be allowed to become the principal organ for the pursuit of economic cooperation. New organs should be discouraged as much as possible and existing intergovernmental organizations should be streamlined so as to avoid the diffusion of effort and the dissipation of energy. Unfortunately, various intergovernmental organizations discussed in the ECA report were prepared to fight at national and sub-regional levels in order to preserve their independent existence. The community would still need to make hard decisions on this issue.

In all, the Nigerian government expressed great satisfaction with the outcome of the ECOWAS summit in Lome.[6] All the vacant statutory posts in the community were filled. The heads of state decided, in a closed meeting, that ECOWAS members which had not previously provided senior officers to the community should be given opportunity to occupy the vacant posts. For instance, Sierra Leone was to provide the next Executive Secretary of ECOWAS. Mr. Monu was accordingly appointed to that post. The summit also took decisions which strengthened the ECOWAS Fund and endorsed the establishment of ECOBANK as a commercial banking concern with the objective of speeding up economic and commercial integration.

Notwithstanding this general satisfaction with the outcome of the 1984 summit, Nigeria found itself on the defensive, especially on the issue of her border closure. General Buhari had to appeal for the understanding of those member states adversely affected by our decision. Although he agreed to assume chairmanship of ECOWAS following the 8th summit of the community, also in Lome, in July 1985, General Buhari was made fully aware of the great expectations that other members continued to entertain about Nigeria's positive role in ECOWAS.

It will be difficult to sustain such expectations if Nigeria continues to adopt national policies, however defensible at the time, which nonetheless appear to weaken her commitment to ECOWAS. This is perhaps why there is a need to develop a strong support group or fairly widespread constituency for ECOWAS within Nigeria. The implementation of the ECOWAS treaty and protocols has immediate, medium-, and long-term consequences for the socioeconomic and political life of Nigerian citizens, in which case, it should be possible to mobilize support for ECOWAS issues among the informed public that could serve as a pressure group on the government. At present, there is a National Commission on ECOWAS but this is a restricted body dominated largely by government officials. A larger body consisting of nongovernmental people (from business, labor, and academe) needs to be established. Such an enlarged and more diversified group would be better placed to make imaginative recommendations to the Nigerian Government, and may also assist in moving our country toward greater regional community-mindedness without sacrificing our national interests.

In a widely publicized article on Nigeria's role in ECOWAS, written in May

1978, the point was made that our country was merely paying the community piper without questioning the tune.[7] This was rather simplistic, because the leadership role in an international organization does not necessarily confer the right always to dictate the tune. Moreover, Nigeria appears rather unsure of what tune to call for ECOWAS, even after several years of the community's existence. In any case, the problem of our country's policies toward ECOWAS in the 1980s appears to be one of paying the community piper but sometimes singing discordant tunes. A serious re-thinking of what Nigeria expects to give and receive from ECOWAS must be made in official and private circles.

Finally, it is possible to say that there are forces inside West Africa quietly working toward a stronger ECOWAS. Such forces, which include national planning ministries, central banks, private investors, and sporting organizations, attempt to build on creative compromises that arise from clashes between the national interests of member states, while taking a forward-looking approach to the problems of our sub-region. These forces cannot, however, be taken for granted; they must be supported and carefully nurtured. Nigeria has to be at the forefront of such positive forces, not only for our long-term interests but also for the survival of the community as a model for African unity and cooperation.

From these West African sub-regional concerns, we may now move to an examination of continental African issues, beginning with the perennial problem of Chad.

Notes

1. See, for instance, the pioneer work by Jacob Viner, *The Customs Union Issue* (New York: Carnegie Endowment for International Peace, 1950) and Peter Robson, *The Economics of International Integration* (London: George Allen and Unwin, 1980).
2. See I.A. Gambari, "The Relevance (or Poverty) of Traditional Theories of Integration to Developing Countries," presented at the 10th Annual Conference, Nigerian Society of International Affairs (National Institute for Policy and Strategic Studies, Bukuru, Jos, 26–28 April 1982).
3. See "ECOWAS: Seventh Anniversary," in *West Africa*, 24 May 1982.
4. Ibid.
5. Ibid.
6. General Buhari, "Annual Foreign Policy Address, Annual Patron's Dinner, Nigerian Institute of International Affairs" (3 December 1984).
7. I.A. Gambari, "ECOWAS: Time for National Appraisal," *Daily Times* (Lagos), 6 May 1978.

PART 3

Continental Issues

7

Chad and Relations with Libya

The Republic of Chad has been discussed earlier in the context of Nigeria's relationship with neighboring countries. Here, we shall examine Chad as a continental trouble spot which requires our country's involvement. Nigerian involvement in the Chadian conflict has taken several forms, including military interventions and bilateral and multilateral diplomacy aimed at ensuring peace in that war-torn country.

Unfortunately, Nigeria's efforts in Chad have not always yielded lasting results. Probably out of frustration, some domestic critics of our country's policy have concluded that Nigeria's diplomacy toward Chad has been a total failure. Some critics suggest that an alternative diplomacy would be to pick a faction in Chad which would share our interests and then act decisively to put it in power. These and related views were expressed during the Special Seminar on Chad which, at my request, was organized by the Nigerian Institute of International Affairs, Lagos, in March-April 1984, for brainstorming by a mixed group of academic experts and diplomats from the External Affairs Ministry.

However attractive unilateral intervention in Chad might be in theory, it presented several serious problems in practice. First, we tended to be quite deficient in information regarding the balance of politico-military forces on the ground in Chad. This had been the case despite Chad's contiguity to our northeastern state of Borno and notwithstanding Nigeria's previous engagements during our national as well as the OAU's peacekeeping operations in Chad. Second, no one had seriously defined our national interests inside Chad to make us equal with France or Libya—two countries which invest huge financial, military, and political resources to support their favored factions.

Third, we continued to deal with several personalities, leaders, and factions in that unhappy country—all of them engaged in complex and shifting alliances without appearing to be fully committed to the destiny of Chad. Finally, once Nigeria concluded that all non-Chadian troops must be withdrawn from that country as one of the preconditions for peace and national reconciliation, we could not then unilaterally inject our own troops into Chad. Apart from the hypocrisy of such an act, the likelihood of achieving lasting success on the ground within Chad would be very slim indeed.

Soon after assuming power, the Buhari administration synthesized the national objectives which Nigeria was to pursue toward the attainment of peace in Chad. These included:

(i) support for a politically united Chad under an acceptable representative government;
(ii) prevention, for our national security interests, of the emergence of a political leadership hostile to Nigeria;
(iii) frustration of meddlesome activities of extra-regional and extra-African powers, whose intentions toward Nigeria as well as the sub-region might not be honorable or friendly.

Out of these general objectives, and drawing upon the lessons of our previous involvements in Chadian affairs, we developed several options for policy decisions. The Buhari administration shunned direct unilateral action and, instead, sought to associate France, the former colonial power, as well as the immediate neighbors of Chad, while attempting to find essentially African solutions through the OAU. The experiences of KANO I and II and the Lagos Accords on Chad, reached as a result of our country's initiatives and the failure of our unilateral military intervention in Chad in 1979, pointed to new approaches.

Therefore, the following options were considered as being more worthy of further considerations:

(i) Support the de-facto partition of Chad. This would follow the example of the legalization of the military stalemate and the consequent divisions into north and south parts in Korea and Vietnam. The problem with this option would be the legitimization of occupation by forces external to Chad contrary to OAU principles. Such partition, reminiscent of the fateful division of the African continent by alien European powers, might not prevent the kind of ideological rivalry which eventually led to serious war in Vietnam. This was clearly not something we should countenance.
(ii) Support the choice of a new leadership for Chad. This is the so-called "third option"—i.e., influence the emergence of a new political leader in Chad who would overshadow or eliminate Habre or Ouaddei. This option appeared attractive to the Libyans,

largely because it would lead to the exit of their foe, Hussein Habre. Libya appeared willing to sacrifice her friend, Goukouni Ouaddei, if that was the price to be paid for the removal of Habre. Apart from the fact that this option would contravene one of the cardinal principles of the OAU, it may have been too late to arrange at the time of Buhari's rule in Nigeria.

(iii) Allow the present combatants to fight it out and only intervene when a military solution was near. In the first place, a military solution would not be the same thing as a political solution and would not be lasting. Moreover, peace need not wait until overwhelming destruction has taken place. In addition, a protracted war of attrition could invite further escalation of the level of violence, with a high probability of extra-African interventions.

(iv) Continue the search for peaceful solutions through multilateral diplomacy, particularly the OAU, but also through skilful bilateral diplomacy, taking advantage of the considerable goodwill which Nigeria appeared to enjoy among the various parties to the conflict.

The last option was selected by the Buhari administration as our point of departure. Our immediate task was to get a general consensus behind a set of principles which we believed would govern the attainment of peaceful solutions to the conflict in Chad. The first of these Four Principles, in our view, was to accept the fact that much as other interested parties could assist in solving the problem, the key was always held by the Chadians themselves. Second, only a political solution could bring lasting peace. However attractive the military solution to the conflict, all attempts should be made to bring the various factions together for political discussions. We noted, for example, that Habre and Ouaddei were northerners and that the interests of southern Chadians would need to be represented by groups or individuals with firm roots in that section of the country. Third, the process of national reconciliation was unlikely to commence or be pursued seriously unless all non-Chadian troops were removed. As long as each of the major parties believed that they could rely upon military support from outside, they would not be inclined to go to the conference table. Fourth, the political and national reconciliation talks should commence and proceed under the auspices of the OAU, the only continental organization and the most neutral in terms of multilateral attempts to find lasting solutions to the Chadian problems.

Having defined the broad objectives and identified the most suitable options available, our administration undertook several diplomatic initiatives. We began extensive consultations with both Habre and Ouaddei as well as some other factions in Chad. We commended the acceptance of the Four Principles which, in our view, could bring about an end to the conflict. The most delicate negotiations, at this level of direct contact with major Chadian parties, took place in Abuja (the new capital city being developed for Nigeria) with Hussein Habre on 5 May 1984; it was characterized by tough negotiations between the two delegations.

The visiting president and his team were left in no doubt about the Four Principles, which we strongly believed would assist the peace process. However, the Chadians were more concerned about the issue of the Libyan presence in Chad. We emphasized our point that all non-Chadian troops needed to be withdrawn so that Chadians could establish peace among themselves. We also promised to do all we could to talk with the French and Libyans about the wisdom of this position. The direct bilateral issues between our two countries were raised and resolved within two hours. One issue was the Chadian request that relief items from Europe and petroleum products be allowed to cross our border (which remained closed) from Maiduguri (capital of Borno state) into Chad. This request was immediately granted by General Buhari. He was, however, unable to grant the other request by Chad, to have a new consulate opened in Maiduguri, since that might have posed additional security problems for Nigeria.

In their interaction, General Buhari and President Habre were tough as nails and shrewd as foxes. They had led or directed military forces which fought in the border clashes involving their respective countries in 1981. Although Nigeria was in a dominant position during the discussions in Abuja, because we had in our power to do what the Chadians wanted, the Chadian leader did not conduct himself as someone who was operating from a position of inferiority. Although General Buhari included some senior men in the Nigerian delegation who had actually fought against Habre's troops along the border or inside Chad, he also wanted accommodation with Habre.

While it is true that it took almost five months of persuasion by me before General Buhari agreed to meet with Habre, once the summit began, there was a guarded spirit of give and take. Unlike any other summit meeting in which I participated, General Buhari insisted on chairing the formal discussions from beginning to end. At the conclusion of the Buhari-Habre summit it was clear that some gains were made in solving bilateral problems and clarifying the positions held by both sides on the larger issues. It was also quite clear that although the two leaders did not appear to like one another very much they respected each other's toughness and control.

Immediately after Habre departed from Abuja, General Buhari instructed me to proceed to Tripoli and thereafter to Niamey, Niger Republic, to brief Col. Gaddafi and President Kountche on the summit and hold further consultations with them on the Chadian situation. I was scheduled to leave Lagos for Tripoli the following day, Wednesday, 16 May 1984, at 11 a.m. However, to my dismay, the Nigerian government plane detailed to convey my delegation and me to Tripoli was nowhere to be found at the Murtala Mohammed Airport. Apparently, someone from the Ministry of External Affairs had told the Air Force officers there that the trip was cancelled, and therefore the plane was sent on another mission. After contacting several senior Air Force officers, we were able to have the plane re-routed in mid-air to Lagos, and we then left for Tripoli at 4:30 p.m. Further investigations of this incident were to reveal that some people within my ministry opposed any dealings with Libya. Unfortunately, we could not locate the individual who made the unauthorized telephone call to the Air Force base.

Although we were several hours behind schedule, our delegation was met at the Tripoli airport by the Libyan foreign minister (Secretary for Foreign Liaison, in their official parlance), Dr. Ali Abdulsalam Treiki. He introduced me to a fairly long line of senior Libyan officials amidst extensive television and media coverage. We were later greeted by the entire diplomatic corps representing the African countries accredited to Tripoli at a dinner party organized in honor of our delegation but which took place several hours behind schedule.

Actually, this was the second opportunity for intense discussions and bargaining on Chad between Nigeria and Libya since Buhari came to power. The first occasion was provided through a visit to Lagos by Major Abdulsalam Jalloud (second-in-command to Col. Gaddafi), accompanied by Dr. Treiki. During that visit, several hours were consumed in drafting the joint communique, largely because the Libyans wanted reference to extra-African foreign troops only and we insisted on calling for the withdrawal of all non-Chadian troops from Chad. The visiting delegation reluctantly conceded this point although the Libyans denied having their soldiers in Chad in the first place.

The two major events since the Libyans' visit to Lagos were the contacts which the Libyans made with France over the withdrawal of all troops from Chad and our own direct contact with Habre. We briefed one another on the outcome of these initiatives. It appeared as if Libya was not too pleased that we had received Habre in Nigeria, thereby according their mortal enemy international legitimacy. Our position, however, was that we had a duty to talk to all parties in the Chadian conflict, including extra-African powers that had an interest in the matter.

Col. Gaddafi was particularly interested in knowing what Habre wanted in relation to the conflict in Chad; whether he was interested in political reconciliation under OAU auspices and what Habre thought of Goukouni Ouaddei. As far as we could observe, Habre wanted withdrawal of Libyan troops from Chad and was not particularly enthusiastic about an OAU-sponsored political reconciliation. As for Ouaddei, Habre regarded him as no more than the leader of an opposition group. Col. Gaddafi assured our delegation that he was not as concerned about staying in or withdrawing from Chad as he was about Nigeria playing a strong and decisive role in Chad. However, he warned against being too close to either France or Habre, since both were well known for their duplicity and anti-Libyan role in the Chadian conflict.

From Tripoli, my delegation went to Niamey to brief President Kountche on our consultations with Habre and the Libyan leadership. Niger has an interest in this issue because Chad and Libya are neighboring countries. We shared this concern with Niger and we also believed that President Kountche, well regarded among his francophone colleagues, could sell them our ideas regarding a settlement. Kountche had made a very good impression on General Buhari during his maiden state visit to Lagos early in our administration. The two leaders felt that they could work closely together on bilateral, sub-regional, and continental issues and should therefore keep in close contact in the best tradition of Niger-Nigerian amity. President Kountche expressed his deep appreciation of Buhari's gesture in keeping him informed about the outcome of Nigeria's initiatives over Chad. He supported our efforts and promised to encourage his francophone colleagues to endorse the Nigerian approach based on consultations with Habre, the Libyan leaders, and their supporters in Chad.

As part of our efforts to involve the OAU in the peace process, I went to Addis Ababa in June 1984, almost immediately after returning from Tripoli and Niamey, to deliver a special message from General Buhari to Col. Mengistu Haile Mariam, who was currently the chairman of the OAU. Outwardly ascetic, Col. Mengistu seemed to be trying hard to conceal a tough, passionate, and almost volcanic interior. He listened to my elaboration of the principles which we believed could ensure peace in Chad. Col. Mengistu was particularly interested in having our assessment of the state of mind of Gaddafi and Habre. I also conveyed General Buhari's feeling that, much as we were not opposed to proposals regarding a new meeting for political reconciliation among the Chadian factions scheduled to take place later in 1984, in the Peoples' Republic of the Congo, we believed that there would be greater merit in holding the proposed meetings under the auspices of the OAU with the chairman of our continental organization presiding.

The chairman of the OAU replied that he was willing to swallow his personal pride and that of the organization if, by so doing, any reconciliation arrangement involving the Chadian factions had greater chances of success. He recalled the efforts which he had made in achieving the twin objectives of peace and reconciliation in Chad both on behalf of his government and in his capacity as chairman of the OAU. He appeared to be impressed with Nigeria's initiatives on the matter and expressed the hope that the injection of new energies by Nigeria on this matter would bring solutions to the Chadian conflict closer to realization. Although Col. Mengistu was sharp in his probings, shrewd in his analysis, and deep in his commitment, his overall attitude to the Chadian problem still appeared to be one of sorrowful skepticism.

The next target of Nigeria's diplomatic efforts on Chad was France. Actually, in February 1984, we did receive Claude Cheysson, the Foreign Minister of France, in Lagos on an official visit. The problem of Chad naturally dominated the discussions between our two countries. Cheysson's visit, coming so early in the life of the Buhari administration, gave us a unique opportunity to exchange views with the French as we were developing our own policy toward Chad. By the time of my official return visit to France in September 1984, our views on Chad had crystallized and the correctness of our approach to the conflict appeared to have been affirmed. Indeed, just as we were entering the plane in Lagos to depart for Paris on 17 September, I received messages from France and Libya that were identical in content. They contained advanced information on the troop withdrawal agreement from Chad which the two countries had signed. Following the arrival of my official delegation in Paris, I tried to reach the highest levels of my own government to share this information.

Why did the French government not consult with us earlier or wait until my arrival in Paris before making the agreement public? Apparently the French believed that the agreement could not have been reached if it was not kept secret from all except the two contracting parties. The September 1984 Franco-Libyan agreement on mutual troop withdrawal from Chad was obtained by keeping Habre and the United States government in the dark about the negotiations until the very last moment. The agreement later failed, partly because Habre and the Americans were not committed to its success. It was also not clear that Gaddafi was really interested in withdrawing his troops from Chad. Nonetheless, the French government attached great importance to our visit. An unprecedented guard of honor was mounted to receive our party, which was also escorted throughout the visit by police outriders and security men. During the first meeting with my French counterpart, Mr. Cheysson, we had a tete-à-tete alone for more than 45 minutes, at which details of the troop withdrawal agreement were disclosed. On behalf of the French and Libyan governments, Cheysson requested the Nigerian government to allow Kano to be used by a mixed Franco-Libyan Military Monitoring Unit, whose role would be to resolve any dispute arising from the observance of the troop withdrawal agreement. The unit was expected to work from 25 September until 8 November 1984. Transit permission for Senegalese and Beninois observer groups was also requested from Nigeria. These were, of course, new proposals which had to be considered at the highest levels of government in Nigeria. Nonetheless, I sensed great impatience on the part of Cheysson, who appeared to believe that any delays in making the delicate agreements operational might scuttle the entire effort, in which he seemed to have great personal and political stakes.

I commended the French and Libyans for taking this important step of troop withdrawal, which was a key element in our own proposals for a peaceful solution to the Chad crisis. Therefore, I assured Cheysson that Nigeria would do all that it could to assist the peace process in Chad. Meanwhile, we pressed the French government to make new efforts on the political front by having Chadian leaders move to the conference table for national reconciliation talks.

Unknown to me, some senior bureaucrats and other high government officials back at home attempted to use these views expressed to the French government against me. Although my statements were consistent with our administration's private and public positions on Chad, they were deliberately misrepresented as a unilateral decision on my part to commit Nigeria to a course of action which had not been fully examined and decided upon at the highest levels of government. Fortunately, General Buhari and his number-two man, Idiagbon, supported my position. It was widely known that once general policy positions were cleared with General Buhari, he often gave his ministers considerable room in negotiations that took place in overseas missions. In any event, I did obtain General Buhari's approval in principle for the Franco-Libyan monitoring unit proposed for Kano, pending receipt of operational details, and I accordingly informed the French Foreign Minister. I advised Cheysson to embody such operational details in a prompt formal application to the Nigerian government for permission to use Kano as a staging station for the monitoring groups.

Upon receipt of such a formal application from the French government, the Federal Military Government promptly deliberated on the entire situation. Since the troop withdrawal agreement was considered to be consistent with our own policy toward Chad and the request for the use of Kano was made jointly by France and Libya, the Nigerian government formally approved the request. However, the Nigerian government was dissatisfied with the undue pressure which appeared to have been applied by France to obtain approval for the monitoring unit to begin work within a day or two of the formal application. The urgency of the Franco-Libyan agreement notwithstanding, the haste in trying to install the Franco-Libyan group in Kano appeared to be less than justified in our government's view. Later on it became clear that the French government, or more precisely Cheysson, was far more committed to the agreements than was Libya.

Brigadier Joshua N. Dogonyaro, who later became famous as the announcer of the military coup that overthrew Buhari's regime, was appointed as commander of the Host Liaison Group with headquarters at Bagauda, Kano. He was assisted by Air Commodore N.O.O. Yusuff as deputy commander, by Ambassador Deinde George from the Ministry of External Affairs, and by senior security officers. Communications and command requirements were determined and installed. The French liaison group was first to arrive in Kano and their Libyan counterpart joined them a day later. Although difficult at the beginning, the work of the monitoring groups proceeded fairly well, with Brigadier Dogonyaro using all diplomatic and military skills at his disposal to prevent a breakdown of the entire operation. Several disputes occurred between the Libyan and French delegations. The most serious and acrimonious ones concerned the precise language and text of the agreement, the pace of troop withdrawals on the ground in Chad, the simultaneous withdrawal of Zairian troops which operated alongside the French in Chad, and the involvement of Benin and Senegalese observers in the monitoring operations at Kano.

With respect to the last issue, France formally notified the Nigerian government that following further diplomatic consultations between Paris and Tripoli, a decision was reached on 21 October by both governments to substitute Beninois and Senegalese observers with French and Libyan observers. Still, the program of troop withdrawals from Chad and the work of the monitoring unit were not proceeding according to schedule and there were fears expressed that an extension of time would be needed. Nigeria refused to countenance extension of the completion date for the work of the monitoring unit, largely because an open-ended process would not encourage both countries (France and Libya) to deal squarely and promptly with the issues surrounding troop withdrawal. It was at this point that I made a brief, business-like visit to Bagauda on 29 October to reiterate the Nigerian government's position directly to the French and Libyan monitoring groups and to encourage both sides to conclude the program of action for monitoring the withdrawals.

The high hopes generated by the Franco-Libyan accord for mutual withdrawal did not lead to a successful conclusion by the date of expiration, 12 November 1984. For domestic political and external diplomatic reasons, the French were more interested in pulling out of Chad than Libya was. And for the same reasons it was more in the French interest to implement the agreement and to bend over backwards to insure that Libya did the same. Nigeria's role in the entire exercise was deliberately limited to providing the facilities requested by both parties and serving as a catalyst. Two positive results nevertheless came out of the operations. The level of violence and the temperature of the conflict within Chad were lowered. Moreover, the involvement of the Nigerian officials, military as well as civilian, in the operations at Bagauda, Kano, enriched their experience and improved upon their knowledge of the internal situation and the minds of non-Chadian parties in the conflict. This could be of great advantage to Nigeria in any future involvement in Chad.

The next forum for the articulation and engagement of Nigeria's position on Chad was at the 20th summit meeting of the Organization of African Unity, which convened in Addis Ababa on 13 November 1984. Along with the issue of Western Sahara, Chad had been threatening the survival of our continental organization. The failure of the OAU summit meeting scheduled for Tripoli in 1982 was attributed in part to an inability to reach a quorum of members present during a discussion of Chad. Therefore, one of the major tasks of the Nigerian delegation to the 20th summit (led by General Buhari, who was making his first journey outside Nigeria since coming to power) was to diffuse the issue of Chad within the organization.

Accordingly, General Buhari proposed the establishment of an OAU conciliation commission on Chad. Membership of the commission would, of course, include the People's Republic of Congo, which had taken the initiative on Chad, as well as other members with positive concern for the restoration of peace and stability in that country. He further reiterated Nigeria's views regarding the prerequisites for peace and national reconciliation in Chad and, in this regard, welcomed the Franco-Libyan agreement on the withdrawal of non-Chadian forces. The summit endorsed all of Nigeria's efforts and positions except for the creation of the conciliation commission. Instead of such a commission, the OAU renewed, for another year, the mandate earlier given to President Denis Sasso Nguesso of the Congo to promote national reconciliation among the various factions within Chad. Apparently the OAU preferred to tread the old road under President Nguesso than embrace yet another structure for the promotion of peace in Chad.

As the various agencies and ministries in Nigeria grappled with the problem of Chad in all its many dimensions, it became clear that we needed a focal point of analysis and coordination. There were frequent and occasionally alarming security reports about Habre's hostile intentions and proposed negative actions against Nigeria. We also had the perennial border problems, and in addition, we were engaged in intensive diplomatic efforts with OAU members and also with extra-African powers with interests in the Chadian debacle. In view of the multidimensional and increasingly complex nature of the situation and our policy toward it, I proposed the reactivation of the Inter-Ministerial Task Force on Chad which had been established by the civilian administration. General Buhari accepted this recommendation, and under my chairmanship the committee met several times to analyze the rapidly changing situation and propose options to the Federal Military Government. The task force was found so useful that its mandate was extended to cover the issue of our relationship with Cameroon as well.

One of the key dimensions of our policy toward Chad was Nigeria's relationship with Libya. During the Buhari administration, Nigeria was one of the very few African countries which could talk freely and frankly with Libya. This was due, in part, to the respect which the Libyan leadership had for General Buhari. As an illustration of the high regard which the Libyan government had for Nigeria during the Buhari administration, Dr. Ali Treiki requested our good offices to mediate the disagreement between his country and Britain. The disagreement, which arose following the shooting of a British policewoman, allegedly by a Libyan diplomat, during demonstrations near the Libyan Embassy in London, led to Britain breaking off diplomatic relations with Libya. During my official visit to Tripoli, the Libyan Foreign Minister expressed the desire to have Nigeria attempt mediation between the two feuding countries with the possibility of restoring diplomatic relations. Actually, we were to have a serious diplomatic row of our own with Britain a few months later.

Moreover, the Libyans had the perception that under Buhari, Nigeria would pursue external policies which were nationalistic and perhaps more truly nonaligned in content, unlike the predecessor Shagari regime. The Libyans believed that the Buhari administration was unlikely to endorse wholesale, if at all, French intentions and U.S. policies in Chad. Furthermore, having fought the military troops of Habre while commanding the Third Division of the Nigerian Army, General Buhari was perceived as unlikely to be soft toward the Chadian president in any subsequent dealings with him.

The Libyans wanted to have pressure applied against Habre from southern Chad so as to lessen pressures on their own southern flank. Hence Libya continued to look upon Nigeria as a key country which could act as a positive force in promoting a settlement in Chad that would not lead to the establishment of an overtly anti-Libyan government.

On their part, successive governments in Nigeria tried to promote a settlement of the Chadian conflict without being openly pro- or anti-Libya. It is a tightrope, indeed, and some governments more than others have been better able or more willing to walk it. Their success has depended on their different conceptions of the national interests to be promoted in Chad and toward Libya, in relation to the defense of our other national interests in dealing with the Western powers actively involved in Chad. The margin of our diplomatic maneuverability on this and other issues in which Western powers have direct interests tends to be less during periods of worsening economic conditions in Nigeria.

General Buhari's government walked the tightrope fairly well. We refused to be drawn into French and U.S. attempts to settle old or new scores with Libya. At the same time, the Buhari administration retained a healthy skepticism about Libya's long-term intentions toward Chad and its neighbors. Libya has a tendency of entering into agreements with other countries and then trying to outwit the other parties. The troop withdrawal agreement with France in September 1984 was one illustration of this. Previous accords with Polisario (Western Sahara) and later Morocco were other examples. The question was then raised as to whether one would not be made to look foolish after reaching a political understanding or signing agreements with the Libyans. For instance, when it was becoming sadly obvious to us that Libya's appreciation of and commitment to the troop withdrawal agreement were negative, Foreign Minister Cheysson wrote us on 6 November 1984 to express the appreciation of the French government for Nigeria's contribution to the success of the work of the Military Monitoring Groups in Kano. Cheysson further stated that the withdrawal of the Libyan and French troops from Chad was well advanced. He also assured us that the time limit envisaged in the agreement would be adhered to and that members of the French group had commenced their departure, a process which would be completed within the time initially fixed. Could this have been a case of Libyan bad faith or self-deception on the part of Cheysson? In any case, the work of the Military Monitoring Groups was a failure. The French but not the Libyan troops were withdrawn from Chad. Cheysson was to lose his job in part because of this negative outcome.

Nonetheless, Nigeria is not to be equated with France in Libyan eyes. On the contrary, successive Nigerian governments could deal constructively with Libya, not only on Chad but other important continental issues at the Organization of African Unity and elsewhere. The challenge is to identify and pursue the right mixture of friendship and cooperation with healthy criticism. Success in meeting that challenge is important not only for Nigerian-Libyan bilateral relations, but for possible resolutions of continental issues in the wider context of Afro-Arab relationship, especially at the OAU.

Finally, there was an observable consistency between Nigeria's diplomatic actions taken with regards to the Chadian conflict and the concepts and principles underlying them as articulated by the Buhari administration. Other than injecting our military forces into Chad, which had solved no problems in the past and was unlikely to do so in the future, there was nothing else the Buhari administration could have done but failed to do in trying to bring about peace in Chad. Nonetheless, our efforts received very limited success. This can be explained by the fact that the decisive cards in

Chad were not exclusively ours to play, but our administration worked hard to influence the players that appeared to possess stronger hands in the politico-military card game that was being played out in Chad.

8
Efforts to Resolve the Western Saharan Conflict

Although the Western Saharan issue, even more than Chad, almost broke up the Organization of African Unity, it began as a straightforward case of decolonization, handled initially by the United Nations. In 1966, the United Nations castigated Spain for her failure to implement the General Assembly resolution of 1960 regarding the right of self-determination of peoples under colonial rule. The pressure of the international community on Spain was intensified in the 1970s. Spain was repeatedly urged to hold a referendum to determine the true wishes of the people of Western Sahara. The presumption was that in a free and fair referendum conducted under the auspices of the United Nations the people would opt for independence.

The International Court of Justice at the Hague also delivered an opinion on the matter, declaring that "Morocco and Mauritania . . . do not have any right to claim the Western Sahara as part of their territories," and recommending instead that the Saharawis should enjoy the right of self-determination. The UN General Assembly endorsed this opinion in December 1975, and called upon Spain, Morocco, and Mauritania to respect the self-determination of the Saharawis. This position was meant to delegitimize the 14 November 1975 Tripartite Agreement between Spain, Morocco, and Mauritania, in which the colonial power ceded Western Sahara to the other two parties.

There was therefore this peculiar situation whereby a territory emerging from the process of decolonization was, by consent of the former colonial power, falling into the greedy jaws of already independent African neighbors that intended to annex it (Morocco and Mauritania) or control or subordinate it (Algeria and later Libya). The Algerian and Moroccan attitudes to Western Sahara can best be understood in the context of a rivalry for power which occurred amidst contending notions of the state and across the long border between them.[1] Although the border dispute which led to war in 1963 had been somewhat resolved by 1972, the decolonization of Western Sahara exacerbated the conflict between Algeria and Morocco.[2]

Morocco's claim over Western Sahara was irredentist. The absorption of Western Sahara into the ancient Sharifian Empire, whose dynasty stretched back some three hundred years and whose structure as a state went back another one thousand years, would complete the historical process. This old conception of the Moroccan state ran counter not only to the modern idea of self-determination but to Algeria's support for an independent Western Sahara which would be subordinate to Algeria while blocking Morocco's path to the south.[3] Mauritania, itself a product of national self-determination, joined Morocco and Algeria in the respective policy of annexation and subordination of Western Sahara, just emerging from the decolonization process.

The problem faced by the embryonic Western Sahara liberation movement, territory, Polisario (Popular Front for the Liberation of Saqiet al-Hamra and Rio de Oro), was that it had to fight on several fronts at once. The colonial power, Spain, was one, Morocco was another, and Mauritania was the third. The OAU resolutions passed since 1972, which expressed solidarity with the people of Western Sahara, were comforting but not sufficient for sustenance at the diplomatic or military levels.

These resolutions, however, signalled the beginning of the transfer of the Western Sahara issue from the United Nations to the OAU—a process which appeared complete by 1977. In any case, Polisario declared a Saharawi Arab Democratic Republic (SADR) on 26 February 1976. In support of Polisario's act of self-determination was Algeria, the UN General Assembly Resolution of December 1975, subsequent resolutions of the OAU, and Libya—although Libya's role was complex. Opposed to the independence of SADR were Morocco, France, the United States, several conservative African states (largely from the francophone group or those afraid of Libya's real sub-regional motivations), and Mauritania. However, Mauritania later dropped out of the conflict and renounced its territorial claims on Western Sahara when the war, which did not enjoy popular support at home, became an unbearable economic burden. In an agreement signed on 5 August 1979, Mauritania stopped the war against Polisario, thus leaving the liberation movement to concentrate on fighting Morocco.

The sophisticated weapons and supplies acquired from its Libyan benefactor did not enable Polisario to prevent the advance of Morocco's military machine. Indeed, by the end of 1983, the Moroccan forces had succeeded in cutting the territory of Western Sahara by half.[4] Fortunately for Polisario but unfortunately for Morocco, the balance of military forces on the ground did not automatically translate into diplomatic success at the OAU and in the international community. Indeed, the more successful Morocco was militarily in Western Sahara, the weaker her position became at these international bodies. Sensing blood, the supporters of Polisario, led by Algeria, passed for full recognition of SADR by the OAU.

In a highly controversial action by the Secretary-General of the OAU, at a regular budgetary session of the Council of Ministers meeting in Addis Ababa in February 1982, SADR received a seat as a member of the organization. This act nearly destroyed the OAU when several member states staged protest walkouts.[5] Subsequent OAU meetings were boycotted by one side or the other, depending on whether SADR was present or absent at the particular meetings. The most dramatic walkout made the 1982 OAU summit meeting in Tripoli a non-event.

Before this impasse was reached at the OAU, several mediatory attempts had been made to settle the Western Saharan issue. The 1978 summit of the OAU created an ad hoc committee (the so-called Committee of Wise Men) of five member states—Guinea, Mali, Nigeria, Sudan, and Tanzania—to harmonize the claims of Morocco, Mauritania, and Polisario and recommend appropriate solutions for the conflict. During the summit the following year in Monrovia, the committee's recommendations were endorsed, including the withdrawal of both Morocco and Mauritania from Western Sahara and the establishment of an immediate ceasefire, to be followed by a free and fair referendum supervised by the United Nations with OAU collaboration. Mauritania agreed to withdraw from the territories she occupied. However, Morocco not only boycotted all the meetings of the ad hoc committee but objected to its recommendations and walked out of the 1979 summit. Morocco then occupied the areas which were vacated by Mauritania.

The next OAU summit to take up the question of admitting SADR into full membership took place in Freetown in 1980. In spite of overwhelming sympathy for SADR, the summit accepted Nigeria's proposal that the issue be deferred so that the intentions of King Hassan of Morocco to show some flexibility on the SADR problem could be ascertained at the 18th summit of the OAU, scheduled for Nairobi. Apparently sensing the momentum toward recognition of SADR, King Hassan appeared to give his consent to a referendum. The OAU then seized upon this apparent demonstration of reasonableness and converted the ad hoc committee into an Implementation Committee charged with implementing their own recommendations on Western Sahara.

The first meeting of the Implementation Committee at the ministerial level took place in Nairobi in August 1981, followed by a second one in February 1982. The second meeting was followed by another at the level of heads of state and government of members of the committee. As a direct consequence of extensive discussions, detailed recommendations were made in connection with a cease fire, the establishment of an interim administration in Western Sahara, and the compilation of voter registers in preparation for the referendum. The high hopes generated at the February meetings were later dashed because, once again, Morocco reneged on the referendum, reemphasized her non-recognition of Polisario as a party, and insisted that Mauritania and Algeria were the real parties to the conflict. For Morocco, the admission of SADR to the OAU by Edem Kodjo ruined the chances for a referendum. Polisario insisted on direct negotiations with Morocco and confirmation that the warring parties in Western Sahara were Morocco and Polisario.

It was only a few days after the meeting of the Implementation Committee, at the summit level of its members, that OAU Secretary-General Edem Kodjo announced the seating of SADR at the opening of the 38th ordinary session of the OAU Council of Ministers on 22 February 1982 in Addis Ababa. His rationale for taking this unprecedented action was that the matter was his administrative responsibility under Article 28 of the OAU Charter on Adhesion and Accession. Since the majority (albeit a simple majority) of member states meeting at the Freetown summit appeared to support the seating of SADR, Edem Kodjo reasoned that his action was in order, especially following the pressure from some member states which had previously recognized SADR.

Neither the current chairman of the OAU nor the Council of Ministers of the organization had been consulted by the Secretary-General before the announcement of his decision to seat SADR at the Addis Ababa meeting. This unilateral act by Kodjo did not go down well with those member states which did not support SADR's admission. They argued that SADR was neither sovereign nor independent and therefore did not fulfill the conditions for membership as required by Articles 4 and 28 of the charter. Nineteen pro-Morocco member states of the OAU immediately decided to boycott the sessions of the Council of Ministers in which Edem Kodjo had seated SADR. They were Djibouti, Equatorial Guinea, Gabon, Guinea, Ivory Coast, Liberia, Mauritius, Morocco, Senegal, Somalia, Central African Republic, the Comoros, Gambia, Sudan, Cameroon, Tunisia, Upper Volta, and Zaire. Nigeria did not boycott the session but her representative at the meeting was also displeased with the Secretary-General's unilateral action.

The 19th OAU summit, scheduled to take place in Tripoli in 1982, failed because Morocco and her supporters on the SADR issue refused to attend, thus making it impossible for a quorum to be formed in accordance with the charter. The politics of Col. Gaddafi on continental African issues and the prospect of his becoming the next chairman of the organization were also contributing factors to the failure of Tripoli I and II—the summits that never materialized. The 19th summit then had to be reconvened in the "neutral" venue of the headquarters of the organization at Addis Ababa in

1983, where it met only because an agreement was reached with SADR leaders to withdraw voluntarily from participating in the work of the summit in return for a resolution calling for direct negotiations between SADR and Morocco. This promise was kept and Resolution 104 on Western Sahara was passed by the summit.

Resolution 104 called for direct negotiations between Morocco and Polisario. It also requested the Implementation Committee to work out the implementation of the ceasefire and the conduct of the referendum by December 1983. Realizing, however, that Morocco still refused to meet alone with SADR, the OAU Chairman, Col. Mengistu, dispatched his foreign minister and the OAU Acting Secretary-General to Morocco and Algeria with the aim of arranging a face-saving formula which would allow the contending parties to attend the Implementation Committee meeting scheduled for 21 and 22 September 1983 at Addis Ababa. It appeared as if both the Moroccan king and the SADR leaders, who were consulted in Algeria, had agreed to the formula whereby the two parties would not meet alone but sit together with all members of the Implementation Committee around a table. When the committee actually met in Addis Ababa, however, Morocco refused to participate in any meeting with what she described as the "illegitimate Polisario front."

Nigeria stepped in to break the deadlock and, supported by Sudan, Mali, and Sierra Leone, proposed that each party be called in separately to meet with the committee. However, Ethiopia and Tanzania, which had previously recognized SADR, opposed the formula. At the urging of President Nyerere, Chairman Mengistu abruptly adjourned the Implementation Committee meeting. It may well have been that the pro-SADR group within the committee had arranged this outcome in order to force the issue of admission at the next OAU summit. At least this was the feeling of the pro-Morocco members of the same committee. Nigeria remained neutral but appeared dissatisfied with both the attitude of Morocco and the rather high-handed way in which Chairman Mengistu adjourned the meeting of the committee.

This was the situation when the Buhari administration came on the stage in Nigeria and began to formulate a position on the SADR issue. One of the task forces which was established almost immediately after my assumption of office was to examine the Western Sahara question and recommend new options for the government. The task force headed by Ambassador E.O. Fowora submitted its report on 1 February 1984. The report observed ominously that the failure of the last meeting of the Implementation Committee, due in large part to Morocco's intransigence, posed a great danger to the continued existence of the OAU, whose 20th summit might not be held as scheduled in Conakry. SADR had recently announced that her leaders would indeed attend that summit, a decision likely to lead to a deadlock similar to that which plagued the abortive Tripoli summit.

Although Nigeria had recognized Polisario as a liberation movement, she had not recognized SADR as a sovereign state and government. This half-way policy was deliberately pursued to allow our country to continue her nonpartisan role within the Implementation Committee. There was a growing feeling within the Ministry of External Affairs, however, and among informed Nigerian opinion that our government would need to take its support for the principles of self-determination to a logical conclusion.

The continued intransigence of Morocco and the reality of the threat to the survival of the OAU appeared to be grounds for serious consideration of new options on the Western Saharan issue. As a leader on the continent, Nigeria could hardly continue to maintain a middle position after others had taken stands on opposite poles of the issue. Unless Morocco would change her mind and agree to cooperate fully with the Implementation Committee in order to execute the various components of OAU Resolution 104, Nigeria would have to act to save the OAU and resolve the Western Saharan issue one way or the other.

The report of the task force on Western Sahara was debated extensively within my ministry, and we were then able to present a position paper on the subject to General Buhari on 8 May 1984. In it I recalled that our country decided in 1975 to recognize MPLA and took further steps which ensured the admission of Angola into the OAU. The decision was generally hailed then as it continued to be hailed now as the high mark of Nigeria's foreign policy, a commendable show of leadership and independence. Of course, we were now in 1984 and our national economic circumstances could not be compared with those of almost a decade before. Nonetheless, citing a portion of Alfred Lord Tennyson's poem, *Ulysses*, I urged a new and decisive action on SADR and the related question of the future of the OAU:

> Though we are not now that strength
> Which (in old times) moved heaven and earth
> What we are, we are
> One equal measure of heroic heart
> Made weak by time and fate
> But strong in will
> To strive, to seek, to find and not to yield

It was time for Nigeria to "bite the bullet" and make up its mind on the Western Sahara, based on the general principles which had consistently guided our country's foreign policy since independence. These included support for the exercise of the indivisible right of self-determination; opposition to colonialism in whatever form or by whatever power, and commitment to the preservation of the Organization of African Unity.

The history of the conflict and the arguments for and against recognition were presented to the head of state along with an examination of the various options available to Nigeria. The options were basically as follows:

(a) Remain a member of the Implementation Committee, continue the role of neutral mediator, and refuse to recognize SADR. This status-quo position might not advance the cause of self-determination and would be clearly out of tune with the views of informed Nigerian opinion.

(b) Remain a member of the Implementation Committee but recognize SADR, just as Ethiopia and Tanzania had done, on the basis that Morocco remained intransigent on the issue of Western Sahara.

(c) Withdraw from the Implementation Committee and later recognize SADR (or threaten to do so unless Morocco fully cooperated with the committee to implement Resolution 104).

Clearly the third option would be more direct and it had the additional advantage that it could be implemented in stages. Such a course of action might also present Nigeria as a country that avoided reckless diplomatic actions and instead served notice on others to change their own policies before taking final decisions on major issues. The withdrawal from the Implementation Committee would be aimed at giving the correct signal to Morocco and some of her friends, such as Saudi Arabia and Guinea, which were also our potential or actual friends.

General Buhari, though impressed by the arguments presented to him on this issue, asked incisively why the Arab League members and Maghreb states, which shared cultural, religious, and ethnic affinities with Morocco and Western Sahara, had not directly addressed the problem in the organizations. It was pointed out, in response to this query, that the Arab League had shied away from the Western Sahara issue because it could only cause friction, as it had already done within the OAU. Even without being formally seized with the problem, there was already a clear division within the league, with Algeria, Libya, Syria, and possibly Iraq backing Polisario while the generally more conservative states, such as Saudi Arabia and Kuwait, supported Morocco. Egypt and Sudan also supported Morocco, perhaps as a consequence of their uneasy relationship with Libya. The Arab were therefore happy to have the OAU continue to handle the subject of Western Sahara. Now, precisely because the Arab League members would not wish to allow the Western Sahara issue to destroy their own Organization, we felt that the OAU should also handle this issue without allowing it to destroy our own continental organization.

With regards to the Maghreb, the situation was even clearer. Of the five states of the Maghreb—Mauritania, Morocco, Algeria, Libya, and Tunisia—three had recognized SADR, namely, Algeria, Libya, and Mauritania. They had also provided Polisario with arms, ammunition, and diplomatic cover to prosecute the war. Polisario was using Algerian territory as a base of operations.

The sharp pro- and anti-Polisario divisions within the Maghreb and Arab League had made both organizations weak in finding solutions or undertaking serious mediatory roles on the Western Sahara issue. While it is true that the OAU was similarly divided on the issue, the fact that our organization continued to be occupied with the Western Sahara problem, with the blessing of the United Nations, put it in a better position to address the problem.

Although the Buhari administration was evidently trying to make up its mind on the issue of recognizing Western Sahara, no final decision had been made by the government by the time of my public lecture at Ahmadu Bello University, Zaria, on 25 July 1984. Therefore I was only able to tell the audience that while we recognized Polisario as a liberation movement, our administration was not yet in a position to recognize SADR as a sovereign state in view of our membership in the OAU Implementation Committee. Nonetheless, I gave a not too subtle hint of the direction in which our mind was moving by saying that, unless Morocco showed more flexibility, Nigeria would reassess her continued membership in an OAU Implementation Committee which did not meet and was therefore not in a position to implement anything. Furthermore, Nigeria was committed to Resolution 104 and called on all parties, including Morocco, to respect that resolution. The integrity and survival of the OAU must, in our view and determination, be defended at all times.[6]

Gradually, however, our position on the Western Sahara was hardening. We felt that having voluntarily withdrawn from participation in two meetings of the OAU (the 19th summit and the last OAU Council of Ministers meeting in Addis Ababa in February-March 1984), Polisario could not morally be asked to withdraw again from the forthcoming 20th OAU summit, unless we could offer them something substantial in return. Without the voluntary withdrawal of Polisario and without real progress toward solving the Western Saharan issue, the 20th summit might be doomed. The survival of the OAU was, in our view, paramount.

Nigeria then took the next step to convince the OAU chairman to convene another meeting of the Implementation Committee. We also called on the King of Morocco to show the kind of flexibility which would make a success of a reconvened meeting. General Buhari sent a special message to Col. Mengistu, chairman of the OAU, pointing to the grave dangers inherent in allowing the problem of Western Sahara to remain unresolved, especially following reports of resumed and intensified hostilities between Polisario and the Moroccan armed forces. The Nigerian head of state therefore urged the OAU Chairman to convene a new meeting of the Implementation Committee to consider all aspects of the Western Saharan issue prior to the 20th summit.[7]

However, the chairman of the OAU did not convene a meeting of the committee as we had requested. In his consultations with members of the committee and the OAU secretariat, Col. Mengistu may have concluded that, in the absence of any movement on the part of Morocco, such a meeting would be pointless. Nigeria then decided formally to withdraw from any further participation in a committee that could not meet let alone fulfill its mandate to implement Resolution 104.

The options were getting narrower as the Buhari administration approached a final decision on the recognition of SADR. By withdrawing from the Implementation Committee, we had clearly served notice on Morocco that her failure to show greater flexibility on this issue threatened the very existence of the OAU. We were actively considering adding our weight to the majority of member states which had already recognized SADR.

At this juncture, a meeting of an informal consultative group on foreign policy, established under my stewardship as Foreign Minister, was held on 5 November 1984. The group examined most of the issues which were to preoccupy the Nigerian delegation at the 20th summit, scheduled to take place a week later, and came down firmly in support of the recognition and admission of SADR into the OAU. The group further decided that in order to be true to our commitment to the principle of self-determination and in deference to informed domestic opinion on the matter, the Nigerian government should go ahead to recognize SADR and save the OAU.

This position was conveyed through me directly to General Buhari, who welcomed advice from the intellectual community and informed public opinion. My own position in the bureaucracy of the Ministry of External Affairs and within the decision-making process in the government as a whole was no doubt strengthened by the recommendations of the informal consultative committee.

Before leaving for the 20th summit, the Nigerian delegation, headed by General Buhari himself, was given wide latitude by the Supreme Military Council to take decisions on the Western Sahara which would best ensure the survival of the OAU and also serve our national interests. The delegation received authority to choose the best strategy for realizing these objectives at the OAU and for timing the announcement of the Nigerian decision. Timing proved to be almost as important as the decision itself. Had we announced our decision before the delegates of other countries were to arrive in Addis Ababa, the supporters of Morocco and those who opposed the admission of SADR might have been able to organize or lobby enough member states to stay at home to prevent a quorum from assembling. In that case, Nigeria would bring about the very outcome which our country wanted to avoid with regards to the survival and health of the OAU.

When the summit finally convened at Addis Ababa on 12 November 1984, it was not preceded by the usual meeting of the Council of Ministers, out of fear that a pre-summit deadlock at that level on Western Sahara or Chad would be a bad omen. As a consequence, the heads of state and government who came for the summit had to engage in far more substantive consultations on the divisive issues facing the organization than was perhaps ever the case in a pre-summit atmosphere. General Buhari, who was attending a summit for the first time as Nigerian head of state, took full advantage of the situation favoring extensive consultations with his counterparts. Such consultations confirmed the wisdom of Buhari's decision that the time had indeed come for Nigeria to recognize SADR and support its sitting as the 51st member of the OAU.

It was my historic duty to announce the decision to the international press on 11 November 1984—the day preceding the summit. "The Federal Military Government," I told members of the international press corps assembled at the Nigerian Embassy, "after very careful consideration of all aspects of the Western Sahara problem which has bedeviled our Organization over the past few years, has decided to recognize the Saharawi Arab Democratic Republic."[8] Our view was that the seating of SADR at the summit was central to the success of the summit and to the survival of the organization.

"For the past few years," I continued, "we have all watched helplessly as our continental Organization, the OAU, has been paralyzed over the seemingly intractable problem of Western Sahara [which] has led to the abysmal neglect of other pressing challenges facing Africa [including] the devastating drought, famine, the continued deteriorating economic situation of our continent as well as political problems such as the disturbing developments in Southern Africa."[9] In order that we might put the diplomatic aspect of SADR's recognition behind us and allow the OAU to address other pressing economic and political issues, we then appealed to "all OAU member states in the higher interests of Africa, to attend this Summit; and also urge them to participate fully and thereby ensure the success of this 20th Summit." In conclusion, we threw a face-saving device to some member states by declaring that "as we are all aware, international usage permits nations attending conferences with other nations which they do not recognize."[10]

This solemn announcement caught Morocco and her supporters off balance. During the opening ceremonies the next day, SADR formally took its seat. It appeared too late for Morocco and her supporters to organize walkouts by enough members of the OAU to prevent the summit from proceeding. However, we did not leave this to chance. The Nigerian official delegation was divided into small sub-groups, each headed by a senior member of the delegation, and each was given the task of lobbying members of other delegations to support our most recent decision on SADR. Our diplomatic efforts and lobbying activities were targeted at those countries which had earlier threatened to withdraw from the OAU if SADR was allowed to take a seat as a full member of the organization at that summit.

Air Vice-Marshall Muazu, then military governor of Kaduna state and, next to General Buhari, the most senior member of the delegation, led the small group that worked on Zaire. Chief M.S. Adigun, Minister of National Planning, took charge of the efforts directed at ECOWAS countries attending the summit. Major-General Hannaniya, ambassador-designate to Ethiopia, was detailed to convince Somalia and the Comoros that our position was justified in order to save the OAU, while Major-General Joseph N. Garba, former Foreign Minister and Permanent Representative of Nigeria to the United Nations, assisted by Ambassador Metteden, who had spent several years of his diplomatic career in and around Southern Africa, was assigned to the frontline states. Ambassadors Hamzat Ahmadu and Peter Afolabi, directors-general of African Affairs and International Economic Cooperation, respectively, in the External Affairs Ministry, lobbied Central African Republic. The Attorney-General of the Federation and Minister of Justice, Mr. Ofodile, assisted by Dr. Musa Yakubu, Dean of the Faculty of Law, Ahmadu Bello University, Zaria, had the least enviable task of trying to convince Morocco not to walk out of the OAU despite the seating of SADR as its newest member. Ambassador Jim Blankson, a veteran of the OAU and Director of Intra-African Affairs in the External Affairs Ministry, worked on the draft statement announcing Nigeria's decision on Western Sahara and also joined the efforts to lobby Zaire to accept the seating of SADR without walking out of the summit.

The brief containing the lobbying instructions given to the various sub-groups within the Nigerian delegation, highlighted the rationale for our country's position as follows:

(a) commitment to the principle of self-determination by the people of territories which experience colonial domination;

(b) overriding concern for the survival of the OAU and its continuing relevance to important African problems;

(c) urgent need to resolve the Western Saharan issue so that the current and subsequent OAU summit conferences could address other pressing matters, such as;

(i) the severe drought and famine being experienced by several African countries,
(ii) the delay in granting independence to Namibia within the framework of UN Security Council Resolution 435,
(iii) the serious and sustained threat posed by South Africa to the peace, security, well-being, and territorial integrity of the frontline states,
(iv) the desperation of the regime in Pretoria as repeatedly demonstrated by new acts of intimidation, oppression, and repression of black peoples inside South Africa.

In his address to the summit, General Buhari confirmed the essence of this rationale for Nigeria's position on Western Sahara.[11] He further declared that "no member state [should] walk out of the Organization because such an action would achieve nothing but merely please the imperialists and other detractors of our Organization."[12] Only Morocco left the organization as a consequence of seating SADR at the summit; Zaire, although joining Morocco in a walkout, was careful to declare that this action did not mean her leaving the OAU itself.

This was a great victory for the principle of self-determination, for the OAU, and for Nigeria's diplomacy. Clearly, Nigeria's decisions tipped the diplomatic scale in favor of seating SADR, although Morocco then left the organization. As an observer aptly put it, "the deadlock [over Western Sahara] was complete. One party had recognition but no territory; the other had the territory but no recognition."[13] The rest was left essentially to the battlefield and further diplomacy; hence the United Nations and the OAU have not really seen the last of this matter.

Nigeria gained two diplomatic bonuses from this issue. During his visit to Saudi Arabia immediately after the summit, General Buhari appeared to have convinced King Fahd and the Saudi government that our decisions over Western Sahara were based on the need to save the OAU. He told the King what was later shared with the Nigerian public and the diplomatic community in Lagos, that the recognition of SADR notwithstanding, Nigeria wished to maintain and strengthen her relations with Morocco, but that "it is in the interest of Morocco and the over-all interest of our continent for Morocco and SADR to work towards a peaceful solution to the Western Sahara problem."[14] Morocco did not break diplomatic relations with Nigeria following our decisive support for SADR at the summit.

Of all the Buhari administration's endeavors in the external realm, the decision to recognize SADR and seat it as a full member of the OAU probably enjoyed the most popular support within Nigeria. It was happily reminiscent of General Murtala Mohammed's courage and vision in recognizing the MPLA and ensuring its membership in the OAU. Although times were different, for a brief moment it seemed as if, diplomatically at least, Nigeria was born again.

NOTES

1. See the excellent analysis of the background to the conflict in Western Sahara and the contending forces in I. William Zartman, *Ripe for Resolution: Conflict and Intervention in Africa* (New York: Oxford University Press, 1985).
2. Ibid.
3. Ibid.
4. Ibid.
5. Ibid.
6. These nuances of our developing policy on Western Sahara seemed to have been missed by some members of the academic community. Indeed, a former student of mine, Alache Ode, who was present at that lecture, pointed to the contrast between the apparently hesitant posture taken on behalf of the government and the unequivocal positions on foreign-policy issues which used to emanate from me while I was a lecturer at the university. In response, I recalled my own former teacher, late Professor F.S. Northedge of the London School of Economics, who used to say that the view of the foreign-policy road often changed as one moved from the back seat to the driver's position and held the steering wheel. The fact was that, at the time of my public lecture at the ABU in July 1984, the government of which I was spokesman had not yet decided to go farther on the Western Saharan issue.
7. This message was delivered by me in person in Addis Ababa in June 1984.
8. "Statement by Dr. Ibrahim A. Gambari, Minister of External Affairs of the Federal Republic of Nigeria on SADR" (Addis Ababa, 11 November 1984).
9. Ibid.
10. Ibid.
11. General Buhari, speech at the 20th summit of the OAU (Addis Ababa, 12–13 November 1984).
12. Ibid.
13. See Zartman, *Ripe for Resolution*.
14. General Buhari, "Annual Foreign Policy Address, Annual Patron's Dinner, Nigerian Institute of International Affairs" (3 December 1984).

9

Revitalization of the OAU

When the Buhari administration came to power and for almost twelve months afterwards, the fate of the Organization for African Unity truly hung in the balance. That situation was caused largely by the organization's obsessive and almost suicidal concerns with political issues such as Chad and Western Sahara, as discussed in the last two chapters. There was, in addition, a more intangible but no less serious threat in the lack of serious attention devoted by the organization to the economic problems of the African continent. It was becoming quite clear that unless the inattentiveness was reversed, the pan-African organization would become irrelevant to the needs of the over five hundred million people of our continent. Therefore, the Buhari regime worked very hard to help rescue the OAU from its debilitating preoccupations with political matters, while attempting to move it toward serious consideration of Africa's economic crisis and the crisis of development.

In his concise but sobering analysis of Africa's economic and social crises made at the 20th summit of the OAU, General Buhari highlighted the devastating impact of the global economic recession on Africa's growing food crisis, the virtual stagnation of industrial production, rising external debts, and balance of payments difficulties while export commodities earnings were in sharp decline.[1] Development assistance to Africa had declined tremendously in real terms. The result was a virtual halt in the export of primary products, while African states were being forced, more as a result of severe drought, to increase imports of consumer goods, especially food, to feed their rapidly growing populations. Furthermore, African nations were forced drastically to reduce their importation of capital goods, a situation which retarded the growth of the industrial sector and generated higher unemployment.

General Buhari then appealed to the international community, especially the financial institutions, not so much to shoulder Africa's economic burden but to institute policies which would hasten global economic recovery.[2] He called upon them to address African economic problems with urgency, flexibility, and greater understanding, something that would entail, among other measures, an increase in the flow of capital and financial resources from the West to Africa, balance-of-payments support, lower interest rates, and fair-trade practices that would grant easy access to the world market for export commodities.

Turning the searchlight inside, General Buhari pointed out to the summit that while "we all hailed the Lagos Plan of Action and the Final Act of Lagos as the Economic blueprint for Africa, based on the philosophy of self-reliance and self-sufficiency, most of our countries have only paid lip-service to both documents."[3] It must be pointed out that the unfavorable international economic environment since 1980, when these documents were adopted, had dampened the enthusiasm that underlined the resources and commitment to implement the economic blueprint.

Nigeria then proposed at the summit that African governments should organize an economic summit to consider new collective strategies for attacking economic problems. The severe impact of drought and other natural disasters and the debt issue required attention at the highest levels of authority. The proposed summit would provide an appropriate forum to examine and give political backing to the special memorandum produced by the 10th Conference of Ministers of the Economic Commission for Africa (ECA) and adopted by the ministers in May 1984. The memorandum had suggested a framework for dealing with our continent's economic crisis, while making recommendations for emergency, short-, medium-, and long-term solutions. A special economic summit would also buttress the "Declaration of Africa's External Indebtedness" adopted by the conference of African finance ministers in June 1984.[4]

The only way that the entire global community would respond to our appeals was to show that African states were themselves seriously preoccupied with finding solutions to the economic problems. As General Buhari concluded, "we cannot expect the United Nations Secretary-General to take all initiatives on our behalf regarding our dismal economic situation only for us to fail to follow up such initiatives or give due encouragement to them. His credibility will be undermined by our seeming indifference and so will hope for new resources to be transferred from developed countries."[5]

General Buhari's remarks and the specific recommendations for action presented by the Nigerian delegation were accepted with tremendous applause and later included in Resolution 4 (XX) Rev. I. The specific Nigerian recommendations were in two parts:

(a) the holding of an economic summit the following year to review the progress made in the implementation of the Lagos Plan of Action and the Final Act of Lagos adopted by the O.A.U. in Lagos, Nigeria, in 1980, and the formulation of an emergency program for Africa including immediate measures in the priority economic areas, particularly the agricultural and food sectors, and

(b) the setting up of a steering committee consisting of Algeria, Ivory Coast, Tanzania, and Zimbabwe, to begin preparing the documents for the special summit.

The Algerian president suggested, and it was endorsed by the summit, that Nigeria and Senegal be included among members of the Steering Committee. As a prime mover of the very idea of an economic summit, Nigeria was expected to play a major role in ensuring its success. Senegal was also included in order to maintain the geopolitical balance in francophone West Africa. Cameroon was also added to the list of committee members.

Another related proposal which Nigeria presented to the summit was the creation of a special fund for the relief of drought and famine. This fund would be under the operational control of the OAU, and members would be asked to make voluntary contributions to it. Establishing the fund would demonstrate a willingness to make sacrifices in order to assist countries that were worst hit by the incidents of drought and famine. Such a demonstration of collective self-help on the part of African states might induce outside powers to make further contributions toward solutions for the continent's economic crisis.

This initiative was also endorsed by the summit, which in Resolution AHG/133 (XX) established the Special Emergency Assistance Fund for Drought and Famine in Africa. Algeria pledged $10 million, as did Libya. Nigeria later pledged $5 million; Tanzania, Zimbabwe, Ghana, and Ethiopia pledged $500,000 each. By June 1985, the total pledges had risen to $25 million when several other members of the OAU joined in making pledges.

On the return of the Nigerian delegation to Lagos, General Buhari briefed his colleagues on the National Security and Defence Council, which often served as a standing committee of the Supreme Military Council when dealing with external relations. He later briefed the nation on the outcome of the summit, which he declared "was the most successful OAU Summit in recent years."[6] He pointed out that Nigeria had exerted her energies in a determined bid to shift the focus of the organization from diversionary political issues that tended to threaten its very existence to the crucial problems of economic and social development. He concluded by saying that he "perceived a new realism and commitment on the part of the OAU member states to work together to act upon Africa's endemic problems in a vigorous, rational and appropriate manner."[7] Most participants in, or observers of, the summit would have had no difficulty in agreeing with the evaluation and conclusions made by General Buhari.

In order to sustain the momentum generated by our country's proposals on the economic summit, I proposed that the Steering Committee should commence work immediately and hold a minimum of two meetings prior to the Council of Ministers' full meeting, which would precede the summit scheduled for July 1985. My further suggestion concerned the need to have the Ministry of External Affairs coordinate the inputs of all relevant home ministries in preparation for the 21st summit of the OAU. We were also to contact the Algerian authorities, who shared similar views with Nigeria on this matter and might wish to host the preparatory meetings of the Steering Committee. These recommendations were approved by General Buhari on 6 December 1984.

The Steering Committee commenced its work at ministerial level on February 11, 1985 in Addis Ababa. Officials and experts of the Steering Committee had met from 4 February to prepare the agenda for the full ministerial meeting. With the able assistance of my colleague, the Minister of National Planning of Nigeria, Chief M.S. Adigun, I succeeded in amending the Steering Committee's agenda so as to have better focus on our assignment. We identified the immediate economic problems facing Africa and amended the draft agenda submitted by the expert group accordingly. The revised agenda then had the following main themes:

(i) The Lagos Plan of Action (LPA) and the Final Act of Lagos (FAL): assessment of measures taken so far and new efforts for their accelerated implementation. Under this item, there would be a progress report on the implementation of LPA and FAL by member states, African and international organizations, and the secretariats of the OAU and ECA. There would also be an examination of the economic situation in Africa from 1980 to 1985 and a revised practical program attaining the objectives of LPA and FAL.

(ii) Special Program of Action for Implementation of the Food Situation and the Rehabilitation of Agriculture in Africa. This would consist of emergency, medium-term, and long-term measures.

(iii) External Debt. The growing problem of Africa's indebtedness would be analyzed and measures recommended for dealing with it.

(iv) Proposals for a Common Platform for Action. We would recommend measures for collective action by OAU member states at the sub-regional, continental, and international-community levels.

Following extensive discussions of these items, the Steering Committee decided to hold its next meeting in May 1985, to be preceded by a meeting of experts. The reason for this apparently long interlude was to give the forthcoming 41st session of the OAU Council of Ministers, which was to meet jointly with the economic ministers, additional opportunity to react to and offer any new proposals on the agenda. There would also be the ECA Conference of Ministers in April 1985, which would be required to pronounce on the agenda as proposed by the Steering Committee.

At its 41st Ordinary session, between 25 February and 5 March 1985 at Addis Ababa, the Council of Ministers agreed with the draft agenda for the economic matters to be discussed by the 21st summit of the OAU as prepared by the Steering Committee. This was a clear testimony to the thorough work done by the Steering Committee. On the Special Emergency Assistance Fund for Drought and Famine in Africa, the council decided that there would be a Policy Committee of twelve members, the management of the fund would be assigned to the African Development Bank (ADB), and a special unit within the OAU would be created with no additional budgetary expenses on the OAU or the fund. The mechanism by which a member state applying for assistance could be assessed for the grant from the fund was also agreed upon.

After a lengthy debate on the nature of the proposed disbursements, the Council of Ministers decided that both loans and outright grants should be considered. The criteria for such disbursements were the nature of the emergency and the use to which the resources would be made. Loans, the council agreed, should be on very easy terms. The only aspect of the fund left for the 21st summit to consider concerned the statute establishing it.

By the time the Council of Ministers met again just before the 21st summit, two main documents had emerged from the various stages which the agenda for the economic summit had gone through. One was the "Report of the First Meeting of the Steering Committee" on Africa's economic problems, as endorsed by the OAU Council of Ministers at the February-March 1985 meeting in Addis Ababa. Second was the "Recommendations of the ECA Conference of Ministers Concerning the Economic Issues on the Draft Agenda of the 21st Session of the Assembly of Heads of State and Government of the OAU."

At this point it may be of interest to note the rivalry that often characterized the relationship between the ECA and the OAU secretariats. The ECA, a United Nations body, deals almost exclusively with socioeconomic matters affecting Africa from the perspective of the world body. It has competent staff with professional economic backgrounds and a good reputation for producing sound analyses. For historic reasons, the ECA shares the same physical facilities with the OAU, especially the venue for ministerial and summit meetings of the pan-African organization. The OAU secretariat, on the other hand, has dealt largely with political issues, and its competence in socioeconomic analyses is not as advanced as that of ECA. Nonetheless, the OAU secretariat has often claimed jurisdictional supremacy over economic and social matters, whenever summits have requested both secretariats to work together in producing joint reports and documentations. The inevitable rivalry and sometimes unbecoming jockeying for positions on such matters were not abated by the fact that, for some years at least, both the OAU interim Secretary-General, Peter Onu, and the Executive Secretary of the ECA, Prof. Adebayo Adedeji, were Nigerians!

The document emanating from the ECA, which fleshed out the report of the OAU Steering Committee on Africa's economic problems, contained five major segments. Part one dealt with LPA and FAL; the assessment of both documents and new measures for accelerating their implementation. It also gave an overview of the African economic and social performance between 1980 and 1985, as well as a sector-by-sector analysis of the LPA and practical measures for the accelerated attainment of objectives. Part two of the report examined the Special Program of Action for Improvement of the Food Situation and Rehabilitation of African Agriculture. Part three was devoted to a consideration of the external debt issue. In part four, proposals were made for a common platform for action. Finally, part five contained recommendations for the follow-up and monitoring of decisions to be taken by the African heads of state and government. As one can observe, the original contributions made by the ECA Conference of Ministers were in the areas of data, evaluation, follow-up, and monitoring. Otherwise the substance of the work of the Monitoring Committee and the Council of Ministers' contributions to the draft agenda on Africa's economic problem remained almost intact. And for the second time, the Council of Ministers endorsed the package put together by the Steering committee but took due cognizance of the improvements made on it by the ECA.

This was the progress made prior to the commencement of the crucial 21st summit of the OAU. Two creative suggestions were made and agreed upon which facilitated the summit's consideration of the agenda on economic matters. First, the heads of state and government of the Steering Committee members met at Addis Ababa before the main summit began its work. The mini-summit considered the report prepared by the Steering Committee at ministerial level. The small group of heads of state endorsed the report and agreed to commend its adoption to the full summit meeting. Second, it was decided that, in order to properly focus on the issues contained in the draft agenda, national delegations attending the summit would be requested to avoid reading lengthy speeches and instead would directly intervene on specific agenda items. Meanwhile, the heads of state and government of the Steering Committee members would each choose an agenda item and lead the discussion about it in the plenary sessions of the full summit. These were unprecedented schemes of work, and, except for one or two deviations, their implementation facilitated the consideration and adoption of recommendations on specific aspects of Africa's economic problems.[8]

Nigeria decided to speak on the agenda item the "Special Program of Action for Improvement of the Food Situation and the Rehabilitation of African Agriculture." The Steering Committee had suggested establishment at the national level of an early-warning system based on objective parameters, such as crop conditions, while also advocating the need to address the market situation and nutritional requirements. It recommended creating a Fund for National Emergencies and emergency-related institutions; an increase in the proportion of national budgets earmarked for agriculture; the coordination of nation measures at the sub-regional level; and, at the continental level, early implementation of the newly created Emergency Assistance Fund for Drought.

In the short-term, the Steering Committee recommended that general assistance be given to farmers to raise funds, purchase and maintain equipment, and distribute products at remunerative prices. It suggested that provision be made for institutions to maintain equipment and infrastructure as well as better to utilize water resources. For medium-term measures, the committee recommended that countries should concentrate on food production, promote better resource utilization, and conserve forest resources. National animal production as well as fishery production would need to be improved through better management, expanded veterinary services for livestock, and the establishment of fishing corporations at the regional and continental levels. For the long term, the committee emphasized structural measures, the need to improve research, technology, and distribution. In addition, the committee urged improvements in the training of skilled manpower while raising the living conditions and improving the infrastructure of rural areas. They also recommended developing other economic sectors in tandem with agriculture. Finally, at the sub-regional and regional levels, they suggested cooperation in the agricultural sectors and food production.

On the problem of drought and desertification, the committee recommended strategies such as national policies that emphasized effective utilization of vegetation, the protection of ecosystems, and an intensified development of water and energy resources. Other recommendations included the need for information and data exchanges, development of the Sahelian green belt, implementation of relevant OAU/ECA resolutions, and improved South-South cooperation at the sub-regional and continental levels.

The Nigerian delegation endorsed these recommendations and also emphasized the need to find ways to achieve internal self-sufficiency in food production, thereby reducing Africa's dependence on the outside world while conserving foreign exchange for other developmental needs. General Buhari highlighted the need to implement programs of integrated rural development and the provision of infrastructure finances, and general mobilization of the rural population to encourage farmers to embark on meaningful agricultural production. Nigeria also proposed that the African Centre for Fertilizer Development should commence operations immediately so that farmers could be assisted in achieving their goals of increased production.

Recommendations relating to small irrigation schemes such as earth dams, the need locally to fabricate small agricultural equipment, adequate storage facilities, and the establishment of early-warning systems and permanent mechanisms for coping with emergency situations were also endorsed by Nigeria. The head of state further emphasized the need for member states to cooperate in the control and eradication of livestock diseases, which do not respect national borders.[9]

At the international level, General Buhari proposed that a strong appeal to the World Bank, specialized agencies of the United Nations system, and all other donor countries be included in the final declaration to channel funds for African drought, famine, and economic recovery through existing sub-regional and regional groupings, such as cooperative efforts in agriculture and food production.[10] It was Nigeria's view that such assistance would eliminate the need for further feasibility studies and additional staff that would consume scarce funds. Support for ongoing projects and programs already designed and approved by these sub-regional groups would eliminate further delays in getting international assistance directly to the people.[11]

On the external debt issue, Nigeria fully endorsed the call for an international conference. A collective African position on this issue would strengthen our bargaining position with creditors over the means of alleviating the crushing debt problem. Although Africa's total external indebtedness was estimated at just over $170 billion through the end of 1985 and represented a relatively small proportion of the external indebtedness of all Third World Nations, this remained a deceptive situation. The debt-service burden on the African countries remained quite alarming because it swallowed up to 27 percent of the continent's total export earnings. Moreover, Africa's level of industrial output and foreign-exchange earnings from non-commodity exports remained very low. The deteriorating terms of trade had also harmed even the traditional commodity exports, which led to a substantial reduction in foreign exchange earnings.

While African countries would continue to request assistance from the international community in pursuing their development goals, Nigeria reiterated the point made earlier that "the major responsibility for our social and economic development rests squarely on us and we should demonstrate a high sense of commitment to our regional development programs."[12] General Buhari pointed to various avenues for promoting economic and technical cooperation among African states for the improvement of their economies, but also observed that the level of cooperation had not been impressive.[13] New measures would also need to be taken to strengthen existing platforms for consultation and negotiation in the various international fora, so as to enchance Africa's bargaining position. Nigeria further suggested that the secretariats of the OAU and ECA should cooperate more fruitfully and promote the attainment of Africa's development aspirations.

These proposals were incorporated in the conclusions of the 21st summit of the OAU. In addition, the summit approved the establishment of national monitoring units which would also prepare regional and international conferences, while incorporating common regional objectives into national programs. Furthermore, the Department of Economic Cooperation in the OAU was to be strengthened. High-level machinery to coordinate and prepare the positions of African states in negotiations at various international fora was to be established by the OAU.

Nigeria played a pioneering, sustained role in the efforts that resulted in a successful OAU summit devoted largely to a consideration of Africa's economic problems. Under the leadership of the senior officials in the Ministry of External Affairs, several other home ministries and relevant agencies of the Nigerian government also made highly commendable contributions which enhanced the participation of the Nigerian delegation. The wisdom of strengthening the capacity of the Ministry of External Affairs in the coordination of Nigeria's international economic cooperation was also vindicated. The Directorate of International Economic Cooperation in the Ministry of External Affairs gave a good account of itself, although the input of the Department of Intra-African Affairs was no less significant in the preparation of final briefs for the summit delegation. Due recognition should also be given to the crucial roles played by the Ministry of National Planning under the leadership of its minister, Chief M.S. Adigun, and his indefatigable Permanent Secretary, Alhaji Abubakar Alhaji.

The Informal Consultative Committee on foreign policy also had an opportunity to review and comment on the draft agenda and outline of the positions to be taken at the summit. The committee's suggestions were brought to the attention of General Buhari, who found them particularly useful in his own consultations at Addis Ababa before and during the summit. Since that was the second time General Buhari had attended an OAU summit, and because the very idea of an economic summit originated from him during the previous year, he was more relaxed than he was at the previous summit. He demonstrated considerable confidence and a great grasp of the issues. His views were welcomed and eventually endorsed by his colleagues.

There was, however, one major hurdle to cross by the summit delegates, and that concerned the election of a Secretary-General for the organization. It would certainly have derogated from the accomplishments of the African leaders who gathered at Addis Ababa if the summit failed, once again, to elect a Secretary-General, whose job was to facilitate the implementation of their decisions on the continent's economic problems. Actually, there had been no new Secretary-General of the OAU since the forced departure of Edem Kodjo in 1983. During the 19th summit, Gabon and Mali presented their respective foreign ministers as candidates for the post, but neither one secured the two-thirds majority needed for election. Dr. Peter Onu, a Nigerian diplomat who was also the longest-serving of the assistant secretaries-general of the OAU, was appointed Secretary-General *ad interim*.

As the 20th summit approached, Nigeria announced its position regarding the office of the Secretary-General.[14] Since independence, we explained, it had been our policy not to nominate a Nigerian for the post, in the same way that the Great Powers did not put up their nationals for the post of Secretary-General of the United Nations.[15] However, Nigeria had always worked to obtain the post of one of the assistant secretaries-general in the OAU, and in this we had succeeded thanks to the general cooperation of member states in the West African sub-region. Dr. Peter Onu was a beneficiary of the success of this policy of retaining an assistant secretary-general post for Nigeria.

The Buhari administration intended to be consistent on this matter and therefore declared its intention not to put up any Nigerian as a candidate for Secretary-General at the 20th summit. Our commitment to the OAU would transcend personnel considerations, such as having a citizen of Nigeria as head of the secretariat. This policy decision was made without prejudice to the situation whereby Dr. Peter Onu could continue in office if that was the wish of other OAU members.

At the summit, member states needed six ballots to elect a new Secretary-General. Both Gabon and Mali presented the same candidates who had failed to get elected to the post during the previous summit. Once again, neither candidate secured the two-thirds majority. After the third ballot the summit recessed and all the heads of delegations went into private consultations. When the summit resumed, the Malian candidate, Mr. Beye, withdrew from the contest and voting was resumed for the single candidate from Gabon, Mr. Okumba. Still, after three more ballots, he failed to secure the mandatory two-thirds majority. The deadlock was becoming embarrassing to the African leaders, who then went into a second recess. The chairman,

President Julius Nyerere, and the bureau of the summit went into private consultations and after heated arguments concluded that the stalemate could not be broken. It was therefore suggested by the bureau, and endorsed by the summit as a whole, that Dr. Peter Onu should continue for another year as Secretary-General *ad interim*. Our policy statement made earlier on this issue was vindicated almost to the letter.

However, the situation had changed somewhat by the time the 21st summit had convened. The pressures to elect a substantive Secretary-General were then more insistent. Moreover, the previous summit had appealed to the governments of Gabon and Mali to withdraw their candidates before the 21st summit. Gabon did so but Mali remained equivocal on the issue. Meanwhile, Niger had formally intimated to the OAU secretariat and, through it, to all member states, its intention to present Ide Oumarou as a candidate for the post. In addition, Niger had sent envoys to most African states, including Nigeria, to canvass for their candidate.

Niger was perhaps the most peaceful, understanding, and friendly of all the neighboring countries of Nigeria. President Kountche had made a highly successful state visit to Nigeria early in the life of the Buhari administration. Both President Kountche and General Buhari developed excellent rapport and laid the foundation for a mutually beneficial interaction between our two countries. As a matter of deliberate policy, Nigeria had no intention of presenting any candidate of her own for the post of Secretary-General. Moreover, no other country besides Niger had asked for Nigeria's support in the upcoming contest for the post. It was therefore not surprising that Nigeria pledged to support the candidate of Niger, Idi Oumaru. Nigeria was not alone in endorsing the Nigerien candidate.

However, some other members of the OAU were not as enthusiastic at the prospect of Niger's candidate for the post. Tanzania suspected that France was behind the Nigerien nomination. Algeria and the so-called "radical states" within the OAU also had reservations, not so much about the personal competence of Mr. Oumarou (he performed competently as chairman of the 40th Council of Ministers meeting at Addis Ababa in 1984) but about the independent foreign policy positions of Niger and especially her failure to recognize SADR.

Armed with instructions from the Federal Military Government, I preceded the Nigerian delegation to the 21st summit and used the pre-summit Council of Ministers meeting to persuade my colleagues to elect a substantive Secretary-General. We worked on ECOWAS member states to agree that a single candidate from our sub-region should be supported in the coming election. We also made it clear to the foreign ministers of other member states that Nigeria was not playing any diplomatic games and would not provoke another deadlock so that Dr. Peter Onu would be retained as acting

Secretary-General. There was in fact a rather malicious publication in the French journal *Jeune Afrique*, alleging that Nigeria wanted to create such a deadlock. For the good of the OAU and the credibility of the organization's new focus on economic concerns, a new Secretary-General was needed.

Notwithstanding the arguments advanced by Nigeria and our delegation's efforts at seeking more votes for the candidate who had our firm support, the eventual election of the Secretary-General by the summit was not easy. The Malian government continued to give the impression that the candidature of its foreign minister, Blondin Beye, had not been withdrawn since it was initially submitted in a communication with the OAU secretariat dated 10 June 1983. This hurdle was scaled when the Malian president was prevailed upon to withdraw Beye's candidature. Then, after three straight ballots, the single candidate, Oumaru, failed to obtain the two-thirds majority. At that point the heads of state went into private session.

Upon their return to the open session, three additional ballotings took place and Oumarou still failed to get elected. There was a general feeling that the key to breaking the deadlock was in the hands of President Nyerere and the so-called "radical member states." Several delegations appealed to the determined minority to the effect that, having made their reservations known, they should allow the overwhelming majority to have its way. And when the seventh ballot took place, Idi Oumarou finally received 37 votes with 8 opposed, 3 abstentions, and 1 void ballot. He was thus elected the new Secretary-General of the OAU for a four-year term, as stipulated by the charter of the organization.

The OAU emerged from that summit in much better shape than a year or two before, when it appeared to be at the point of collapse and, even worse, irrelevance to Africa's real problems. The OAU had succeeded in diffusing the issue of the legitimacy of the leadership in Chad and also resolved the Western Sahara issue in favor of Polisario—at least on the diplomatic front. A new Secretary-General was elected and the attention of member states had been shifted to economic concerns. Finally, the summit adopted the document *Africa's Priority Program for Economic Recovery 1986–1990*, which had a realistic approach to obtaining the resources for its implementation.

It was to the credit of skilful African diplomacy and the soundness of the recommendations contained in that document that the United Nations later decided in its General Assembly Resolution 40/40 to convene a special session to consider the critical economic situation in our continent. In that special session, scheduled for 27 to 31 May 1986, the General Assembly was to focus "in a comprehensive and integrated manner, on the rehabilitation and medium and long-term development problems and challenges facing African countries with a view to promoting and adopting action-oriented and concerted measures."

In all these positive achievements made by the OAU prior to and during the 21st summit, Nigeria played important roles. Hence the Nigerian delegation, under the leadership of General Buhari, returned to Lagos after the summit justifiably proud that our country had contributed to the revitalization of the OAU.

NOTES

1. Address by General Buhari to the plenary session of the 20th summit of the OAU, Addis Ababa, 12 November 1984.
2. Ibid.
3. Ibid.
4. Ibid.
5. Ibid.
6. General Buhari, "Annual Foreign Policy Address, Annual Patron's dinner, Nigerian Institute of International Affairs" (3 December 1984).
7. Ibid.
8. General Buhari, contributions to the plenary session of the 21st special summit on Africa's economic problems, Addis Ababa, 18–21 July 1986.
9. Ibid.
10. Ibid.
11. Ibid.
12. Ibid.
13. Ibid.
14. Public lecture at Ahmadu Bello University, Zaria, 26 July 1984.
15. Ibid.

10

For Liberation in Southern Africa

A revitalized Organization for African Unity was capable of championing African liberation with greater respect and credibility in the international community as a whole. Therefore, our administration in Nigeria paid particular attention within the organization to the liberation issue. My own baptism in practical diplomacy on this issue occurred shortly after my taking office as foreign minister at the 40th ordinary session of the OAU Council of Ministers.

The Nigerian delegation to that meeting was invited to co-sponsor a draft resolution seeking the full support of the council for diplomatic initiatives taken by Angola and Mozambique, which had made special arrangements with South Africa, known respectively as the Troop Withdrawal and Nkomati Accords. We declined to do so. Instead, Nigeria joined Ghana and Benin to express strong reservations about what was tantamount to "dialogue" with the racist South African regime. Our reservations contributed to the eventual outcome, whereby the council merely "expressed sympathy and deep understanding" with those frontline states which felt the necessity to reach some kind of understanding with South Africa. However, Nigeria and other members of the OAU Council of Ministers reaffirmed their commitment to the continued struggle for the independence of Namibia and the dismantling of apartheid. We also reiterated our collective support for the frontline states and paid special tribute to Angola, Mozambique, Lesotho, and others in the sub-region for their continuing sacrifices in the face of South Africa's repeated acts of aggression and destabilization.

It is perhaps necessary to put Nigeria's attitude in the wider context of our policy in that sub-region. Nigeria has always believed that South Africa constitutes one of the greatest threats to her national interest. Since independence we have mounted a sustained campaign of destabilization against the racist regime. In return, South Africa has identified Nigeria, the most populous black African state with the greatest potential ability to undermine apartheid, as a prime target for possible retaliation. Nigeria, by maximizing the advantages inherent in holding chairmanship of the United Nations Special Committee against Apartheid, sought to expose the monstrosity and moral poverty of apartheid before world opinion. As a result, even the friends of South Africa in the Western world have been forced to denounce apartheid in various international fora.

Actually, before the inauguration of the Reagan administration in the United States in January 1981, the racist regime had been generally put on the defensive internationally. The sudden collapse of the Portuguese colonial empire in the Southern African sub-region exposed the futility of erecting so-called impregnable defenses. When Mozambique and Angola became independent in 1975, it was clear that Rhodesia would soon become transformed into the sovereign state of Zimbabwe. Namibia's own independence, which looked decades away, suddenly became achievable when the UN Security Council adopted Resolution 435 in 1978 and laid down the procedures and processes for the decolonization of that territory, illegally occupied by South Africa. An international arms embargo placed on the racist regime in 1977 appeared to signal that the international community was responding positively to the repeated calls that only through strong and effective sanctions could the racists be brought to their senses.

After 1981, however, things began to change, and for the worse. The early part of the Reagan administration coincided with a worldwide economic recession, which hit the Third World nations particularly hard. For Nigeria, the resulting oil glut adversely affected traditional earnings from oil exports. The share of that income available for foreign policy pursuits fell sharply. In addition to the effects of the global recession, the frontline states suffered from other economic ailments, such as drought, famine, and flood; they were also the victims of intense and sustained criminal attacks from South African military forces in flagrant violations of their sovereignty and territorial integrity. Given the prevailing climate, it was not surprising that the Reagan administration gained the upper hand in promoting the idea of so-called constructive engagement with South Africa. A policy initially billed as one of "carrot and stick" later became all carrots and no sticks.

Meanwhile, Mozambique had signed a non-aggression pact with Pretoria and Angola concluded troop withdrawal agreements with the racist regime. These could not have been signed out of choice but out of necessity, imposed by the horrendous economic and security problems faced by these frontline states with hardly any assistance from sister African states. Nonetheless, the agreements with South Africa endangered the sanctuaries of the South West African Peoples' Organization (SWAPO) in Angola and threatened the operational bases of the African National Congress (ANC) in

Mozambique. In that sense, the two sets of agreements with South Africa constituted serious setbacks to the process of liberation.

It was largely because of these unfavorable developments that the Federal Military Government decided that I should proceed on an intensive tour of the frontline states. The tour began on 20 May 1984, the first stop being Dar es Salaam, in Tanzania, and ended on 4 June 1984 at Addis Ababa, where our delegation briefed the chairman of the OAU, Col. Mengistu of Ethiopia. There were four main objectives for the trip. First was to gain an on-the-spot assessment of the situation and of developments in Southern Africa, with special emphasis on the accords and agreements signed by some of the frontline states with Pretoria. Second, we were to assess the effects of those agreements on the decolonization efforts in Namibia and on the operational activities of the liberation movements—the ANC and SWAPO. Third was to exchange views with the leadership of the frontline states on the situation in Southern Africa, other continental issues, and bilateral matters. Finally, and perhaps most important of all, was to express solidarity with the frontline states and the liberation movements in Southern Africa.

In addition to Tanzania, our official delegation visited Mozambique, Zimbabwe, Zambia, Botswana, and Angola before going to the OAU headquarters in Addis Ababa and finally returning home. We had informative and highly rewarding conversations with the presidents, heads of government, and foreign ministers of these countries, whose remarks contained several common threads.

First, South Africa's economic and military predominance in the subregion had increased the vulnerability of all the frontline states to destabilizing acts. Second, the increasing dependence on goods and services from South Africa had threatened the economic survival of the frontline states, especially Mozambique, Lesotho, and Botswana. Third, the U.S. policy of "constructive engagement," which rolled back the rising tide of liberation in Southern Africa and bought time for the racist regime, had promoted the signing, almost under duress, of the troop withdrawal and non-aggression pacts by some frontline states. Fourth was the need for the liberation movements, particularly the ANC, the frontline states, and Africa as a whole to adopt new strategies to deal with the realities and challenges rapidly unfolding in Southern Africa.

These developments and the fresh perspectives gained from the tour led to a reexamination of our own policy and postures. As a result, the following decisions were taken. First, we felt that the accords signed by some of the frontline states amounted to a renewed dialogue with the racists. Any kind of dialogue had been decisively rejected by Nigeria and other members of the OAU in the 1970s, and we should continue this opposition to dialogue in any form or variant. In addition, Nigeria would mobilize the support of other African countries for our view that the racist regime should first engage in meaningful dialogue with its own people, including authentic black leaders such as Nelson Mandela, who was still imprisoned in Robben Island. The searchlight of world opinion should, in this way, be placed squarely on South Africa's domestic situation.

Second, and notwithstanding the recently concluded accords, Nigeria would maintain support for the liberation movements through a combination of strategies such as:

(a) making substantial financial and other material contributions to the ANC and SWAPO, and, to a much lesser extent, to PAC (Nigeria made monetary contributions to some of the frontline states to assist them in consolidating their national economies and their military capabilities);

(b) encouraging the ANC to rethink new strategies of operations within South Africa itself. Although this would now be possible only at greater risks than before, the ANC should be emboldened by the desperation of the racist regime and increased support from Nigeria and other African states;

(c) increasing consultations with Eastern bloc countries with a view to improving their assistance to the liberation movements;

(d) on the wider international scene, identifying and working actively with influential groups such as religious organizations and anti-apartheid groups to increase world attention directed at the evils of apartheid;

(e) obtaining international support for the frontline states through the Non-Aligned Movement, the UNO, and OPEC, so as to strengthen their economies and reduce their dependence on South Africa.

At the level of the Organization for African Unity's Coordinating Committee for the Liberation of Africa, Nigeria fully participated at the 43rd and 44th ordinary sessions, at Accra and Arusha, Tanzania, in January and July 1985. The Nigerian delegation to the session in Accra, led by me, proposed that the 45th session of the committee be held in Lagos as a further demonstration of our commitment to the liberation issue. That session also endorsed our proposal that a high-level delegation from the OAU, preferably led by the current chairman and his bureau, should be sent to Washington to convey Africa's feelings against the U.S. policy of "constructive engagement."

The Liberation Committee went on to reject the United States' linkage of the right of independence of the Namibian people to the withdrawal of

Cuban troops from the sovereign state of Angola. In order to break the stalemate on the implementation of UN Security Council Resolution 435, another meeting of the Security Council was to be sought. To ensure maximum success, it was agreed that such a Security Council meeting should be preceded by meticulous preparations and receive a high level of representation by African countries. Finally, the committee commended the decision of the government of New Zealand to close down the South African consulate in that country, but expressed grave concern over the plan made by a New Zealand rugby team to visit South Africa toward the end of that year, in violation of the Commonwealth agreement to prohibit sporting contacts with racist South Africa. The New Zealand government later took positive steps to have the rugby tour stopped.

The Liberation Committee held its 44th ordinary meeting in Arusha, Tanzania, between 4 and 6 July 1985. The meeting was attended by the foreign ministers of Ghana and Tanzania, and myself, two ministers of state from Uganda and Zambia, two vice-ministers from Mozambique and Kenya, as well as representatives of the liberation movements, the ANC, SWAPO, and the Pan-African Congress (PAC). The Acting Secretary-General of the OAU, Dr. Peter Onu, was also in attendance. This was clearly one of the best attended meetings of the OAU liberation movement.

However, the biggest attraction of the session was the presence of Mwalimu Julius Nyerere, then president of Tanzania, who opened the meeting. In a real sense, President Nyerere's address was a public farewell speech on liberation in Southern Africa, because a few months later he stepped down as the head of state and government of his country. Therefore his analysis of the situation in Southern Africa took an additional significance. According to Mwalimu Nyerere, Africa now faced the hard core of a racist and colonialist power. He analyzed the situation in Namibia in detail and showed how the Reagan administration's policy of constructive engagement had emboldened South Africa to defy world opinion about granting early and genuine independence to Namibia. He also noted that the apartheid regime had installed a puppet interim administration in Windhoek, capital of Namibian territory. SWAPO therefore had no alternative but to intensify the armed struggle to force the implementation of United Nations Security Council Resolution 435.

With regards to South Africa itself, President Nyerere recalled that peaceful means to effect change in that republic started as far back as 1912, but successive racist governments had responded with greater acts of repression. African states had no choice now but to support the struggle of the majority in South Africa. President Nyerere recalled the murderous attacks of the regime against its own citizens and neighboring states. He put at $7 billion the cost of South African aggression against other states, and he concluded by calling upon Africa and the world to assist the frontline states, because the principles which they were defending were universal principles relating to the equality and dignity of man.

Nigeria was later unanimously elected to chair the 44th ordinary session of the Liberation Committee. As leader of the Nigerian delegation, I then presided over the rest of the session. The election of Nigeria was a further recognition of our country's foremost role in the liberation struggle. Nigeria was often regarded as a frontline state, not in the geographical sense, obviously, but in its commitment to the struggle. Nigeria was also to chair the next session of the Liberation Committee, scheduled for Lagos in early 1986.

There were two sensitive issues which Nigeria addressed at the 44th session. In my closing speech, I touched on need for member states to pay the arrears of financial contributions to the Liberation Committee:"The test of our commitment to the struggle is the payment of contributions when due,"I said, "otherwise it rings hollow to denounce apartheid but fail to bear a modest financial burden to speed up the collapse of the racist regime."[1] Our economic difficulties notwithstanding, African states could not be excused for continued failure to pay their contributions.

There was also the issue of dialogue. Having observed that Africa had firmly rejected dialogue with the racists a decade and a half previously, I pointed out that the 20th summit of the OAU included in the Declaration on Southern Africa the prohibition of links with the racist country, except for those member states whose historical links and geographic location unavoidably tied them to South Africa.[2] We in Nigeria felt extremely disturbed by reports of economic and other ties with the regime. In our view, "no economic plight or potential benefits could justify such links," and we therefore called upon those states to dissolve those ties, because such connections undermined morale and made a mockery of efforts to isolate Pretoria.[3]

Nigeria effectively used the forum provided by the Non-Aligned Movement. At the extraordinary ministerial meeting of the Coordinating Bureau of the nonaligned countries on the question of Namibia, which took place in New Delhi, India, 19–21 April 1985, Nigeria reiterated her support for SWAPO as the sole and authentic representative of the Namibian people. The Delhi meeting happily coincided with the 25th anniversary of SWAPO. The Nigerian delegation also condemned the latest South African attempts to circumvent UN Security Council Resolution 435 by promoting an internal settlement through the so-called Multi-Party Conference. South Africa was also pronounced guilty of wrecking the Namibian independence talks held in Lusaka and Mindelo in 1984 through an insistence on introducing elements extraneous to the resolution.

Putting the responsibility for the unfortunate state of affairs in Namibia squarely on the major Western countries, which had intensified their collaboration with Pretoria in the nuclear, military, economic, financial, and technological fields, contrary to the resolutions of the United Nations, the Nigerian delegation demanded a change of heart from them.[4] On the part of the Non-Aligned Movement, while the members should be commended for keeping the Namibian issue very much alive, the Nigerian delegation wanted declarations of support for SWAPO to be translated into concrete actions. The determination of the Non-Aligned Movement to make sacrifices and display singleness of purpose to help bring freedom and justice to Namibia would powerfully complement SWAPO's intensification of the armed struggle.

As leader of the Nigerian delegation to this meeting, I made a recommendation which, if adopted, would enhance the movement's diplomatic support for SWAPO. The meeting was called upon to request "all members of the Non-Aligned Movement and indeed all developing countries as well as friends of our Movement which still maintain diplomatic links with South Africa to sever them without further delay as a sign of their disgust at the continued subjugation of Namibia and the perpetuation of apartheid."[5] This proposal was endorsed in the final documents that emerged from the Delhi meeting.[6] Nigeria also joined other delegations in mandating the bureau of the Non-Aligned Movement to request an urgent meeting of the UN Security Council to discuss the Namibian question. The bureau then designated the foreign ministers of Nigeria and selected African countries to participate at the Security Council meeting.

It was also decided that the chairman of the Coordinating Bureau should remain in constant touch with the UN Secretary-General and the representative of the chairman of the OAU, as well as with the president of the United Nations Council for Namibia and SWAPO, with a view to coordinating efforts aimed at expediting the attainment of Namibian independence. Since the year 1985 marked the 40th anniversary of both the consideration of Namibia by the United Nations and the establishment of the world body itself, appropriate programs of activities were to be undertaken to highlight the Namibian cause.

The bureau further requested the UN Council for Namibia and SWAPO to implement its Decree No. 1 for the Protection of the Natural Resources of Namibia in order to reaffirm its validity under international law and to put an end to the unceasing plunder of Namibia's natural resources. In addition, the bureau requested the council to consider steps toward establishing an exclusive economic zone for Namibia in order to safeguard and assert Namibian sovereignty over its offshore and marine resources.

Pending the imposition of mandatory sanctions against South Africa under Chapter VII of the UN Charter, the bureau urged member states and other nations to sever all links and dealings with South Africa, in accordance with UN General Assembly resolutions to that effect. The measures were to include:

(i) observance of an oil embargo;
(ii) disinvestment and a stop to new investment;
(iii) withholding of overflight and landing facilities to aircraft and docking rights to ocean vessels;
(iv) prohibition of the sale of krugerrands and all other South African coins;
(v) strict observance of the sports and cultural boycott; and
(vi) ratification and implementation of the International Convention on the Suppression and Punishment of the Crime of Apartheid.

The bureau urged the United Nations to strictly enforce, and member states to scrupulously observe, the mandatory arms embargo imposed against South Africa by Security Council Resolution 418. Member UN states were also urged to implement Resolution 558 (1984), forbidding import of armaments from South Africa. In more concrete terms, the bureau urged nonaligned countries to contribute generously to the Non-Aligned Solidarity Fund for Namibia and directed the fund's board of directors, in consultation with SWAPO, to propose to the Coordinating Bureau in New York appropriate uses of the available resources.

The final document of the bureau's Delhi meeting also called upon parliamentarians, nongovernmental organizations, media representatives, academics, intellectuals, and peoples of the world to "raise their voice, severally and collectively in support of the Namibian cause," because the mobilization of world public opinion and pressure remained particularly crucial in "countries whose policies and practices are at variance with relevant United Nations resolutions and decisions."[7]

These conclusions and outcomes were gratifying to the Nigerian delegation. It was also commendable that throughout the meeting, representatives of the frontline states including Nigeria met constantly to plan strategies and present a coordinated perspective on the Namibian question. The focus of the perspective later moved from the Non-Alignment Movement itself to the international community as a whole.

The diplomatic battlefront was then shifted, as agreed, to New York and to the special session of the UN Security Council. In view of the growing informed public within the United States, the Reagan administration appeared particularly careful not to veto a Security Council resolution passed by wide consensus. The decision facing the African delegations to the special session was whether to present a strongly worded draft resolution, which the United States would almost certainly veto, or to be satisfied for the time being with a relatively weaker version that the United States government could support. This was not an easy decision and there were several strong arguments on both sides of the question.

The Nigerian Permanent Mission to the United Nations in New York hosted several strategy sessions involving the frontline states' foreign ministers and myself. These sessions and the conclusions reached were particularly useful for harmonizing positions before the debate in the Security Council commenced. They also testified to the increasing regard with which Nigeria was held on this issue. The consensus of the strategy session was to go for a resolution that would strongly condemn the U.S. policy of constructive engagement and linkage, while also calling for comprehensive and mandatory sanctions to force South Africa to implement the process of Namibian independence.

Several other meetings took place at the OAU office in New York to discuss the issues with a wider group of African states, and later at the United Nations headquarters itself, where we met with the Non-Aligned Movement as a whole. By the time the Security Council debate commenced, the solidarity of members of the Non-Aligned Movement was strengthened, their bargaining position was enhanced, and only a veto by the United States, alone or in conjunction with Britain and France, stood between them and new resolutions calling for the immediate implementation of Resolution 435 and the imposition of sanctions against South Africa.

The 2583rd meeting of the Security Council, convened for the special consideration of the Namibian issue, was very well attended. Under the presidency of Mr. Mahaber of Trinidad and Tobago, all the permanent and other members of the Security Council reiterated their well-known positions on Namibia. The president also called upon the acting president of the United Nations Council for Namibia and SWAPO, Sam Nujoma and the Indian Minister of State for External Affairs, Khurshed Alam Khan, to address the council. The three speakers reviewed the analysis and conclusions of the Coordinating Bureau's meeting at New Delhi. Several other ministers and delegations spoke before the South African delegate, Mr. von Schirnding, addressed the council.

Mr. von Schirnding's contribution was truly astounding. As usual, he blamed the victims of South Africa's racism at home and aggression abroad for the worsening situation in Southern Africa. According to him, the problems of Southern Africa should be solved on a regional basis, precisely the environment in which the racists have overwhelming military and economic advantages. He reaffirmed the linkage of Namibian independence with the withdrawal of Cuban troops from Angola and commended for international approval the internal settlement arrangements made for Namibia by South Africa. Finally, Mr. von Schirnding identified the ANC members not as freedom fighters but as people whose actions posed a "direct threat to the people of South Africa and southern Africa."[8]

By a strange coincidence, I was invited by the Security Council president to speak immediately after the South African representative. Taking advantage of the coincidence, however, I ad-libbed the statement that "the racists have just spoken before this Security Council and [we can all see how] their evasions, their diversions and their lies have multiplied."[9] The stalemate over the implementation of Security Council Resolution 435 gave the impression, I said, that the issue of Namibian independence was no longer a subject of decolonization but a pawn in the ideological chess game invented by South Africa to draw a superpower to its side. What was needed, in our view, was "not a new plan, not bilateral negotiations brokered by outside power, but the will of the international community, and particularly the United States of America, to prevail upon South Africa to cooperate with the Secretary-General in ensuring the implementation of Resolution 435(1978) without any further delay."[10] Meanwhile, Nigeria reiterated her total opposition to South Africa's attempt to circumvent the United Nations by promoting an internal settlement as part of an imposed settlement that would leave the people of Namibia in perpetual bondage.[11] In conclusion, I said that "the Security Council cannot continue to spare the rod and spoil South Africa. The recalcitrant child, which apartheid South Africa has proved to be, deserves to be chastised with the full weight of the Council's authority. And [Nigeria] stands ready to assist the Council fully in enforcing any sanctions the Council may impose [while we continue] to assist SWAPO to intensify its armed struggle against the forces of oppression, until total liberation of its fatherland from illegal occupation by a racist, brutal colonial regime."[12]

At the end of the Security Council meeting, a resolution was passed that rejected the linkage idea and endorsed voluntary sanctions against South Africa along the lines earlier passed by the General Assembly and reaffirmed by the Coordinating Bureau of the foreign ministers meeting of the Non-Aligned Movement in New Delhi in April 1985. A limited victory, this was nevertheless a significant milestone in what had, unfortunately, become a rather long road to the attainment of independence for Namibia under the leadership of SWAPO.

NOTES

1. Closing speech by the Nigerian Foreign Minister and chairman of the 44th ordinary session of the OAU Coordinating Committee for the Liberation of Africa, 6 July 1985.

2. Ibid.
3. Ibid.
4. Speech by the Foreign Minister of Nigeria, at the Extra-Ordinary Ministerial Meeting of the Coordinating Bureau of the Non-Aligned Countries on the Question of Namibia (New Delhi, India, 19–21 April 1985).
5. Ibid.
6. See "Final Documents, Extra-Ordinary Ministerial Meeting of the Coordinating Bureau of the Non-Aligned Countries on the Question of Namibia" New Delhi, India, 21 April 1985.
7. Ibid.
8. "Provisional Verbatim Record of the Two Thousand Five Hundred and Eighty-Third meeting of the Security Council held at Headquarters" (New York, S/P, 2583, 10 June 1985), p. 101.
9. Ibid., p. 107
10. Ibid.
11. Ibid., p. 111.
12. Ibid., p. 112.

PART 4

Dealing with the West

11

Bargaining with the United States over Southern Africa

Two major instruments for the advancement of liberation in Southern Africa had emerged. They were the intensification of armed struggle and the effort to seek the abandonment of the policies of linkage and constructive engagement pursued by the Reagan administration. Nigeria had found it easier to make substantial financial and material contributions to the liberation movements in Southern Africa than to persuade the Reagan administration to change its policies and join the growing international pressure to impose comprehensive sanctions against South Africa.Nonetheless, our country had not relented in the efforts to bargain with the United States and show that her long-term interests would be better served by ostracizing South Africa than by collaborating with it.

The United States is a global superpower, whereas Africa has no raw power with which to bargain with the United States. However, the basis for mutually beneficial interaction and interdependence does exist between Africa and the United States. The United States cannot responsibly ignore Africa's abundant raw materials and valuable minerals, which her industrial and military establishments require, while Africa could use American technology and expertise in the agricultural and food sectors, and in the exploitation of mineral resources and the industrial base. This interdependence is even more real in the dealings between United States' allies in Europe on the one hand and Africa on the other, and it creates the basis for seeking changes in American policies.

With specific regard to Nigeria-United States relations and the prerequisites of fruitful interaction, there are several commonalities between the two countries. First, Nigeria has an economic system that is basically premised on "free enterprise." We share similar democratic spirits and our two countries contain the largest concentrations of black people in the world. With a population of about 100 million, Nigeria has the market potential to attract investments from international companies with headquarters in the United States and Western Europe. As an important country in the West African sub-region and in the OAU, Nigeria can hardly be ignored by the United States on political matters affecting the African continent. It is for these reasons that bilateral relations with the United States have great potential, irrespective of changes of regime and administration in either Nigeria or America.

Nonetheless major irritations between the two countries had arisen from sharply differing perceptions of the political problems in Southern Africa. United States Assistant Secretary of State for African Affairs Dr. Chester Crocker noted that these have constituted the only "nuisance" in Nigeria/U.S. relations, a nuisance that could be removed if the differing approaches to the liberation issues in Southern Africa could be reconciled or at least sharply reduced. The task of Nigerian diplomacy was to use the interdependence between the two countries to steer the United States away from the unhelpful positions taken by the Reagan administration.

We began bargaining in January 1984 by stressing the areas of agreement. Both countries shared the view that apartheid remained an evil system which must be eradicated, and that Namibia must receive independence. However, that was where agreement stopped. Nigeria was committed to the international isolation of South Africa in political, diplomatic, athletic, and cultural fields. For example, at the Commonwealth of Nations, South Africa lost her membership in 1961 as a result of the combined efforts of Nigeria and other member states. Nigeria also led the efforts by the Supreme Council for Sports in Africa to champion boycotts of South Africa in sporting contacts at the Commonwealth Games, the Olympics, and inter-club competitions involving other countries.

South Africa made unsuccessful efforts to break out of the international isolation imposed on her throughout the decade of the 1960s and early 1970s. It was the United States which tried particularly hard to help South Africa escape that isolation. Under the Nixon and Ford administrations, and later under President Reagan, the United States took steps which were designed to "buy time" for the racist regime in Pretoria and confer a kind of international respectability on her through the policy of constructive engagement. This attempt to promote contact and dialogue with South Africa was strongly opposed by Nigeria and the OAU. What would be the value of such dialogue, we asked, when the racist regime refused to engage in meaningful dialogue with its internal opponents?

With regard to Namibia, the United States had introduced the issue of the presence of Cuban troops in Angola, which we maintained was extraneous to the right of self-determination in Namibia. The Reagan administration was obsessed with a perceived Communist hold on Angola. Nigeria, however, believed that there should be no preconditions outside the terms of UN Resolution 435, which ought to be implemented without further delays. On the one hand, following his reelection in 1984 for another four-year term, President Reagan declared his intention not to change his policies on Southern Africa. On the other hand, no government in Nigeria could publicly declare its intention to compromise on the basic issues of anticolonialism and opposition to apartheid. Therefore, these fundamental differences remained between Nigeria and the United States, especially under the Reagan administration. Nonetheless, there were several more positive developments inside the United States. Opinion on college campuses, some board rooms of multinational corporations operating in South Africa, inside Congress, and among religious and civic groups throughout the United States was clearly becoming more enlightened about South Africa. A wave of demonstrations in major American cities against racism and in favor of disinvestment by American companies in South Africa called for tougher sanctions against the racist regime. Even more poignantly, more than 30 Republican congressmen registered their open dissent from the administration's Southern African policy by serving notice that they could no longer support President Reagan's policy of constructive engagement and the related aspect of pursuing "quiet diplomacy" with South Africa. The Congressmen pledged to join their Democratic counterparts to obtain legislation which would impose diplomatic and economic sanctions against South Africa if the latter continued to be intransigent.

President Reagan could hardly ignore this revolt within his own party. Accordingly, he felt compelled to declare on International Human Rights Day that South Africa must abandon apartheid, and called on the regime "to reach out to its black majority." Although it must have been difficult for him to admit this, he said that "there are occasions when quiet diplomacy is not enough . . . and that is why the United States calls for all South Africans to advance the democratic process and work towards a system of government based on the consent of the governed." Still, these were mere words and the administration remained unconvinced about the imposition of tough sanctions.

Taking advantage of these positive developments, Nigeria sought to convince the Reagan administration that she was sensitive to the concern over the perceived Communist domination of the cape route in Southern Africa, which the Western Powers regarded as crucial to their strategic interests. During the first ministerial-level contact between the Buhari administration and the United States, in Washington on 15 March 1984, the Southern African situation was discussed in full. Minister of Defense Major-General Domkat Bali and I told Secretary of State George Shultz that the problems could not be solved by a fixation on the fine points of ideological commitment or alignment, but rather by examining how to mitigate the debilitating consequences of continued black subjugation by the white minority regime. We argued that just as the socialist government in Angola did not endanger the interest of Western companies in the Cabinda oil fields, a free South Africa would respect legitimate Western interests.

Mr. Shultz was, of course, more concerned about the Soviet and Libyan involvements. We countered, however, that it was not always helpful to impose East-West conflicts on local issues in Africa. The Americans commended the signing of the non-aggression pact between Mozambique and South Africa. We expressed the view that any development which could bring peace to Southern Africa and halt the mass killings of blacks was desirable. However, the real threat to peace remained the Republic of South Africa's policies of destabilization, its illegal occupation of Namibia, and the violence of the apartheid system itself. Unless these policies were changed, the solid foundations for peace in Southern Africa would remain elusive. The meeting ended with no converts on either side, but we agreed to continue high-level discussions.

The next opportunity came during the 39th session of the United Nations General Assembly, when Secretary Shultz and his officials met with my staff and me at New York in October 1984. Once again, the bilateral issues between us were quickly discussed and we moved to a further round of talks on Southern Africa. And, once more, neither side changed its position on the liberation issues, but it appeared to us that while we were pushing our views with greater conviction, the same could not be said for the Americans. In any case, the United States government was, at very high levels, patiently listening to further clarifications of strongly held Nigerian views.

During the next meeting, between Dr. Crocker and myself in New York on 30 November 1984, we went over the same ground but perhaps with more heat from both sides. Dr. Crocker thought that Nigeria had ceased to have an open mind about the United States' efforts to bring early independence to Namibia. He pointed out the package deal that the United States had urged South Africa to embrace included UN Resolution 435 and the withdrawal of Cuban troops from Angola. Dr. Crocker also mentioned the troop-disengagement meetings between Angola and South Africa held two weeks earlier and noted that a second one was planned soon. He stressed that the United States had also expressed great concern to the South Africans over the wave of unrest there and the spate of detentions. All these efforts by the United States, said Dr. Crocker, appeared to be ill-understood by Nigeria and by African and some other Third World countries.

My team, which included Major-General J.N. Garba, Permanent Representative of Nigeria to the United Nations, and Ambassador Olu Adeniji, director-general of International Organizations in the Ministry of External

Affairs, expressed regret that the United States continued to oppose simple, routine resolutions proposed or passed by the United Nations on South Africa, even when the language and provisions of such resolutions had been significantly modified to take account of American sensitivities. As a result, the Nigeria government felt that it was not getting enough response from the United States on the Southern African question.

We assured Dr. Crocker that the Reagan administration's efforts on Namibian independence were appreciated but that we felt the United States could do more on this issue and push harder for real democratic change in South Africa. The policy of constructive engagement was producing the opposite effect, and in any case, the feeling of frustration by Nigeria could be easily explained by the fact that the UN Resolution 435 had been passed in 1978 and we were no closer to its implementation. We wanted evidence that the United States would serve notice on South Africa that the racists could no longer count on automatic U.S. support at the United Nations, and we could not see any indications in that direction.

I wrote directly to Secretary of State Shultz prior to the Security Council meeting on Namibia scheduled for 10 June 1985. I reiterated Nigeria's views and our preference for the employment of measures against South Africa under Chapter VII of the UN Charter, with the hope that they would meet with U.S. concurrence. Mr. Shultz declined to embrace the imposition of mandatory sanctions against South Africa but promised to continue to work with Angola, South Africa, Nigeria, and other interested parties to achieve Namibian independence. He reiterated the American position that the resolution of the Namibian problem had to take into account some regional security considerations which the Angolan and South African authorities were trying to resolve with U.S. mediation.

The apparently conciliatory tone of Shultz's letter created a more favorable climate for the next meeting between Dr. Crocker and myself, in New York at our Permanent Mission to the UN, on 12 June 1985, during the special session of the Security Council on Namibia. Dr. Crocker briefed us on the result of U.S. consultations on Namibia since our last meeting. He lamented that the Angolans and South Africans had not reached a compromise on the security issues dividing them, but he condemned the recent South African raid of Cabinda as an unacceptable action which had badly damaged South Africa's international stance. He in response to our query, Dr. Crocker also said that the multi-party proposal for Namibian settlement by South Africa was unacceptable to the United States and the international community.

We informed Dr. Crocker that we had joined the foreign ministers of the nonaligned states on a draft Security Council resolution which might incorporate Chapter 7 of the UN Charter and impose mandatory sanctions against South Africa. Dr. Crocker confirmed the point made earlier to me by Secretary Shultz, that the United States would oppose such language in the resolution, but his comments revealed some flexibility when he appeared to suggest that his side would be prepared to accept elements and language of the Security Council statement of 3 May 1985 and the Security Council resolution of October 1983 on Namibia. We then inquired whether the United States would commit itself to the implementation of Resolution 435 while other regional issues were handled separately. We pressed the view that, after all, the U.S. efforts since 1983 to settle regional security issues concurrently had not succeeded. In response, the Assistant Secretary of State said that Nigeria and the United States should work for a consensus resolution by the Security Council which would leave no one in doubt about the culprit in Southern Africa, but that the United States would never condemn or reject its own diplomacy in Southern Africa.

During the Buhari administration, we felt that we could use improved bilateral relations with the United States to achieve Nigeria's objectives in the areas of national security and economic interests and also to nudge the Americans to work more closely with us on the issues of Namibia and apartheid. We decided to revive the bilateral talks begun in the 1970s, which had been a useful forum for the discussion of joint as well as international issues. These talks, which were held annually in rotation between Lagos and Washington, involved very senior officials of both governments. In the civilian-government period in Nigeria, the talks were held at the vice-presidential level. It was our turn to host one in 1983, but it was postponed to the next year because of the arrangements for national elections in Nigeria; and then it was postponed again because the new military government needed more time to prepare. The time had come to resume these useful discussions in 1985.

There were definitely many bilateral issues to talk about. Evidence showed that the drastic reduction in American purchases of Nigerian petroleum was not due to high oil prices alone or even to the undeniable switch by many refineries in the United States to heavier crudes. It appeared to have resulted from deliberate policy. Moreover, Nigeria could use American technology and investments in both the agricultural and industrial sectors. The United States could also be positively involved in Nigeria's major petrochemical and liquified natural gas projects through the injection of much-needed capital investment and technical expertise. We could also discuss the problems which we were having in our negotiations with the International Monetary Fund (IMF) and the difficulties which its terms would create for our nation.

Numerous discussions and communications with Secretary of State Shultz and Assistant Secretary Crocker left me in no doubt that much could be gained on both sides by improving our bilateral relations. The extreme U.S. sensitivity to Nigeria's criticisms of her policies in Africa and some other world regions might well indirectly indicate the importance she attached to our opinions and positions on major issues. A concrete illustration of the regard in which Nigeria was held at the diplomatic level was embodied in a message received on 20 June 1985 from the United States government, which asked our support over the holding of more than 30 American citizens in Beirut as hostages in return for some 700 Shiite prisoners (Amal faction) imprisoned by Israel.

Of course, events in the Middle East changed so rapidly that we had no real leverage. Nonetheless, we felt we had to respond to the request for assistance, and we had to go on record as supporting the safety of all innocent airline passengers and opposing the detention of innocent prisoners as hostages. To be evenhanded, we expressed solidarity with all the Lebanese people and we condemned the Israeli government's disregard of the Geneva Convention when she moved the Shiite prisoners across international boundaries into Israel.

In the spirit of improving upon bilateral relations, and consistent with our policies concerning the Middle East, we dispatched urgent messages from General Buhari to the heads of state and government of Egypt, Syria, and Lebanon, requesting them to use their good offices to seek the release of the American hostages in Beirut. We also used the media to brief Nigerians about the American request and our response.

There was definitely a growing perception within the Buhari administration that if the two countries moved closer to each other we could skillfully use the improved relation to nudge the Americans toward substantial progress on the Southern African issue. We even proposed that General Buhari should make an official visit to Washington toward the end of 1985, when he was to be in the United States to attend the 40th anniversary of the creation of the United Nations. Such a visit would seek concessions from the United States and would complement the efforts of the chairman of the OAU, President Diouf of Senegal, who was to attend the UN General Assembly to present Africa's united views on what the continent expected on Southern African issues.

We were quite aware of the sharp limitations in our capability to make the U.S. government radically change its policies. The heady years of our country's oil boom and the use of oil as a diplomatic instrument were probably over. Our economy was in such a poor state that we were even more dependent on the Western world than before. The consumption pattern of our national elite and the need to regenerate industrial output required imports from the West which we were not in a position immediately to pay for. We wanted these countries to reopen their credit lines and meanwhile agree on some rescheduling of trade arrears and other external loans. At the same time, the creditor nations insisted on our getting the international badge of respectability (i.e., signing an agreement with the IMF) as a precondition for rescheduling and new credit lines.

It was a credit to Nigeria's diplomacy that, notwithstanding our seriously weakened economic position, we refused to be subservient; rather at every opportunity, in conversations with high government officials in the United States, at the OAU, at the United Nations, and in communiques issued during state visits to Nigeria, we expressed total opposition to apartheid and to the United States' linkage and constructive engagement policies.

However, we did realize that the diplomatic exchanges between Nigeria and the United States and the articulation of our views on Southern Africa to American officials and the rest of the world were useful mainly to clarify issues and apply pressure on the Reagan administration. They could not make that administration change its policies in Southern Africa for a change could come only within the United States itself. We therefore needed to develop useful contacts with prominent American politicians, black and white, Republicans and Democrats, and private individuals such as businessmen and journalists. The American political system and the processes of policy formulation operate not only through the administration but also through strong lobbying efforts and the involvement of influential individuals and pressure groups. Accordingly, we decided to supplement diplomatic contacts with direct interaction with nongovernmental groups and individuals. Major-General J.N. Garba of our Permanent Mission in New York received a special role because he had, in his other role as chairman of the United Nations Special Committee against Apartheid, developed the necessary communication lines to such groups, organizations, and individuals.

As a start, we extended an invitation to the Reverend Jesse Jackson to visit Nigeria to deliver some lectures and meet with high-level government officials, as well as anti-apartheid organizations. On his return to the United States, Reverend Jackson would undoubtedly be an important resource person for our continuing efforts to change the Reagan administration's posture on Southern Africa. We also had our eyes on Randall Robinson, executive director of the TransAfrica Foundation, the black group largely responsible for organizing the wave of anti-apartheid demonstrations in major American cities; David Rockefeller, and Anthony Solomon, the recently retired president of the Federal Reserve Bank of New York, who had remained a lover of African, and especially Nigerian, art. The companies earmarked for contact were Gulf, Mobil, Kellogg, and Bechtel, which were to serve as additional channels of communication with Americans.

It was perhaps a fitting end to my tenure of office as Foreign Minister that my last official duty under the Buhari administration was to recieve visiting

United States Congressman Stephen Solarz in Lagos on 22 August 1985, to discuss the situation in Southern Africa and press for a change in United States policies. Congressman Solarz, Democrat from New York, was one of the key opponents of the Reagan administration's policy of constructive engagement. Prior to visiting Nigeria, the congressman had been to South Africa, but he left five days before President Botha had made one of his famous speeches which proved, once again, to be a big disappointment to those expecting movement toward real change in the apartheid system. Our view was that the disappointment generated by Botha's speech could fuel the anger of blacks and that peace could only come with the rule of law and majority rule. Nigeria remained committed to the imposition of mandatory economic sanctions and to the immediate and unconditional implementation of UN Security Council Resolution 435 on Namibia.

The visiting Congressman replied that Nigeria had an important role to play in the Southern African problems and declared his hope that the negotiated settlement recommended by the United Nations in Resolution 435 could be achieved soon. He reiterated his opposition to apartheid and expressed delight at the growing sentiments within the United States against racism in Southern Africa. It was an interesting coincidence that in that same week, Mrs. Winnie Mandela, wife of jailed South African black nationalist leader Nelson Mandela, spurned an American offer of aid to rebuild her Brandfort home, which was destroyed by arsonists believed to be agents of the racist regime.[1] Turning down a State Department donation of about £10,000 as part of a fund-raising drive to rebuild her home, Mrs. Mandela said that she could not accept money from a government whose so-called policy of constructive engagement supported a regime that brutalized her family and people.[2] Well, *a luta continua*!

NOTES

1. See the *Guardian* (Lagos) 23 August 1984, front page.
2. Ibid.

12

Deterioration of Anglo-Nigerian Relations

Nigeria shares with Britain the use of English as the official mode of communication, but the two countries rarely speak the same language on political issues. In spite of close historical, economic, trade, cultural, institutional, and other ties between independent Nigeria and the former colonial power, serious political discord has seldom been far from the surface. During the Buhari administration, the relationship between the two countries deteriorated almost to the point of diplomatic rupture. That unsatisfactory state of relations derived from the attempted kidnapping of a former Minister of Transport and Aviation of the Second Republic, Alhaji Umaru Dikko, who was in exile in London; competition between petroleum from Nigeria and Britain's North Sea in the international oil market; and Margaret Thatcher's uncompromising policies on Southern Africa.

Sir Abubakar Tafawa Balewa, Nigeria's first Prime Minister, made a famous statement on independence day celebrations that "we know the British first as masters, then as leaders, finally as partners, but always as friends." In reality, it was an unequal partnership and not always a friendly one. As a colonial master, Britain assumed an identity of interests between the colonies and herself. However, the British wanted to govern at minimum cost and therefore instituted cash-crop economies to help defray administrative expenses, and established a system of indirect rule through local chiefs.[1] When Britain adopted a policy for colonial development, the main objective was concerned with metropolitan needs. When the British economy sneezed, the colonies caught cold or were forced to help prevent the cold from worsening in the mother country. Colonial aid, when given at all, was meant to benefit ailing British industry through export production, keeping profits high and her work force employed.[2] The trading system and colonial budgetary and market mechanisms were organized to insure British producers favorable access to colonial markets and to encourage self-sufficiency and balanced budgets in the areas of British rule.[3]

The record of British colonial development in the area of secondary economic structure (i.e., processing and marketing) was even worse. Indigenous middlemen were eliminated or discouraged and market prices were artificially lowered on commodities for the benefit of British firms. These deliberate policies were largely responsible for the relatively low level of industrialization and tertiary economic activities in most African states at the time of their independence.[4]

As the colonial power in Nigeria, Britain also dominated other sectors of the economy, such as banking, insurance, and shipping—the lucrative items of invisible trade which often reduced the need for high-level British capital investment in the colony. As late as 1963, three years after Nigeria's independence, the total value of British investments was little more than £90 million. In 1974, Britain decided that she would cease to extend capital aid to Nigeria, because of the latter's rising status as a major producer and exporter of oil within OPEC.

Nigeria's trading relationship with Britain had been quite extensive. We exported to Britain traditional commodity items, such as cocoa, groundnuts, cotton, natural rubber, timber, hides, and skins. In return, Britain exported to us a wide range of products, such as pharmaceuticals, textiles, glassware, motor vehicles, and heavy machinery. Although the content of Nigeria's export to Britain has changed somewhat, largely because of the dwindling quantity and value of traditional exports and the rise in the export of crude oil, Nigeria has remained one of Britain's ten largest markets outside Western Europe and the United States. Even when Britain ceased to import large quantities of Nigerian crude oil, she managed to retain her position as Nigeria's largest supplier of goods and services, capturing more than 20 percent of our domestic market in 1982. One consequence of this was that by 1981 Britain had a favorable balance of trade of about N1,200 million, whereas in previous years the situation used to be the reverse; in 1974, for example, the balance favored Nigeria to the tune of N575 million. Sooner or later, the Nigerian authorities would resort to measures to reduce British exports, to correct the imbalance in trade and payment. This has been one source of friction between the two countries irrespective of regimes or administrations.

Another source of concern was the number of private- and government-sponsored Nigerian students in Britain and the rising costs of providing for them. Estimates ranged from 12,000 to 50,000 Nigerian students enrolled in British institutions of learning in 1985, of whom at least 5,000 were sponsored by either the federal or state governments. At a time of dwindling national foreign exchange earnings and reserves, it was estimated that Nigeria had to remit about £500 million per annum to support the private students. The sum of N82,075,235 was actually released in foreign exchange to cover the tuition and living expenses of state- and federal-government-sponsored students.[5] However, there was a sharp reduction in total foreign-exchange remittances to private students from N335 million in 1983 to N123 million in 1984, as a result of the decision by the Buhari administration to abolish foreign exchange remittances for students seeking courses which were available in Nigerian universities and other domestic institutions of higher learning.

Under Margaret Thatcher, the British government had not seen eye to eye with Nigeria over Southern Africa. Indeed, the British government had been most supportive of the South African government, and in spite of overwhelming appeals from Nigeria, some other Commonwealth countries, and nongovernmental groups in Britain itself, Margaret Thatcher allowed President Botha to visit Britain on 2 June 1984. Mrs. Thatcher appeared quite content to ignore worldwide pressures to impose sanctions against South Africa, and as late as 25 April 1985 the British government completely rejected the Labour party's demand that Britain stop bank loans and investments to South Africa. Whenever the Pretoria regime announced cosmetic changes in the apartheid system, Prime Minister Thatcher's government would be quick to declare that these were "significant and promising developments." Since Nigeria had always been at the forefront of the anti-apartheid movement, this British attitude was an enduring source of political confrontation.

Another point of conflict has been petroleum. North Sea oil and Nigeria's light crude compete in the international oil market. Unlike Nigeria, Britain did not join OPEC and therefore her North Sea Oil has never come under the production quota and prices imposed by that organization. However, when the British National Oil Corporation (BNOC) and the Norwegian oil company Statoil cut their official posted prices by $1.35 per barrel in October 1984, for instance, Nigeria had to follow suit. Nigeria had to cut the price of her crude oil by the same amount when Britain reduced the price of North Sea oil by $3.00 per barrel in 1983. The informal contacts and consultations established between the energy officials of both countries have not really succeeded in reducing or eliminating competition in oil production and pricing.

Finally, there was the feeling in Nigeria that Britain did now show much interest in Nigeria's economic recovery. On the contrary, Britain was believed to have taken unhelpful stands both at the European Creditors Group and the IMF regarding Nigeria's negotiations for a new credit line, rescheduling of trade arrears and other debts, and new loans. The perception was that as the beneficiary of a favorable balance of trade with Nigeria, Britain was not doing enough to aid the Buhari administration's efforts to revamp our country's ailing economy. This perceived failure was attributed partly to the expenditure in Britain of billions of pounds sterling which fugitive Nigerian politicians were alleged to have obtained through corrupt enrichment and then repatriated to the safe haven of British banks.

These were the underlying sources of discord when the now famous Dikko affair suddenly intruded into the language of Anglo-Nigerian diplomacy. The affair began on 5 July 1984, when four men, one a Nigerian, attempted to kidnap Alhaji Umaru Dikko, former Minister of Transport and Aviation in the defunct Shagari administration, from a street near his home in Bayswater, West London. The men apparently wanted to return Alhaji Dikko to Nigeria, to face criminal charges in connection with the alleged misuse of office to enrich himself and his party, the National Party of Nigeria. The abduction attempt failed when, acting on a tipoff by Dikko's personal assistant, Elizabeth Hayes, British security men intercepted two wooden crates which were to be placed in a plane chartered from Nigerian Airways, apparently bound for Lagos. When Scotland Yard detectives opened the crates they found Alhaji Dikko, bound with rope and apparently drugged unconscious, and one other person. In the other crate, the security men found two more men who were unbound and conscious and later identified as Israelis.

Margaret Thatcher was reportedly infuriated by the attempted abduction of Alhaji Dikko, largely because it came only months after another diplomatic furor, caused by a gunman in the Libyan embassy in London who fired on protesters outside and killed an English policewoman. The police were instructed to make a thorough investigation of the entire episode and prepare charges against anyone involved in the attempted abduction of Alhaji Dikko. Accordingly, a total of 17 people, including the three men found with Dikko in the crates, were arrested by the police and interrogated. None of the arrested persons claimed diplomatic immunity at that point.

In his brief statement to the House of Commons on 6 July 1984, the Home Secretary, Leon Brittan, gave further details of the Dikko incident. He stated that members of the Nigerian High Commission in London were already at Stansted Airport, allegedly to handle the crates before they were to leave for Nigeria, and one of them, a Mr. Edet, was invited to inspect the crates once the security men forced them open. What the Home Secretary did not tell Parliament was that British authorities had detained the aircraft belonging to Nigerian Airways as well as its crew, supposedly to assist in the investigation.

On the same day that the Home Secretary made his statement to Parliament, the British Foreign Secretary summoned the Nigerian High Commissioner, Major-General Hannaniya, to the Foreign Office. While there, the High Commissioner was told that Her Majesty's government took an extremely serious view of the developments at Stansted Airport. Major-

General Hannaniya denied that the Nigerian government or his High Commission were involved in the incident. Sir Geoffrey Howe then requested that the High Commissioner himself and two other staff members of the commission submit to police questioning on the incident. The questioning could take place within the building of the High Commission in London. Such a request by the British authorities would have amounted to a waiver of diplomatic immunity and was therefore considered unacceptable.

In addition to confirming that our government had nothing to do with the kidnap attempt in London, my reaction was reported in the British *Sunday Telegraph* as follows: "We are determined not to allow the matter to get out of hand. The British government feels much the same way but they have a Parliament and public opinion to worry about. [Although] we do not have a Parliament [at this time] we surely have a vocal public opinion, too. What remains now is the matter of the detained (Nigerian Airways) aircraft and crew members."[6]

Meanwhile, the Nigerian government had ordered a British Caledonian plane, which was already airborne on its regular flight from Lagos to London via Kano, to return to Lagos. Although the plane was put under detention, the passengers were treated as special guests and put up in a comfortable state-owned hotel in fashionable Victoria Island, contrary to the reports in the British press that they were not well treated. However, once the Nigerian Airways plane and its crew were released, the British Caledonian plane and its crew and passengers were allowed to fly out of Nigeria. Both the Nigerian Airways and British Caledonian flights were soon back to normal.

Still to return to normal, however, were the diplomatic relations between the two countries. The situation took a turn for the worse when the British government concluded that police investigations had established the involvement of members of the Nigerian High Commission in London in the kidnap attempt, and that action against some of our diplomatic staff "would be inevitable." The action contemplated by the British government was the expulsion of two officials of the High Commission. The continued stay in Britain of the High Commissioner, Major-General Hannaniya, was also being questioned by the British government. These issues and the actions which the British government planned to take were conveyed to me through the direct line of communication which was kept open between Sir Geoffrey Howe and myself.

In response, I requested the British Foreign Secretary to postpone his planned statement to the House of Commons, in which he would have announced these actions to be taken by the British government. Such a postponement would enable me to cut short my participation in the International Conference on Assistance to Refugees in Africa (ICARA II) in Geneva and return to Lagos immediately. Sir Geoffrey Howe agreed to do this. However, he informed me that on addressing Parliament a day later, he would then make public the decision to expel Peter Oyedele and Okon Edet of the Nigerian High Commission, on the grounds that they may have "engaged in activities incompatible with their status as diplomats." In addition, the men in police custody had been charged for their attempted abduction of Alhaji Dikko.

Suspecting that if we did not act fast, Major-General Hannaniya himself might well be asked to leave Britain, I informed Sir Geoffrey that our High Commissioner had been recalled to Lagos immediately for consultations. This action was taken, I emphasized, so that we could use his input in the Nigerian government's comprehensive review of the entire situation. I then added that it remained our hope that Sir Geoffrey's statement in Parliament would be made in the spirt of our joint determination, constantly expressed, to limit any adverse effect of the situation on the long-term relationship of our two countries.

The statement in the House of Commons made by Sir Geoffrey was reasonable and the debate that followed was positive in tone. However, at the end of the usual parliamentary questioning that followed, the British Foreign Secretary made the unfortunate remark that "as the extent of the Nigerian High Commission's involvement [in the kidnap attempt] had not been determined, it would be inappropriate for the High Commissioner to return to London after his consultations in Lagos." That off-the-cuff remark amounted to a questioning of the credibility of the Nigerian government in its constant denials of any involvement in the kidnap attempt. We also felt betrayed by the British government for failing to maintain our jointly declared intention to diffuse the crisis. In retaliation, we decided to seek the withdrawal of two members of the British High Commission (J.D. Harrison and S.J.L. Evans) in Nigeria. We told the British that the continued stay in Lagos of the British High Commissioner, Hamilton Whyte, while his counterpart in London had been recalled for consultations, was inappropriate and would soon be regarded as untenable.

Despite intensive communication and efforts by Sir Geoffrey Howe and myself to minimize the damage to Anglo-Nigerian relations, we could not prevent the injuries inflicted on the personal feelings and diplomatic careers of the individuals who were caught up in the tit-for-tat diplomacy that resulted from the kidnap attempt. For many informed Nigerians, that was a small price to pay for the need to show the British that, after almost 24 years of independence, we were no longer content to be treated as their houseboys. Indeed, patriotic feelings were running so high in Nigeria that several calls were made to break diplomatic relations and downgrade our economic relations with Britain.

The public hostility toward Britain was reflected in the media. In a strongly worded front-page editorial, the *New Nigerian* was quoted as questioning British motives in the entire episode.[7] According to the paper, Britain had not tried to disguise the fact that Nigerian prosperity and progress were incompatible with her own national interests.[8] Hence, the imperialists, like Britain, had made the defeat and humiliation of Nigeria a fundamental aim of their diplomacy.[9] The paper commended the Buhari administration for its adroit handling of the British government, and thereby restoring our nation's honor and causing the conspirators in the West to fail in their designs against Nigeria.[10]

Several letters published by the editors of major newspapers expressed righteous indignation over the issue and congratulated the Nigerian government for responding to the actions taken by the British government. Some Nigerians wrote directly to the government on the issue. A typical sentiment was that our foreign policy could never be "enhanced by swallowing insults. And because Nigeria had not initiated any [negative] steps but has applied the legitimate policy of reciprocity over whatever action Britain [had] taken, the Nigerian government's attitude falls in line with the concept of equality of sovereign states."[11] The former secretary to the government of Mid-Western Nigeria (now Bendel state), Andrew Iyere Wilson, wanted an immediate breach of diplomatic relations with Britain on the grounds that she had planted economic saboteurs in Nigeria and collaborated with the Umaru Dikkos to wreck our economy.

In its own press release, the Academic Staff Union of Universities (ASUU), speaking through the University of Jos branch, expressed solidarity with the Federal Military Government over the handling of the Dikko affair and urged the government not to hesitate in taking firm and decisive actions if Britain failed to extradite the Nigerian fugitives hiding there. The press release condemned "the insensitivity of the British ruling class to the tragedy that had befallen every Nigerian family—the tragedy of worsening conditions of existence resulting from four years of looting and robbery of the public treasury by a gang of unarmed robbers led by Umaru Dikko."[12]

There were, of course, relatively muted voices appealing for caution in dealing with the British. Such forces for moderation pointed to the interdependence between our two countries. The federal government was very mindful of this and the Ministry of External Affairs constantly conveyed to the British government the need to put relations between our two countries back to even keel. In return, we received communications from the British Foreign Office seeking the same objectives. There was also considerable evidence that the private sector in Britain was applying behind-the-scenes pressures to modify the usually aggressive posture of Margaret Thatcher's government and improve Anglo-Nigerian relations.

On our side, important figures in the private sector, such as Sir Mobolaji

Bank-Anthony, Chief Jerome Udoji, and Chief E.A.O. Shonekan, chairman and chief executive of the giant United African Company Nigerian Ltd, made positive contributions toward improving the strained relations between Nigeria and Britain. Sir Mobolaji used his considerable contacts with British financial and political circles to nudge the private sectors of both countries to move their governments to better relations. A great patriot, Sir Mobolaji Bank-Anthony even used his own financial resources to organize dinners for British and Nigerian citizens who could help normalize relations between the two countries. This he did in his usual unassuming, quiet, and generous manner. The Chief of Staff, Supreme Headquarters, Major-General Tunde Idiagbon, later learned of Sir Mobolaji's private initiatives and expressed the government's approval and gratitude.

I had extensive private conversations with Chief E.A.O. Shonekan on 25 June 1985, prior to his business trip to Britain at the end of that month. While in London he received an audience with the British Foreign Secretary, and the two men reviewed the obstacles to the normalization of relations. Both promised to report to their respective constituents and work for better relations.

The diplomatic ball was then passed to the British court, especially when we took three further actions to break the stalemate in Anglo-Nigerian relations. First, Major-General Hannaniya was reassigned as the new ambassador of Nigeria to Ethiopia.[13] Our government did this to signal to the British authorities that we expected them to reassign Hamilton Whyte elsewhere. In this way, we could close the chapter on mutual withdrawals of high commissioners which had resulted from the kidnap attempt. The stage would then be set for the appointment of new high commissioners who would be better able to advance the normalization of relations.

Second, we received in Lagos Sir Roger du Boulay, a retired senior member of the British diplomatic service, who visited us as the personal representative of the Foreign Secretary. Sir Roger met with my senior staff and myself and some other senior civil servants on 13 September 1984. He gave details of his delicate mission and reiterated the importance which Britain attached to her relations with Nigeria, not only at the bilateral level but also in the Commonwealth. Realizing the concrete interests at stake for both countries, Sir Roger expressed the wish that we work together to limit the fallout from the Dikko affair. We pointed out that the steps taken so far by the Nigerian government were much more restrained than what our public would want. The reaction of Britain to the extradition of Nigerian fugitives in Britain, and British flexibility regarding Mohammed Yusuf, after the British courts would have given their judgment, would be crucial tests of British commitment to the normalization of relations. Several other meetings took place; Sir Roger was then to report to his government. Finally, the

Nigerian government formally sent a request for the extradition to Nigeria of Alhaji Umaru Dikko to face criminal charges carefully laid out in documents attached to a covering letter dated 10 January 1985, and signed by Chike Ofodile (SAN), Attorney-General of the federation and Minister of Justice.

The road to the normalization of relations remained rocky, however. The specific obstacles were considerable. The trial of the four men (including the Nigerian, Mohammed Yusuf, Alexander Barrak, a businessman, Dr. Levi Shapiro, and Felix Abitbol—all Israeli citizens) involved in the kidnapping attempt opened at the Old Bailey on 11 February 1985. The accused pleaded guilty to charges of abduction and administering stupefying drugs. The presiding judge, Mr. Justice McCowan, said that he accepted that the abduction attempt was not a case of indiscriminate terrorism. The public was not put at risk and the men had all believed that Alhaji Dikko had committed crimes in Nigeria and that he was "the biggest thief in the world."[14] Nonetheless he sentenced the accused to prison terms ranging from 10 to 14 years.

The sentences were regarded as too severe. Many had expected that, at worst, the court would recommend deportation. In the Bow Street High Court, on 8 February 1985, Mohammed Yusuf's attorney had made an application for the release of his client, invoking the Vienna Convention on Diplomatic Immunity. According to the application, Yusuf had come to the United Kingdom on a diplomatic passport genuinely issued by the Nigerian government. He had applied for and obtained a diplomatic visa issued by the British High Commission in Lagos, prior to his trip to London on a diplomatic mission. However, the presiding judge rejected this apparently belated application on the grounds that there was no reason to believe that Yusuf was "a diplomatic agent accredited to Britain."

There was a further complication , and it had to do with a difficult choice the British Home Secretary had to make. Before him were two applications. The first was Alhaji Dikko's application for political asylum, in which he denied the corruption charges made against him.[15] "I am being persecuted", he claimed, "first because I was the only one of the former politicians who came out publicly after the coup [of January 1984] and said that I was in favor of democracy. Second, because I was in charge of two presidential election campaigns in both of which our party was victorious, they see me as a very serious threat."[16] The second was the Nigerian government's request for Dikko's extradition, based on documentary evidence from Nigerian courts that he had received N450,000 from Felix Ayinotu, chairman of a Nigerian company, Hamer Construction. Dikko denied ever meeting Ayinotu and said that no one had accused him of taking a bribe personally, but he admitted being one of those responsible for collecting voluntary contributions from party supporters, which was quite legal.[17]

The Home Office had delayed taking action on Dikko's application for political asylum, probably to gain time to study Nigeria's extradition request and to be able to produce him should he be required as a principal witness in the trial of the men charged with the attempt to abduct him. When the trial was over, the Home Secretary was obliged to give his decision on Dikko's application for political asylum. Should the secretary grant the application, his action was unlikely to improve Anglo-Nigerian diplomatic relations.

On 6 June 1985, the Home Secretary told the House of Commons that he had refused Dikko's application for asylum. He added that he was still considering the Nigerian authorities' application for the extradition of Dikko. This decision was welcomed by the Nigerian government and, as a result, discussions were begun about a visit to Nigeria by Sir Geoffrey Howe, tentatively scheduled for late June or early July 1985. The visit was to promote a thoroughgoing discussion of issues of importance and concern to both countries.

The visit had to be rescheduled, largely because of Nigeria's preparations for the ECOWAS and OAU summit meetings, which took place in July 1985. Some other relatively minor problems had to be dealt with or resolved before Sir Geoffrey's visit. For example, there were a number of consular issues relating to Nigeria's complaint about the treatment of Mohammed Yusuf in prison and British dissatisfaction with the continued detention of two of their citizens in Nigeria. Then there was the theft of a helicopter in Lagos by two British pilots, Angus Patterson and Kenneth Clark, who were arrested in March 1984, freed, and then rearrested. Nigerian security officials complained about the mysterious escape from Nigeria of a British citizen, J. Hurd, whose passport was held in their possession, while investigations continued in the case of the Glauber Company, allegedly involved in abetting the corrupt practices of some highly placed Nigerians and a "British" woman, Mehmet Chambi, through a scheme to launder N15.2 million in the Lagos branch of the Savannah Bank. The escape of Hurd was believed to be impossible without assistance from the British High Commission in Lagos.

There was also the issue of the British government's nomination of M.K. Evans to replace Hamilton Whyte as the new High Commissioner in Nigeria. Britain wanted the nomination to be approved soon, so that Evans could assume his post by the time Sir Geoffrey was to visit Nigeria. The nomination of Evans was carefully examined at the highest levels of government in Nigeria, and it was decided we should agree at the end rather than as part of the process of normalizing relations with Britain.

Finally, British firms operating in Nigeria were facing serious problems arising from the growth of counter-trading (barter) arrangements between

Nigeria and some other countries.[18] The arrangement was necessitated in part by the difficulties that the Nigerian national petroleum company was experiencing in selling oil at OPEC's official price and quota levels. In return for essential goods and machinery at agreed prices and special arrangements, Nigeria shipped oil to the countries that were willing to buy it. There was the much publicized $500 million deal with Brazil. Discussions were also going on with SCOA and the French government about similar counter-trade agreements. Several European Community members, especially France, Germany, Italy, and the Netherlands, with considerable balance of trade deficits with Nigeria, welcomed counter-trade arrangements.[19]

Britain opposed counter-trading in principle and, in any case, was not in a position to use Nigeria's oil. Nonetheless, if the logic of counter-trading was pushed to its logical conclusion, British exports to Nigeria would be seriously jeopardized. This fear and the attraction of counter-trading deals which Nigeria was offering to other takers caused two British firms, it was reported, to become involved in the counter-trade business.[20]

The British Foreign Secretary kept up the pressure on his proposed visit to Nigeria, proposing alternative dates to be considered by Nigeria. Sir Geoffrey expressed the wish that during the visit he would be able to establish personal contacts with me and other senior members of the Federal Military Government, and that the discussions in Nigeria would be a major step in restoring relations between our two countries. The Foreign Secretary also referred to the visit of the Minister of Information, Group Captain Emeka Omeruah, to London for the British-Nigerian Association Concert to mark the 25th anniversary of Nigerian independence. He stated that many friends of Nigeria appreciated the presence of the minister and his positive remarks while there. My recommendation was that the head of state's approval should be given for Sir Geoffrey to visit Nigeria on one of the dates proposed by him. General Buhari gave his consent and preparations for the visit commenced immediately.

As things turned out, Sir Geoffrey's visit did take place, but by then General Buhari and his administration had been ousted in a military coup which brought into power the former chief of army staff, Major-General Ibrahim Babangida. Nonetheless, Sir Geoffrey was gracious enough to point out that it was the Buhari administration which initiated his visit and paved the way for the normalization of relations. However, the British government had not yet made a final decision on the Nigerian government's request for the extradition of Alhaji Umaru Dikko.

What then were the major lessons for Nigeria in the Dikko affair? First, and perhaps foremost, that fundamental conflicts or serious differences between Nigeria and Britain existed prior to, and would probably outlast, the Dikko affair. Would Britain be interested in addressing the issue of her policies toward South Africa and the imposition of comprehensive sanctions against the racist regime, and thus avoid this potentially destabilizing problem in Anglo-Nigerian relations? Would the British government be prepared to show greater sensitivity to our country's concern over the competitive pricing of North Sea oil outside the OPEC constraints under which Nigeria must operate? Could Nigeria expect more forthcoming responses from the British to the requests to have the political refugees in Britain extradited to face criminal charges at home? Would Britain also continue to insist on maintaining her advantages in the balance of trade and payments with Nigeria, and therefore spurn our efforts to redress the situation, such as further reductions of British imports which were not essential for keeping our industries in full production, reducing the number of Nigerians studying in Britain, as well as curtailing frivolous foreign travel by our citizens? Only correct answers to these fundamental issues could smooth Anglo-Nigerian relations.

The second major lesson from the Dikko affair was that we need not deal with Britain from a position of subservience. Britain would always try to maintain its commercial, capital, and political interests in Nigeria. We were the country buying more British goods while they bought little or nothing from us. We could also take positive measures to diversify not only our exports but our sources of imported goods, and thus reduce dependence on Britain. Then both countries could establish the basis for true interdependence. We should never, as an independent country, subordinate our national interests to those of Britain or indeed any other foreign country. Rather, we should work to harmonize conflicting national interests where possible, and to the extent possible, always consistent with mutual advantage, and pursued in the framework of respect for the sovereign equality of states.

Third, a developing country such as Nigeria could not expect to match a much older, traditional country such as Britain in the fine art of diplomatic niceties. The policy of retaliation, which employed advantages in our economic and political arsenal in reaction to condescending or exploitative actions emanating from a foreign power, should remain a credible option. Even the superpowers used such a policy as a bargaining tool in critical international situations. Nonetheless, a serious country would not break diplomatic relations as the first resort.

Although calls by segments of the Nigerian public to break diplomatic relations with Britain over the Dikko affair arose from a deep sense of injured national pride, for the government to agree to such a course of action would have been premature and almost certainly counter-productive. Contingency plans were one thing, but the Buhari administration felt that once retaliatory actions took their full course, we had to keep open the lines of communications for dialogue with the British and work toward normalization of relations.

Finally, Nigeria would continue to be seriously handicapped in the pursuit of an activist, anti-imperialist and truly nonaligned foreign policy until it lessened its dependence on the West in general and Britain in particular. This broad issue will be examined in a later chapter. Suffice it to say here that a credible foreign policy must rest on a strong economic base. We must be willing to eliminate waste, increase domestic productivity to produce more of what we consume, accept the need for greater discipline, and sacrifice even more to restore our economy to real growth and widespread development. With our economic house in order, we may then gain respect in a world increasingly dominated by economic giants.

NOTES

1. See Walter Rodney's general study, *How Europe Underdeveloped Africa* (Washington: Howard University Press, 1982).
2. These issues are well articulated in E.A. Brett, *Colonialism and Underdevelopment in East Africa: The Politics of Economic Change* 1919–1939 (New York: NOK Publishers, 1973). His analysis of the colonial situation in East Africa is largely applicable to British colonies in the rest of the continent.
3. Ibid.
4. Ibid.
5. Central Bank of Nigeria Figures, (Lagos, Annual Report) 1985.
6. *Sunday Telegraph*, 8 July 1984.
7. Report in *Daily Telegraph*, 10 July 1984.
8. Ibid.
9. Ibid.
10. Ibid.
11. For example, the letter from Ambassador R.I. Egbuziem, former High Commissioner of Nigeria to Tanzania, 20 July 1984.
12. Press release on the Dikko affair signed by Dr. A.T. Gana, Chairman, ASUU, University of Jos Branch, Jos, Nigeria, July 1984.
13. Report in *New Nigerian*, 20 October 1984.
14. *The Times* (London), 13 February 1985.
15. As Alhaji Dikko was stressing his innocence, we received anonymous communications which alleged that he had a secret bank account in Switzerland. For a 10 percent finder's fee, the author of the telegram informed us, he could provide the passwords for the account and assist the Nigerian government to recover some hundreds of million dollars recently transferred from a bank in the United States. It was difficult to separate serious offers of assistance from plain hoaxes.
16. *The Times* (London), 13 February 1985.
17. Ibid.
18. See "Balancing Act in Lagos," *Nigeria Newsletter*, No. 163, 3 May 1985.
19. Ibid.
20. Ibid.

13

Other Major Western European Countries: Economics Above Politics?

While the British hold on the Nigerian economy was declining, especially after North Sea Oil removed Britain as a major market for Nigeria's own crude oil, French involvement in our economy was increasing. France had become not only a major importer of Nigerian crude oil but one of Nigeria's most important economic partners. This relatively new French connection was welcomed in some informed circles in our country, but not because of trust in France's political motivations, of which Nigeria has harbored deep suspicions. Some Nigerians believed that France could be a useful counterweight to British influence.

France was one of the first major Western European countries visited by emissaries of the Buhari regime. Led by Alhaji Liman Ciroma, on 15 January 1984, the delegation delivered a message through Foreign Minister Claude Cheysson, to President Mitterand, that explained the reasons for changing the civilian regime of President Shagari and sought French help in the efforts to revamp the badly damaged economy. In an earlier chapter, I discussed Cheysson's visit to Nigeria and my own official return visit to France.

Mr. Cheysson was always more comfortable with discussions of political issues, such as Chad, Western Sahara, and the OAU, and global problems, such as East-West relations and international security. Although Nigeria was also interested in discussing these issues and promoting political cooperation with France, my official delegation in September 1984 was particularly interested in developing new opportunities to advance trade and economic relations.

Nigeria expressed great satisfaction that the French had supported our position in the IMF for an agreement which would modify their straightjacket conditions. We also observed that the bilateral negotiations with

France on rescheduling trade debts had proceeded well. Under the Federal Military Government, a significant contract was awarded to a French company to conduct preshipment inspections of our country's imports from Europe. Counter-trade proposals were made to a major French company operating in Nigeria, and also with the French government to pay for crucial goods and services from that country with our crude oil.

The highlights of my official visit to France in September 1984 were the luncheon given in honor of the Nigerian delegation by the Confederation of French Industrialists (roughly equivalent to the Manufacturers Association of Nigeria) and the meeting with President Mitterand. The president impressed me as a reflective intellectual in government. In the usual graciousness and felicity of language characteristic of French diplomacy, President Mitterand declared that he regarded my visit as the harbinger of new sunshine in Franco-Nigerian relations. He also promised to lend the full weight of his authority to the intensification of that relationship. Speaking on a subject obviously close to his heart, President Mitterand said that he would continue to speak with a voice consistent with our own on the need to reform the present international economic system, especially the IMF and the problems of Third World external indebtedness.

The French leader made the comment that the task facing the leadership of Nigeria in trying to revamp economic and other national problems was not an easy one. This was because of the nation's physical span and the size and diversity of its population. He concluded by wishing the Nigerian leadership all the best and renewed his invitation to General Buhari to visit France as soon as it was convenient for him.

The exchange of official visits at the ministerial level helped to create a favorable political climate; nonetheless, there was more to the Franco-Nigerian relationship than reciprocal visits by two foreign ministers.[1] France is a power in Africa and Nigeria is an African power. Although weaker than France economically, technologically, and militarily, Nigeria has the advantage of being an indigenous power in the continent. When the two major powers (France and Nigeria) in Africa interact in the continent's affairs, there is the possibility of conflict, but also prospects for cooperation. In reality, Franco-Nigerian relations have been characterized by both conflict and cooperation since Nigeria's independence in 1960. On the whole, however, there has been more conflict in the political sphere but more cooperation in economic relations. Would it be realistic for the two countries to continue or intensify cooperation in the economic sphere, while maintaining a state of political rivalry? The next question is: Who benefits more from the economic interaction between the two countries?

France had more colonies in Africa than any other European power. The Fifth Republic in France was rooted in Africa, considering the fact that de

Gaulle and his associates strove to reconquer their fatherland using Africa as a springboard. This historic relationship between Africa and France has been an unequal one. The Africans have been victims of French conquests, subjugation, assimilation, experts, and neocolonial masters. There have been continuing efforts since the presidency of de Gaulle to retain French hegemony in the former colonies. The economic weakness of most of the francophone African countries and dispositions of their leaders make them particularly vulnerable to French desires to assert their authority in Africa.

The reality of the French military presence has been an added dimension to the unequal relations between France and her former colonies. As an illustration, France has defense pacts with eight African countries, Togo, Cameroon, Comoros, Central African Republic, Djibouti, Cote d'Ivoire, Gabon, and Senegal. Seventeen other African countries (including all of Nigeria's immediate neighbors) have military agreements with France. French military aid to Africa grew from about 660 million francs in 1982 to 800 million in 1984. Over 1,700 African soldiers received military training in French academies in 1982, and the number rose to 2,226 in 1983. France also has the Force d'Action Rapide (FAR) of nearly 50,000 troops, ready for action in Africa. To show that the FAR is not a theoretical proposition, France has intervened militarily in Chad, Mauritania, Burkina Faso, Zaire, Tunisia, Central African Republic, Cameroon, and Gabon.

Nigeria's relative power position in Africa grows out of the following factors. Apart from the country's physical size and population, respectively third and first on the continent, Nigeria is endowed with a wide variety of physical and mineral resources, the most prominent in recent times being crude oil, although most are underdeveloped or not developed at all. There has been a growing skill and aggressiveness by our human population. Finally, the country's elite has long believed that Nigeria should, or was in fact destined to, play a leading role in African affairs.

Nigeria has played decisive roles in important African issues, such as: the expulsion of South Africa from the Commonwealth; participation in the UN Peacekeeping Force in Congo (Zaire); the establishment of the OAU and ECOWAS; recognition of the MPLA and the admission of Angola to the OAU; the independence of Zimbabwe under Mugabe's leadership; uncompromising opposition to apartheid and South Africa's illegal occupation of Namibia; interventions in Chad; and the admission of Western Sahara (under Polisario) as the 51st member of the OAU.

There was, perhaps, no better symbol of Franco-Nigerian political relations than the fact that no French president had ever visited Nigeria and no Nigerian head of state had ever made an official visit to France. It was not until 1984 that Foreign Minister Claude Cheysson and myself exchanged official visits and attempted to usher in an era of warmer political relations.

This was followed a year later by the Akinyemi-Dumas exchange of visits at the same level. However, it is also significant that of the four foreign ministers involved in promoting this new warmth, not one had remained in his post by the end of the year 1987.

Several factors harmed Franco-Nigerian political relations, especially during the first decade of Nigeria's independence. First was a general mistrust and skepticism arising from the fact that Nigeria was a British colony towering over all the francophone countries in West Africa and thus capable of reorienting the latter away from France. Second was the stubborn decision of de Gaulle to test atomic weapons in the Sahara despite protests from Nigeria which led to the expulsion of the French ambassador. Third was French attempts to block Nigeria's application for associate membership of the European Economic Community. Finally, there was the French role in the Nigerian Civil War and active support for secessionist "Biafra."

Although political relations between France and Nigeria improved somewhat in the 1970s and early 1980s, there were other strong obstacles to smooth political interaction. The French gave military support for Cameroon, following border conflicts between that country and Nigeria in 1982 that led to the death of five Nigerian soldiers. Furthermore, France has tended to intervene militarily in African politics, which has remained worrisome to Nigerian leaders, given the reality of French military agreements with all of Nigeria's neighbors. Again, France has had close relations with South Africa, especially in the supply of sophisticated military equipment. The coming to power of the Socialists in France in 1981 led to a more rigorous denunciation of apartheid, but President Botha made a visit to France in 1985. Moreover, Prime Minister Chirac has now decided to send back the French ambassador who was earlier withdrawn from South Africa in protest against the policies of the racist government. If France is returning to active support of the apartheid regime, that move would certainly worsen her political relations with Nigeria.

While the tempo of political relations between France and Nigeria moved from bad to worse and then to in-between, economic ties between the two countries moved in more positive directions. Between 1973 and 1985, Franco-Nigerian economic relations grew so much that France became a key economic partner of Nigeria. In the last two years, other than Britain and West Germany, no country in the world has surpassed France in Nigeria's economic and commercial relations. At present over 165 French firms pursue business in Nigeria. In 1985, Nigeria imported French goods to the tune of 4,944 million francs, while Nigeria exported goods (largely petroleum) worth 15,286 million francs. A five-year economic and technical agreement signed in 1979 covers joint industrial enterprises, development projects of common interests in the areas of telecommunications, housing, agriculture, roads, ports, research, consultancy services, feasibility studies, pilot projects in energy, geological surveys, and rural development. France has become the second largest foreign investor in Nigeria with a net investment of over $500 million. Franco-Nigerian enterprises employ over 100,000 Nigerians. French imports from Nigeria consist mainly of petroleum, which represents 99.3 percent of all imports. On the other hand, French exports have been more diversified, consisting of Peugeot CKD parts (35 percent), agricultural and industrial products, building materials, engineering equipment, and commodities such as sugar.

In the banking sector, the French presence has been impressive and growing. Added to the older French banks operating in Nigeria, such as UBA (1949) and IBWA (1959), three more commenced operations in Nigeria: Societé General (1977), Marchant Banking Corporation (1983), and Commercial Bank Credit (1983). Two other banks had representative offices in Nigeria: French Banking Bureau (1974) and Banque Nationale (1979). The aggregate assets of Nigerian banks with French affiliates stood at 7.5 billion *naira* (or 25 percent) of the assets of all commercial banks in Nigeria). Employing over 10,000 people, these banks with French interests hold N6.0 billion in deposits and maintain portfolios of loans and advances worth N2.5 billion.

The impact of French companies in the industrial sector in Nigeria has been tremendous. The two leading French trading firms, CFAO and SCOA, are among the largest industrial and commercial firms in Nigeria. CFAO's shares are held 60 percent by Nigerians and 40 percent by CFAO France. In 1984 it made a net profit of N15 million from a turnover of N302 million. Similarly, SCOA made a net profit of N11.4 million on a turnover of N390 million. SCOA was also designated as the company to handle counter-trade agreements in 1984–85. In addition, the Peugeot assembly plant represents the single largest French investment in Nigeria. In 1984, it made a net profit of N15.4 million on a turnover of N493.6 million. Peugeot France owns 40 percent of the shares in Peugeot Automobile of Nigeria, while the Nigerian government owns 50 percent, with the rest going to some of the company's distributors. Incidentally, by 1979, French cars accounted for 56.2 percent of all cars on Nigerian roads. Michelin, another French company, made a net profit of N2.2 million on a turnover of N60.2 million in 1984.

Although impressive on the surface, French involvement in Nigeria's industrial development has been lopsided. French companies have been more interested in trade and the execution of lucrative government contracts than in investment in meaningful industrial activities capable of enhancing Nigeria's overall industrial development. Compared with the huge turnovers of the trading companies with French connections, the level of French investment in industry has remained low. The proportion of local value added in industrial production involving French companies in Nigeria has also remained very low. Industrial activities by French companies consist largely of the assembly of goods imported from France, and importation consumes huge foreign exchange reserves.

The most dramatic impact of the French companies has been in the construction business. By the end of 1980, almost one-half of the total contracts awarded for the construction of the new federal capital at Abuja were given to French companies, such as Dumez (N170 million for Abuja Airport), Spie-Batignolles (N60 million for a water-supply dam), Societé Auxilliarie Entreprise (SAE) (N27 million for housing) and C.K. Renaud (N426 million for housing). At Ajaokuta Steel Industry, Dumez won a contract for N180 million, Fougerrole another one for almost N330 million, and Sofre-Mines one for N2 million. At Aladja Steel Mills, Dumez won another contract for public buildings and access roads worth N60 million. For building the Ikeja Sheraton Hotel, SEFRI won a contract for N90 million. French National Railways was to get an engineering contract for the Port-Harcourt/Ajaokuta rail line worth N46 million, but this contract was later suspended. However, SGE won over N150 million in various road construction contracts from 1976 to 1978.

The picture of Franco-Nigerian economic relations has been one in which French companies were more successful in obtaining and executing Nigerian government contracts, buying and selling goods, and operating in the banking sector than in long-term or commensurate investment in meaningful industrialization. The apparent objective has been to take as much from Nigeria as the country earns from exports of crude oil to France. This dawned on Nigeria as the French trade deficit with Nigeria began to disappear.

The ethics of the French construction companies have come under serious questioning. The Uwaifo Investigation Panel, after examining the case of Nigerians held on charges of corrupt enrichment, showed that Fougerolle paid kickbacks or bribes worth N21.8 million in return for obtaining a contract of N329 million from the civilian administration under President Shagari. As long as the Nigerian political leadership could be easily bribed, and as long as French companies engaged in the export and import business, France may well have believed that there was little need to improve political relations with Nigeria or to invest significantly in industrialization. Now, however, the era of public accountability has come in Nigeria. Poor political relations between France and Nigeria also have affected economic relations, just as they have in recent Anglo-Nigerian relations.

Three sets of realignments are therefore necessary in Franco-Nigerian relations. First, the level of French investment must be realigned with the level of turnover enjoyed by the French companies operating in Nigeria. This would mean a much more positive action on the part of the French government. Support would also need to be given to research and development toward producing raw materials in Nigeria for manufacture by French companies, as well as other measures to raise the level of local value added to French goods manufactured in Nigeria.

Second, the situation whereby France imports only crude oil must be realigned to diversify French imports from Nigeria. This would require opening up French markets to other export items, especially now that the Babangida administration in Nigeria has been pushing the export of non-crude-oil items as a strategy for diversifying and increasing the country's foreign exchange earnings in the face of falling world oil prices.

Third, political relations between France and Nigeria need to be adjusted to the level of economic relations between the two countries. The election of Prime Minister Chirac and the return of Mr. Foccart (late President de Gaulle's conservative adviser on African affairs) could mean cooler rather than warmer political relations with Nigeria, as both Chirac and Foccart would prefer the safer, closer, and more traditionally neo-colonial relations with the francophone African countries. More ominous still is the prospect of a French return to the situation before the tentative anti-apartheid stand of the government under President Mitterand and foreign ministers Cheysson and Dumas. This would surely put France on a collision course with Nigeria over Southern Africa. Any further deterioration in Franco-Nigerian political relations is bound to affect economic relations. Finally, France, as an imperialist power, which has continued to promote dependency by the francophone African countries, may become involved in political conflicts with Nigeria, a growing African power.

Nonetheless, both countries could work together to solve problems in areas of common political interests, once France redefined its interests in, say, Chad, ECOWAS, and South Africa, in favor of peace, prosperity, and liberation. The greatest challenge facing the French government and private sector is to invest in the future of Nigeria, thereby investing in their own future in Nigeria.

West Germany is another Western European country with which our administration sought to develop enhanced economic and trade ties. The Buhari administration was aware that, as a particularly close ally of the United States, West Germany was not always in a position to take independent political positions on world affairs. West Germany has been a source of military weapons and diplomatic support for the government in Pretoria, and therefore would not favor radical change or mandatory sanctions against the racist regime.

Nevertheless, as an important European power and a segment of the former colonial power in Namibia, where many people of German descent and citizenship still reside,[2] West Germany has often felt a sense of responsibility toward that territory. Perhaps we could attempt to play on those interests to steer the West Germans to support early independence. Indeed, during my talks with the Vice-Chancellor and Foreign Minister of the Federal Republic, Hans-Dietrich Genscher, in Bonn on 21 September 1984, I had the impression that the West Germans were probably doing more than met the eye on Namibia within the Western alliance. Mr. Genscher said that his government was urging the United States to modify its insistence on the linkage of independence with the withdrawal of Cuban troops in Angola.

Mr. Genscher assured our official delegation that the West German government was in direct and constant contact with SWAPO and Sam Nujoma. He believed, however, that SWAPO should develop closer relations with the whites in Namibia, so that together they could press South Africa to leave their country and grant independence. We restated our position that SWAPO was the sole and authentic representative of the Namibian people and that, in any case, the South Africans were more interested in promoting a ruling group of whites and black stooges that would exclude SWAPO. It was instructive that Mr. Genscher made no comments or reply when I told him that Nigeria condemned apartheid in the strongest terms, endorsed the OAU Liberation Committee's resolution calling on all nations not to receive President Botha, and strongly condemned South Africa's illegal occupation of Southern Angola, as well as the regime's acts against neighboring countries.

The heart of the West Germans was more in the discussion of economic issues, mainly the following:

(a) early agreement between Nigeria and the IMF,
(b) a quick conclusion of talks with the West Germans on rescheduling arrangements concerning trade arrears,
(c) the issuance of promissory notes to German creditors and payments to be made on them as soon as possible,
(d) the question of nonpayment of interest on future promissory notes to be issued for rescheduled payments on outstanding debts,
(e) an early resumption of talks with the Europeans on the rescheduling problems.

I assured the West Germans that Nigeria was still committed to an agreement with the IMF which would be satisfactory to both sides. I also assured them that the talks on the rescheduling of debts involving major West European creditors would soon be resumed. When the Foreign Minister gave me a copy of the statistics on the balance of trade, which showed that we were enjoying a favorable balance with the Germans, I pointed out that by buying our crude (which was mainly responsible for the favorable balance of trade), the Germans were assisting our economic recovery and thus our ability to pay for more imports from Germany. I told him that the statistics did not reflect the invisible trade and earnings of German companies, which were responsible for over 80 percent of the civil construction contracts in our country. There were over 250 German companies doing a generally lucrative business in Nigeria. My advice to the German government was to counsel their companies to study the new priority areas of the Federal Military Government's economic program (domestic food production, agro-based industries, liquified natural gas, and steel, among others) and reorient their exports along those lines, as a means of redressing the trade imbalance with our country.

Our overall impression was that the West German government realized it would be unwise to neglect Nigeria's views on political issues, but that Nigeria could affect West Germany's own political positions only through economic and trade cooperation. Even then the West Germans might well try to keep political and economic relations quite separate and independent, while downgrading the former and emphasizing the latter. It would remain our duty not to allow such a dichotomy to operate, but we had to be aware that West Germany, unlike France, was less able and willing to pursue political issues independently of the United States.

Finally, taking both France and West Germany together, it seemed to me that they were beginning to take us very seriously in the trade and economic realms and, to a lesser extent, in political interactions. We should therefore try to take these countries seriously also. This would be in line with the principle of reciprocity, which had always been at the heart of international relations. By dealing with consistency and skill, Nigeria could add to her international constituency, which would be useful in pursuing her national interests, serving to some extent as a balance to her more traditional "friends"—Britain and the United States.[3]

NOTES

1. The substance of this discussion of the historical background, problems, and prospects of Franco-Nigerian relations was contained in my lecture given at the Institute d'Etudes Politiques, Centre d'Etude d'Afrique Noire, Domaine Universitaire, Bordeaux, France, on 16 June 1985. Jibo Ibrahim, a colleague at ABU Zaria, helped to compile some of the statistical data used in that lecture.
2. An estimated 23,000 people of German descent live in Namibia, with about 9,000 of them holding German passports.

3. The new rapprochement between Nigeria and France appeared to have caused some anxiety or curiosity to our traditional "friends." For example, British Foreign Secretary Sir Geoffrey Howe met with our Acting High Commissioner in London, Ibrahim Karfi, and asked him personally to convey an urgent message to me during my official visits to Paris and Bonn. He did and the message was an invitation extended to me to visit London to discuss bilateral issues. Also, United States Secretary of State George Shultz invited me to see him privately in New York during the United Nations General Assembly Session in October 1984.

PART 5

Global Issues

14

The PLO and Peace in the Middle East

The principle of self-determination and the pursuit of international peace and security are inseparable. This perspective has governed our country's foreign policy since independence. We have always felt that Nigeria has to be committed to the principle of self-determination in its universal dimension and application, for it would be hypocritical to push for the liberation of Southern Africa, based on the principle of self-determination, and then fail to support the same principle for the Palestinians in the Middle East. For these reasons, successive Nigerian governments had consistently supported the Palestinian cause.

This steadfastness in commitment has not been without domestic political costs. The major nontraditional religious groups in Nigeria (Christians and Muslims) have often articulated and pursued support for different parties to the Middle Eastern conflict. These differing pulls, based on religious affinities and preferences, have translated into pro-Arab and pro-Israeli groups within Nigeria. The division of opinion has often taken the additional dimension of Northern versus Southern regional divergences concerning the Arabs and Israelis. The details of the difficulties encountered by the federal government in fashioning nonpartisan, even-handed policies in the Middle East, especially during the First Republic, are outside the scope of this study.[1] Suffice it to say here that such a nonpartisan policy under the Balewa administration was largely inoperative in the then largest region of the federation, the North, which was under the tight control of the late Sir Ahmadu Bello, Sardauna of Sokoto and premier of the region, who openly sided with the Arabs.[2]

The Civil War in Nigeria may have weakened political support at the federal level for the Israeli point of view, because that country supported the "Biafran" cause, whereas the support given by Egypt for the Federal Military Government during the Civil War probably enhanced support for Egypt and the Arabs in general in the Middle East dispute. The ill-fated OAU peace mission to the Middle East, which included General Yakubu Gowon, then head of the Federal Military Government, convinced the Nigerian leadership that it was Israel not the Arabs that created greater obstacles to peace.

The 1973 Middle East war, during which Israeli forces crossed the West Bank into Egyptian and hence African soil, provided the rationale for members of the OAU, including Nigeria, to sever diplomatic relations with Israel, which meant Israel's complete isolation within Africa.

The domestic debate in Nigeria about restoring diplomatic relations with Israel has tended to throw more heat on domestic interreligious and interregional differences than light on the Middle East situation. Those who favor resuming diplomatic ties with Israel argue that we should avoid trying to be "more Catholic than the Pope" and therefore follow Egypt's example of establishing diplomatic relations. The resumption of diplomatic relations could also give Nigeria economic benefits and new models of development. The advocates of resuming ties also dismissed the issue of that country's relationship with South Africa as an afterthought which should not guide Nigeria's future relationship with Israel.

As Director-General of the Nigerian Institute of International Affairs, my position was that we should not base our decision on what Egypt did or did not do.[3] Rather, we should rely on our own perceptions, our relationship with the parties to the dispute, and our national interests based on a commitment to certain principles. If there was a coincidence of interests and perspective with Egypt, that was fine, but if there was conflict of interests we should recognize it.

Egypt had in any case become very isolated in the Arab world as a result of Sadat's opening to Jerusalem, yet Egypt had not gotten the concessions from Israel which were supposed to come from the normalization of relations between both countries. The Israelis were still holding on to the West Bank and pursuing policies of dispersal and depopulation of the Palestinians. The whole issue of the homeland for the Palestinians had not been seriously addressed.

On the secondary issue of what Nigeria could obtain from Israel in concrete economic terms, it would be difficult to show how this might be achieved, given the state of the Israeli economy itself. By 1983, Israel's currency had been devalued by about 30 percent, while inflation was running above 100 percent. The Israeli government was also forced to reduce the subsidies given to food and other consumer items by about one-half. Without the billions of United States dollars infused annually into Israel's economic and military machines, the very survival of the country would be in question.

Finally, I argued that the growing Israeli-South African connections were of fundamental importance to us. It was no longer a secret that Israel actively collaborated with South Africa on nuclear weapons development and on the training of South African military forces, enhancing the racist regime's capability to deal with SWAPO forces in Namibia and ANC operations inside the apartheid enclave.[4] A country that befriended our archenemy was not one to restore diplomatic relations with. If, however, Israel were to improve her relationship with neighboring Arab states, withdraw from all territories occupied since the 1967 war, recognize the legitimate right of the Palestinians for a homeland, and end all military cooperation with South Africa, Nigeria could consider the resumption of diplomatic relations with her.[5] After all, as British Foreign Minister Lord Palmerston once said about foreign policy, there are no permanent friends or permanent enemies, only permanent national interests.

In a policy paper approved by the Federal Military Government in June 1985, the Buhari administration decided not to resume diplomatic relations with Israel. Apart from the issue of Israeli collaboration with South Africa, Nigeria felt that the signal should not be given to Israel that aggression ever pays. Israel's record in the Middle East left much to be desired. Provocative policies of establishing new Jewish settlements in the occupied West Bank; the dehumanization of defenseless Palestinian peoples on their very ancestral homes; the systematic and insensitive expropriation of their lands and other properties, and the trampling on their inalienable rights were clear for all to see. Under those circumstances, Nigeria could not understand how a people like the Israelis could seek to establish an identity at the cost of obliterating the identity of a whole people, or try to build their rights on the debris of the trampled rights of others. The subjugation of the Palestinian people had also been followed by brazen Israeli incursions into Lebanon—military occupations and operations which provoked worldwide indignation while threatening the survival of Lebanon as a state.

The objective of Nigeria's policy was to join concerted international action to bring about durable peace in the Middle East. Nigeria had sent a contingent of troops to Lebanon in 1978 as part of the United Nations Interim Force in the Lebanon (UNIFIL), whose mandate was to assist the Lebanese government to reassert its sovereignty in the south. Initially, UNIFIL received a six-month mandate, which was renewed several times thereafter. The failure of the force caused the Nigerian government finally to withdraw its contingent out of deep frustration. Israel was determined to maintain her presence in southern Lebanon, either directly or by proxy, in flagrant violation of Lebanon's sovereignty and territorial integrity.

The Buhari administration was of the view that the Palestinian question lay at the core of the Middle East problem. The road to peace could not be found through military solutions or the imposition of one-sided superpower views, but rather through a negotiated peace which was equitable, fair, and just, and which recognized the inalienable rights of the Palestinians for self-determination, a return to their homeland, and the establishment of an independent state.[6] The decision by the International Conference on the Question of Palestine, held in Geneva in 1983, to call for the convening of a UN international conference on the Middle East was appropriate. Nigeria supported the proposal for a conference that would include the Palestinians themselves, other interested parties in the region, the Soviet Union, and the United States. The Buhari administration urged "the United Nations to arrange such a Conference without further delay and also called on the International Community, particularly Israel and its backers, to respond positively to this challenge of peace under the auspices of the United Nations," and it also warned against the tendency in some quarters to "conclude in advance that such a conference would be unfair to any of the parties [to the dispute]."[7]

The right of Israel to live within secure borders was recognized by Nigeria.[8] However, the Buhari administration stated categorically that Nigeria would not concede to Israel the right to deny the Palestinian people similar rights through its occupation of Arab lands.[9] In his address to the 21st session of the OAU assembly of heads of state and government, between 18 and 21 July 1985 in Addis Ababa, General Buhari noted "with regret" that "while the situation in the Middle East deteriorated, our Organization appeared impotent if not peripheral to the peace efforts in the war-torn region."[10] He attributed this to two main factors. First was the inability of OAU members, separately or collectively, to bring "effective pressure to bear on the Government of the United States of America to change its tactics aimed at seeking separate peace treaties between Israel and some of her neighbors instead of promoting comprehensive peace proposals that would address the crux of the problem in the Middle East."[11] This observation also highlighted the absence of any direct leverage by African states on the state of Israel itself in order to make her change her own policies. As mentioned earlier, the last attempt by the OAU as an organization to mediate in that tragic region ended in complete failure. Israel was polite but remained intransigent over the fundamental issues which the visiting OAU delegation of selected heads of state wanted to discuss. Therefore the OAU was not encouraged to try again. In any case, it was the OAU that resolved that all members should break diplomatic relations with Israel following the 1973 war, and accordingly it could no longer be considered by Israel as impartial in the conflict. Even those African states which had resumed diplomatic relations with Israel, apparently in contravention of the collective OAU decision, were in no real position to exert pressure on Israel.

The second weakness of the OAU was the lack of financial resources to aid the Palestinians.[12] In an organization where several members were in arrears of their regular contributions to the budget and its own Liberation Committee was seriously underfunded, there was little possibility that significant financial resources could be made available to aid the Palestinians. Most member states of the OAU were undergoing serious economic and financial crises, and they were seeking new capital resources from the international community, especially the West.

Nonetheless, the OAU has continued to give diplomatic support to the Palestinians, while endorsing in various international fora the search for genuine peace in the Middle East. But any successful peace proposal must enjoy broad-based support among the Palestinians and the Arab states as a whole. Therefore, Nigeria appealed through the OAU to the Arab states to work for unity, because "in their unity lies their strength and in their collective strength would lie the capacity for their victory over the forces responsible for aiding and abetting the occupation of Arab lands and the oppression and repression of Arab peoples [by Israel]."[13]

The federal government of Nigeria has joined other members of the United Nations to observe the annual International Day of Solidarity with the Palestinian People.[14] We have felt that since 1947, when the question of Palestine was first brought before the United Nations, the Palestinian people have justifiably aroused considerable international sympathy for their plight. Their inalienable right to self-determination in Palestine was endorsed in UN General Assembly Resolution 181 of 29 November 1947, and in Resolution ES-7/2 of 29 July 1980. The United Nations had in 1968 established a Special Committee to Investigate Israeli Practices Affecting the Human Rights of the Population of the Occupied Territories. More recently, the International Conference on the Question of Palestine identified the fundamental elements of a just and lasting settlement of the Middle Eastern conflict.

Unfortunately, appropriate Security Council actions have been frustrated by what we considered as misuse of the veto power, as well as by the extension of indiscriminate military, economic, and diplomatic support and assistance to Israel. The various peace initiatives have been opposed and invariably derailed by one party or the other.

Nigeria has retained the conviction that the issue of Palestinian rights must be the *sine qua non* for a just solution to the Middle East problem. We have also remained convinced that the exclusion of the PLO from any serious negotiations would be an exercise in futility.[15] Rather, the PLO should be invited to participate in any UN-sponsored international conference on the Middle East.

The Federal Military Government seized the opportunity of the International Day of Solidarity with the Palestinian People to "re-affirm its recognition of the

PLO as the sole and authentic representative of the Palestinian people. It commends the role of the PLO in the social, cultural, economic and political development of the Palestinian people and the struggle to attain its political objectives."[16] Nigeria was convinced that, in the long run, the PLO and the Palestinian people would succeed in their war of liberation, because historically all peoples fighting for their freedom had never lost and could never lose a war against their oppressors.

The Federal Military Government went further "to assure the PLO and the Palestinian people that Nigeria would not relent in her efforts in searching for and seeking effective measures which would enable the Palestinian people to attain and exercise their inalienable rights."[17] One act which was within the competence of the federal government was to give diplomatic recognition to the PLO in Nigeria. However, the process of taking that decision was not easy.

Prior to the Buhari administration, PLO leader Yasser Arafat had approached Nigeria to allow his organization to open a representational and information office in Lagos. The request was lost in the bureaucratic process of obtaining the government's consent on the matter. It was clear that some highly placed federal civil servants were not particularly enthusiastic about a PLO presence in Nigeria, with their perception of probable security and political problems that could be caused for our country. The government agencies charged with processing such requests therefore took their time on this one, and whenever inquiries were made about the rather long delays, the need to review the credentials of the proposed PLO office was given as sufficient explanation.

In addition, the Israeli lobby in Nigeria had remained very strong. Several Israeli companies, such as Sonel Bonel, had been engaged in lucrative businesses in Nigeria since our country's independence, despite the absence of diplomatic relations between Israel and Nigeria. The Nigerian partners, directors, and shareholders in the Israeli companies incorporated in Nigeria were natural sources of support for Israel. The previously mentioned religious, ethnic, and regional constituencies sympathetic to Israel were unhappy that the federal government's policies and pronouncements were becoming more critical of Israel. They were also determined to raise the issue of reopening diplomatic contacts with Israel. One of the most tricky actions of the pro-Israeli lobby was the organized and highly publicized visit to Jerusalem by two prominent traditional rulers in Nigeria, the Emir of Kano, Alhaji Ado Bayero, and the Oni of Ife, Oba Sijuwade.

Each traditional ruler also held the public office of chairman of his state Council of Chiefs. Their visit to Israel could legitimately be construed as giving tacit recognition to the state of Israel, contrary to the position of the federal government. The fact that the two rulers were received by high government officials in Israel, and were believed to have addressed the Knesset in Jerusalem, further complicated a potentially embarrassing situation to the Nigerian government. The visit caused a sharp division within the informed public: those who favored resuming diplomatic ties with Israel saw nothing wrong; those who were opposed argued that the rulers had no business fraternizing with leaders who were responsible for the oppression of Arab populations, the occupation of Arab lands by force, and collaborating with the regime in South Africa.

Upon investigation, the federal government discovered that the two traditional rulers had not told their respective state military governors that they were headed for Israel when, as required, they sought permission to go abroad. Had they levelled with the governors, the authorities in Lagos would have been promptly notified and appropriate advice would then have been given to the rulers as to how to conduct themselves while in a country with which we had no diplomatic relations and whose policies in the Middle East and towards South Africa the federal government deeply deplored. After all, several Nigerians visited Jerusalem annually for pilgrimage and religious reasons, and such visits were often made with the full sanction and support of the federal government.

The Buhari administration was therefore compelled to take action against the two traditional rulers for violating established guidelines for official travel outside Nigeria. Each was suspended for six months from chairmanship of his Council of Chiefs. The decision was also made to restrict their movements to within their domains for the same period, the federal government withdrew their passports, and the Emir of Kano was made to forfeit the post of chancellor of the University of Nigeria at Nsukka. These actions reinforced the signal to Israel that her policies in the Middle East and South Africa were unacceptable to Nigeria and that we were not going to reestablish diplomatic relations.

These same actions against the traditional rulers could also be construed as a further endorsement of the Arab/Palestinian cause, in accordance with our country's commitment to the principles of natural justice and fair play in the Middle East. It should be pointed out, however, that the pursuit of these principles had proceeded along with the desire to achieve our own country's national interests in the Middle East. For instance, Nigeria had always expected the Arab states to appreciate and reciprocate our support for their cause. Africa's support for Arab/Palestinian interests in the Middle East was not to be taken for granted. On the contrary, the Arabs had to realize that they had reciprocal obligations to support Africa's political causes as well as the continent's drive for economic development and self-reliance. Any lasting friendship with and support from Africans for the Arab cause had to be based on sovereign equality and mutual respect. These were, some of the concerns often vigorously expressed at meetings or discussion of agenda items devoted to issues of Afro-Arab cooperation under the auspices of the OAU.

Meanwhile, a decision on the establishment of the PLO office in Nigeria could not be postponed much longer. Indeed, Chairman Yasser Arafat had raised this issue, among several others, in the impromptu but rather long discussions he had with our Chief of Staff (Supreme Headquarters) when they both met in Conakry (Guinea) during the funeral ceremonies of the late President Sekou Toure. The Chief of Staff was believed to have indicated to Arafat that favorable action would be taken upon his return to Lagos. More importantly, the Buhari administration felt that it was time to take action within its power and competence to demonstrate in concrete terms the much-declared solidarity with the Palestinian people. The administration had previously demonstrated great courage by announcing the recognition of the Saharawi Arab Democratic Republic (SADR) as a member state of the OAU during the 20th summit at Addis Ababa in November 1984.

General Buhari therefore decided to cut the bureaucratic red tape, overrode domestic political opposition, and agreed to establish an embassy of the Palestinians in Nigeria. After jumping the gun once (that is, before our formal agreement was given in February 1985), the nominee of Chairman Arafat was allowed to return to Lagos as the properly accredited ambassador and representative of the PLO in Nigeria. The ceremony at Dodan Barracks (seat of the Federal Military Government), on 17 May 1985, during which Ambassador-designate Samir Baker Daib presented his letter of credence to General Buhari, was short but impressive. For Nigeria, it signified the keeping of a promise to the Palestinian people. If other nations of the world were to keep their own promises to the Palestinians, perhaps the situation in the Middle East might be different from what it has been so far.

NOTES

1. See Gambari, *Party Politics*, chapter 6.
2. Ibid.
3. I.A. Gambari, interview with Nigerian Television Authority, 24 October 1983.
4. Ibid.
5. Ibid.
6. I.A. Gambari, statement in the general debate, 39th session of the UN General Assembly, October 1984.
7. Ibid.
8. General Buhari, "Annual Foreign Policy Address, Annual Patron's Dinner, Nigerian Institute of International Affairs" (December 3, 1984), p. 7.
9. Ibid.

10. General Buhari, speech at the 21st summit of the OAU (Addis Ababa, July 1985).
11. Ibid.
12. Ibid.
13. Ibid.
14. "Ministerial Address to the Nation on the Occasion of the International Day of Solidarity with the Palestinian People," carried by the Nigerian Television Authority, 29 November 1984.
15. Ibid.
16. Ibid.
17. Ibid.

15

Reaching Out to the East

The greater the frustrations experienced by Nigeria in dealing with the Western countries over their Southern African policies and their attitudes to our economic recovery, the more attractive it became for us to reach out to the East. From there Nigeria could hope to obtain more relevant technology, and seek ideological backing for the attainment of a new international economic order and the continuing struggle against colonialism and racism in Southern Africa.

The initiatives for high-level visits to North Korea and the People's Republic of China (PRC) came from the two countries. It was then agreed that I should make official visits, which would be followed by the Chief of Staff, Supreme Headquarters, Major-General Tunde Idiagbon. A comprehensive tour of the East was then planned to include other countries in the region which had also extended invitations to me for official visits. My delegation began with India and went on to Indonesia, then to New Zealand and Australia, and ended in the People's Republic of China.

The main purpose of the visit to India was to attend the special meeting of the Coordinating Bureau of the Non-Aligned Movement on Namibia, the outcome of which was discussed in an earlier chapter. In addition, however, the Nigerian delegation had the opportunity to meet with the Indian Prime Minister, Rajiv Gandhi, and discussed bilateral issues with him. During the meeting in his office, I conveyed General Buhari's best wishes on the assumption of office following the tragic death of Indira Gandhi. We also briefed the Prime Minister about the efforts being made by the Nigerian government to revamp our ailing economy and the difficulties we were encountering in negotiations with the IMF. Prime Minister Gandhi expressed sympathy and support for the Nigerian government's efforts to deal with the economic situation. He then offered to assist us in the areas of relevant technology, small-scale industries, and agricultural fields in order to work toward self-sufficiency in food production. The Indian Prime Minister pointed out to us that from the previous position of a net importer of food, his country had now attained an enviable self-sufficiency. This was clearly a process which we needed to study closely.

In Indonesia, our next stop, we returned to the themes of ideological affinity and a coordinated approach to the Non-Aligned Movement. We attended the commemoration of the 30th anniversary of the Asian-African Conference, in the historic city of Bandung on 24 and 25 April 1985. The three-hour journey by train from Djakarta enabled the delegates to see the beautiful countryside. Terrace farming was much in evidence and cultivation appeared quite extensive. As far as we could observe, the rural folk appeared to be well dressed, looked rather well, and seemed to live in fairly decent housing. Throughout our visit, we were entertained superbly and all delegations attended magnificent cultural shows accompanied by gracious traditional dances. As Shakespeare would put it, "if music be the food of love," the Indonesian hosts gave the visiting delegations an excess of it during the truly impressive receptions and banquets, without surfeiting our appetites.

The conference itself went very smoothly. Resolutions were passed reaffirming all previous resolutions passed by the Non-Aligned Movement concerning issues of international security, colonialism, and apartheid. In particular, the final declaration of the meeting regretted the fact "that the people of Namibia, having endured a century of colonial bondage, continue to languish under the illegal occupation of the Pretoria regime," and reiterated solidarity with and support for the heroic struggle of the Namibian people to achieve self-determination under the leadership of SWAPO, their sole and authentic representative. The meeting rejected any linkage of Namibian independence with extraneous issues and called for the full implementation of UN Security Council resolution 435.[1]

On South Africa, the meeting "reaffirmed that the eradication of apartheid remains one of the most urgent tasks before the international community," and expressed solidarity and unconditional support for the struggle of the oppressed people of South Africa for a democratic, non-racial unitary state. The delegates unanimously agreed that "the United Nations Security Council should impose mandatory and comprehensive sanctions to compel the Pretoria regime to terminate its policies and practices of apartheid and its illegal occupation of Namibia."[2]

There were similar pronouncements on support for the struggle of the Palestinian people under the leadership of the PLO, and a call upon Israel to withdraw totally and unconditionally from all Palestinian and Arab lands occupied since 1967, including Jerusalem.[3]

On the international economic situation, the meeting observed that "three decades after the Bandung Conference, the just demand of developing countries for the eradication of economic backwardness, domination and exploitation and for the achievement of equitable development and progress is yet to be fulfilled." The meeting then urged the international community to take urgent and effective measures through structural reform of the global economic system, and increased bilateral and multilateral assistance, to support the efforts of the developing countries in general and the African states in particular, which had been hardest hit by global economic recession as well as natural disasters.[4]

The closing session of the meeting was nearly marred by controversies that developed over the remarks made by the heads of the delegations of Iran, Iraq, Afghanistan, and Saudi Arabia. However, the spirit of Bandung, which 30 years before had led to the birth of the Non-Aligned Movement, prevailed once again and the final documents were adopted unanimously. In the vote of thanks given on behalf of all African delegations to the meeting, I emphasized the spontaneous welcome and warm friendliness of the Indonesian people and expressed gratitude to the government for making it all possible.

I also commended the Indonesian Minister for Research and Technology for arranging a demonstration for all delegates at the Indonesian Aircraft Industry, where we witnessed encouraging progress toward the acquisition of high technology.[5]

Finally, I pointed out that whereas only six African states (Egypt, Ethiopia, Ghana, Sudan, Liberia, and Libya) attended the Bandung Conference in 1955, all African states with the regrettable exceptions of Namibia and South Africa were present at the commemorative meeting 30 years later.[6] The "Spirit of Bandung" did influence the winds of change which blew over our continent. We enjoined all the "independent countries assembled there to re-affirm those noble principles (such as world peace, freedom, justice, international cooperation and universal development) which were enunciated at the 1955 Conference in Bandung."[7]

The next leg of the tour took our delegation to Auckland-Rotorua and Wellington. The New Zealand government, under Prime Minister David Lange, who also doubled as Foreign Minister, had aroused deep international interest by sharply disagreeing with the Reagan administration over international security issues and Southern Africa. According to Lange, "New Zealand is a small country with a long way from anywhere. We don't have enemies. We aren't threatened. Because nobody is pointing nuclear weapons at us, we don't see the logic of asking the United States to defend us with nuclear weapons. . . . We don't like nuclear weapons in New Zealand. For that reason, we asked the Reagan administration not to send nuclear weapons to New Zealand."[8]

Nigeria was impressed by the courage of the New Zealand government in standing up to President Reagan, but it was even more impressed by the actions against apartheid. The New Zealand government had closed the

South African consulate—a measure applauded not only in Nigeria but by the Non-Aligned Movement as a whole. Moreover, Lange had made very successful visits to Botswana, Mauritius, Kenya, Tanzania, and Zambia, in which the foundations for constructive relationships with those countries were laid. The New Zealand government was in fact planning to open two resident diplomatic missions in Africa—perhaps in East Africa.

During Lange's visit to Africa in April 1985, he reiterated his anti-apartheid positions. The Prime Minister distanced himself from the United States' policy of constructive engagement and confirmed that New Zealand had no plans to invest in South Africa. Concerning the proposed tour of South Africa by New Zealand's All Blacks Rugby Team (which was actually an all-white group), Lange's government was courageous in trying to have it called off as a sign of solidarity with the liberation struggle in South Africa. Unfortunately, the All Blacks Rugby Team appeared intent to defy pressures from the New Zealand government, parliament, and public opinion and decided to proceed on the tour. Nonetheless, Lange made it very clear that should the All Blacks decide to go on the tour, the New Zealand government would not issue visas to the South African Springboks in 1987 for any return match.

These anti-apartheid policies and actions appeared to be gaining public support within New Zealand. Our visit to New Zealand was therefore aimed primarily at giving encouragement not only to the New Zealand government but also to the leaders of opinion. This purpose was achieved by our visit, which was copiously reported in the local press everywhere we had official engagements.[9]

The bilateral level of our contact with New Zealand was not neglected during our visit. The possibility of cooperation between our two countries on dairy farming and sheep rearing was carefully examined. While visiting a synthetic fuel plant at New Plymouth, I also saw the possibility of Nigeria seriously considering New Zealand's experiment in the conversion of gas to methane and gasoline. Nigeria flared so much gas from the oil wells under production, that if it could be converted into petroleum it could probably be used in domestic consumption without any need for additional refineries. We could then use our full quota of crude oil production as sanctioned by OPEC for export and thus increase our foreign-exchange earnings.

Our visit to Australia from 1–4 May was apparently the first to that country by a Nigerian Foreign Minister. Yet the Australians had sent their Foreign Minister, Andrew Peacock, to visit Nigeria in August 1977, followed by the visit of former Prime Minister Malcolm Fraser in 1979. The visit by my delegation was welcomed by the Australian government not only for reciprocal reasons but as evidence of external support for Prime Minister Bob Hawke's anti-apartheid policies. These policies included the severance of sporting links with South Africa and the overwhelming vote in the Australian parliament to stop a visit by the South African rugby team; closure of Australia's trading office in South Africa, and the banning from the South African routes of Qantas, the national airline.

As an active member of the United Nations Council for Namibia, Australia had extended financial and material assistance to Namibia. In 1984, SWAPO was invited to open an information office in Australia. The country also observed the arms embargo imposed against South Africa by UN Security Council Resolution 418 (1977). Australia often denounced the use of Namibia as a springboard for attacks aimed at destabilizing the frontline states. The Bob Hawke government also rejected the Reagan administration's linkage of Namibian independence to the withdrawal of Cuban troops in Angola and supported the implementation of Security Council Resolution 435 without preconditions.

However, Australia had declined to accept SWAPO as the "sole and authentic representative of the Namibian people," but recognized the liberation movement as "one of the major nationalist groups in Namibia and one which has an essential role to play in the settlement negotiations"; nor had Australia supported comprehensive economic sanctions against South Africa. While Nigeria endorsed the steps taken by the Australian government, our visit was also aimed at encouraging Hawke's government to take further steps.

In our official discussions with the Australian Prime Minister, the chairman of the Joint Parliamentary Committee on Foreign Affairs and Defence, and the Foreign Minister, Bill Hayden, we pressed the Australian government to remove their outstanding reservations about SWAPO and about the efficacy of economic sanctions against Pretoria. It was of course impossible to expect a change of policy after only one visit, but we observed that the Australians held Nigeria in very high regard. They pointed out, for example, that following the recent decision to close down their High Commission office in Accra, for economic reasons, Australia's mission in Lagos was charged with the task of looking after the country's interest in Ghana. The more frequent high-level exchange of views between the two countries, which enjoyed considerable influence and stature in their respective subregions, the greater the understanding between them was likely to be. The two delegations to the various official talks held in Canberra expressed the hope that this would be the case.

On bilateral issues, Prime Minister Hawke expressed a strong willingness to consider an exchange of experts in agriculture and mining, sectors in which the Australians have substantial expertise. In addition to crude oil, Nigeria has been endowed with several other mineral resources, many of which are underdeveloped or not fully explored. The rehabilitation of agriculture and intensified food production were the priorities not only of the Buhari administration but of Africa's new program for economic recovery. Even in manpower and technical training, Australia had been more forthcoming in offering to help, but Nigeria had not in the past made much use of that offer. For example, a memorandum of understanding, similar to the one of 1977, in which the Australian government supplemented the salaries of technical experts recruited to serve in Nigeria, was signed between the two countries on 16 April 1981. Although only one other country enjoyed that kind of arrangement (Papua New Guinea—a former colony of Australia), Nigeria had not fully utilized the opportunities offered to her.

The first point of call during our official visit to China was Shenchen—one of the Special Economic Zones of China. These SEZs were deliberately opened up for the infusion of foreign capital, technology, and expertise. New buildings, hotels, and other construction activities sprang up, as if to prove the success of the thesis "one nation, two systems" being propagated by the Chinese government.[10] This experiment in coexistence between capitalism and socialism was very interesting for us to observe. It must have been even more interesting for the residents of Hong Kong, through which we entered China at the beginning of our visit, who would have to live within that arrangement when the British relinquished their colonial rule in favor of the People's Republic of China by the year 1999.

Prior to my official visit to China there had been high-level contacts between the Buhari administration and the government of the People's Republic. The Minister of Information, Youth, Sports, and Culture, Group Captain Samson Omeruah, had completed a successful trip to China. The Nigeria military had also been negotiating arrangements whereby the Chinese would assist the Defence Industry Corporation in Kaduna in its efforts to manufacture small arms, ammunition, and explosives. The contacts between the two countries on defense cooperation had progressed enough for then Chief of Army Staff Major-General Ibrahim Babangida to go to China to conclude some concrete agreements.

The development of Nigeria's steel production required, among other things, the completion of an adequate mode of transportation of iron ore from the Itakpe mines in Kwara state to Ajaokuta, one of the two main production centers. China was the natural place to go for the construction of a rail link, because the Chinese had accomplished this task before in East Africa, when they built the much more extensive Tan-Zam railways.

Largely to give political backing to the development of these bilateral relations, the head of the Federal Military Government, General Buhari, approved the acceptance of the formal invitation extended to me by the Chinese Foreign Minister, Wu Xueqian, to pay an official visit to China.[11]

Before proceeding to Beijing for the official talks, we had an engagement at Guangzhou (Canton) which was very touching at both the personal and official levels. In a simple but very impressive ceremony at Zhongshan University, the honorary title of professor was conferred upon me. As the first African to be so honored by such a highly regarded university in China, I gave what I considered to be a suitable speech on that occasion, the full text of which is Appendix 3 of this study. The Nigerian ambassador in China, Ade Adekuoye, who was present at the ceremony, later told me that the portion of my speech which dealt with the role of an intellectual in government was totally irrelevant to the Chinese political system, where the party was supreme and intellectuals were barely involved in government. This may be so, but my address was directed to the audience in Nigeria perhaps more than to the Chinese hosts.

The official talks between the Chinese Foreign Minister and his delegation and ourselves took place at the Great Hall of the People on 8 May 1985. Wu Xueqian was very forthcoming throughout the two-hour discussion. There was true identity of views on Southern Africa. We both condemned apartheid, and we agreed to support the liberation movements in that sub-region and to work together to obtain the implementation of Security Council Resolution 435.

The highlight of our visit was, however, the meeting with the Chinese Premier, Zhao Ziyang. A man of about 65, clad in a well-tailored Western-style suit, he seemed at least ten years younger than his age. Articulate and very impressive, Zhao Ziyang seemed to our delegation a man to watch in China's future political arrangements. It was no surprise to me when he later became Secretary-General of China's Communist Party. The Premier was thoroughly informed about the economic situation in Nigeria and urged increased bilateral trade between our two countries, the two most populous nations in Africa and Asia, respectively. He proposed some counter-trade agreements whereby our crude oil would be supplied in return for cotton and rice from China.

Counter-trade arrangements would add a new dimension to the existing bilateral cooperation between Nigeria and China, based largely on projects. Chinese experts were closely involved in agriculture and fisheries, the construction of bore-holes, and irrigation and rice cultivation in the Chad Basin Development Authority area of Borno state and the Itoiki area of Lagos state. Several other projects involving Chinese expertise included the Ode-Ekpe Agricultural Project in the Anambra/Imo River Basin Development Authority and the Bore-Hole Project in Bauchi state.

There was a fairly widespread belief in official circles in Nigeria that the Chinese model of agriculture might be the best for our own program of self-sufficiency. During our official visit, we were very impressed by what we saw at Dali district, not far from Guangzhou, where rice and other agricultural production had increased sharply, as a result, we were told, of the introduction of more scientific farming methods, better fertilizer and seed varieties, greater incentives to peasants following cancellation of the people's commune, and a rigid choice of crops to be planted in each season.

However, those who advocate the adoption of Chinese modes of cultivation for Nigeria should also note that there were some distinct differences in the nature of agricultural production in the two countries. Whereas several new agricultural entrepreneurs in Nigeria now run large farms and use heavy machines, Chinese agriculture has remained labor intensive. In China we saw little or no heavy machinery; moreover, the dignity of labor and discipline in farm work were firmly embedded in the psyche of the Chinese, much more than among Nigerians: for example, the back-breaking work of hand-planting and hand-cultivation of rice in the paddies was simply amazing. Finally, land was owned by the state and no one could sell it. The size of plots for individual or family cultivation was generally small and contract farmers were required to turn in a certain proportion of the yield. The rest of the yield could be sold for profit.

The institutional machinery for the execution of existing projects and the identification of new ones in Nigeria was the Sino-Nigerian Joint Commission. The second session of the commission was to be held in Nigeria between 25 and 28 June 1985. One of the objectives of my official visit to China was to give political backing and obtain the same from the highest levels of Chinese authority for the work of that second session of the Joint Commission. We were successful, and the Joint Commission's second session, which took place later in Lagos, made considerable progress.

To demonstrate the commitment of the Buhari administration to the enhancement of Sino-Nigerian relations and to complete existing projects and agree on new ones, such as the rail link to Ajaokuta and military cooperation through the Defence Industry Corporation, we commenced plans for the Chief of Staff (Supreme Headquarters), Major-General Tunde Idiagbon, to visit China and also North Korea in September 1985. The arrangements were completed and he was to proceed after returning from his pilgrimage to Mecca and Medina in August 1985. As things turned out, however, the overthrow of the Buhari administration took place during General Idiagbon's pilgrimage.

Another visit that never took place was my official tour of the Soviet Union and some of the Eastern European countries, planned for the middle of 1985. We had great difficulties in accommodating the schedule of Soviet Foreign Minister Andrei Gromyko and myself, yet the visits to Czechoslovakia, Rumania, and Poland were to occur after the Soviet one. I did visit the Soviet Union along with General Idiagbon on the occasion of the funeral of

General Secretary Andropov in 1984.

Nigeria-Soviet relations, whose roots stretch back to the mid-1960s, prospered during and after our country's Civil War, and then went into slumber in the early 1980s. The basis for Nigerian-Soviet cooperation may be weaker and more recently established than our country's ties to the West, but it has been real nonetheless. The first government of an independent Nigeria was clearly pro-Western in orientation. Foreign Minister Jaja Wachuku once declared that, in dealing with foreign powers, the Balewa government preferred to move from "the known [Western] to the unknown [Socialist bloc]."[12] Nonetheless, enough domestic pressure was exerted to move the federal government from a marked pro-Western to a more truly nonaligned foreign policy.[13] The needs of Nigeria's economy were being perceived as requiring some diversification in sources of development assistance and export markets. It was for these reasons that Nigeria began to move cautiously toward the Soviet Union and the Eastern bloc.

In July 1963, a trade agreement was signed between Nigeria and the Soviet Union.[14] The value of Soviet imports from Nigeria jumped from slightly more than $250,000 in 1963 to about $4.6 million in 1984.[15] By 1965 the total value of trade between the two countries had doubled. At the educational-exchange level, the total number of Soviet scholarship awards officially accepted by Nigeria was 141 at the end of 1968; by the time the protocol on the equivalency of diplomas was signed in 1973, the number of Nigerians who had received higher or specialized secondary education in the Soviet Union was put at 1,200, while another 500 students and 20 postgraduates were enrolled in Soviet institutions in that year.[16]

The Civil War in Nigeria involved the Soviet Union in the procurement of arms and ammunition for the federal government. Nigeria's "traditional allies or friends," such as Britain and the United States, had earlier refused to sell arms to the federal side. Accordingly, the Soviet Union supplied Nigeria with MiG 17s, Czechoslovakian L-29 Delphin trainers, and other weapons. Soviet technicians also accompanied the deliveries to assemble, test, and later maintain the military hardware. The deliveries in arms and ammunition from the Soviet Union diminished somewhat after the end of the war in 1970.[17] Nigeria paid fully for the Soviet weapons.

In order not to be regarded mainly as a source of supply of military weapons, however, the Soviet Union sought to involve itself in an extensive feasibility study for the long-planned major iron and steel industry in Nigeria.[18] Nigeria responded by announcing that henceforth loan offers from the Soviet Union and the socialist countries would be accepted by the federal government.[19]

One of the key problems was that our country's movement toward the U.S.S.R. was based largely on civil war needs and requirements. We hesitated to approach the Soviet Union for military or economic needs until our relationship with the West had cooled in these areas. The Soviets had tried to maintain an economic foothold in Nigeria beyond the wartime involvement, and even made an exception to the rule whereby they avoided direct dealings with private businesses in developing countries. For example, they joined with private Nigerian businessmen to form the West African Automobile and Engineering Company (WAATECO), to import Russian cars, heavy vehicles, tractors, and agricultural machinery into Nigeria.[20] The accumulation of petrodollars by OPEC members such as Nigeria had also attracted the Soviet Union to "do and sell turnkey projects and set up joint business enterprises, etc."[21] The national iron and steel plant was typical of this approach. When completed, the plant would have a capacity of 1.3 million tons a year (first phase) and a full manufacturing cycle, including rolled steel, with a potential to expand production to an output of 5 million tons a year (third and final phase).[22]

The expansion of economic assistance and trade notwithstanding, there were serious problems that would affect the future of such relations. The structure of the Nigerian economy had not significantly moved away from heavy dependence on the West. There was no serious commitment by the nation's elite to pursue a development strategy which would entail "socialist withdrawal from the international capitalist system which promotes their underdevelopment."[23] Although the Soviet Union had ceased to insist on a Third World country making such a socialist choice before engaging in trade and economic relations, its first preference for aid and economic and military cooperation has tended to be countries leaning toward socialism. To that extent, neither Nigeria nor the Soviet Union would regard one another as "first customers" in serious trade and economic relations. Moreover, as a competitor with developing countries in the international capital market, the Soviet Union might not be able to supply the investment funds needed to modernize and expand Nigeria's industrial development projects, while providing credits for the importation of consumer goods.

The challenge facing Nigeria was to maintain the aggregate increase in the volume of total trade with the Soviet Union, since the expansion of exports in the non-crude-oil sector would surely be to our advantage, especially if we could reduce the unfavorable balance of payments with the U.S.S.R., caused by excessive imports during the period of greater oil revenues in the 1970s and early 1980s. The Soviet Union has remained closely associated with the construction of a blast furnace complex for our steel project at Ajaokuta. Serious delays in completing this project were the fault not of the Russians but of some Western companies which failed to execute their projects according to schedule.

When the Buhari administration came into power it recognized the need to pursue the production goals of the steel mills by the then Minister of Mines, Power and Steel, Alhaji Rilwanu Lukman, and to reestablish high-level contacts with the Soviet Union. The proposed visits to the Soviet Union by myself and later on the Chief of Staff (Supreme Headquarters) were meant to demonstrate our country's political commitment to a joint effort to put Nigeria-Soviet economic and technical cooperation on more urgent and positive footings. Although the visit never occurred, Nigeria could not postpone this line of action without harming her national economic interests vis-à-vis the Soviet Union.

The potential gains of reaching out to the East and the Socialist bloc countries have yet to be fully realized. On the political front, we attained ideological support for our positions on Southern Africa, but at the level of technological transfers and substantial trade and economic relations much more needed to be done on both sides. It would be a long time to come, if ever, for the East to match the West's impact on Nigeria's economy. What we could use right away, however, was greater export and import diversification, which intensified relations with the East and Socialist countries could provide.

NOTES

1. "Final Declaration of the Commemorative Meeting in Observance of the 30th Anniversary of the Asian-African Conference, Bandung, April 24–25, 1985," Rev. III/24–10–1985, p. 4.
2. Ibid.
3. Ibid.
4. Ibid.
5. "Vote of Thanks on behalf of African Representatives at the 30th Anniversary of the Asian-African Conference in Bandung, Indonesia, April 25, 1987," Document E.
6. Ibid.
7. Ibid. A commemorative meeting, the conference was not intellectually demanding, but it was physically exacting. However, there were several cultural displays, artistic performances, musical shows, dances, and state banquets to relieve the physical exertions. For instance, a truly lavish banquet was given in honor of the heads of delegations to round-up the conference. The food and cultural displays were exceptional. I was seated next to Mrs. S. Russan, wife of the Minister of Interior, Republic of Indonesia, who was also formerly in the diplomatic service. She told me that the most beautiful Indonesian women were in Bandung and that I should visit Bali region next time, accompanied by my wife, to be on the safe side.
8. Article by Prime Minister David Lange, *Miami Herald* 1985.
9. In a news conference I warned that Nigeria would join the collective African decision to boycott New Zealand in future games, should the All Blacks Rugby team decide to play in South Africa. I also said that a boycott of the Edinburgh

Commonwealth game was a distinct possibility. "How could sporting bodies say that they wish to 'exercise their individual rights by going to play in South Africa'," I asked, "when that country denied such rights to its own people?" (*The Dominion* [Wellington] 1 May 1985).

10. However, one of the consequences of the new opening to the West became plain during the banquet held in honor of the visiting Nigerian delegation by Deputy Mayor of Shenchen. Mr. Lee looked, dressed and talked like a smooth businessman from the capitalist West.
11. Chinese official hospitality, already legendary, was really lavished on my delegation during our entire visit. Several banquets were given in our honor at Shenchen, Canton, and Beijing, where the Foreign Minister was host, and at the famous Beijing Duck Restaurant where Vice-Premier Tian Jiyun was host. An old Chinese proverb says, "He is not considered noble who has not climbed the Great Wall." We did climb the Great Wall, thanks to the arrangements made by our hosts.
12. See E.A. Ajayi, "Nigeria-Soviet Relations," *Nigeria: Bulletin on Foreign Affairs*, 1, no. 3 (Jan. 1972), p. 4.
13. See I.A. Gambari, *Party Politics*.
14. Robert Legvold, *Soviet Policy in West Africa* (Cambridge: Harvard University Press, 1970) p. 169.
15. Ibid., p. 221.
16. V. Kosenko, *Azia i Afrika Sogdnya* Correspondent in West African countries, "Soviet Nigerian Cooperation" (Date not specified, possibly 1979/80), p. 25.
17. Guy Arnold, *Aid in Africa* (London/New York: Kogan Page & Nichols Publishing Co., 1979) p. 105.
18. Legvold, *Soviet Policy*, p. 319.
19. Ibid.
20. See Christopher Stevens, *The Soviet Union and Black Africa* (London: McMillan, 1976) p. 34.
21. Elizabeth K. Valkenier, "The USSR, The Third World and the Global Economy," *Problems of Communism*, July–August 1979, p. 32.
22. Arnold, Aid in Africa, p. 109.
23. See Garvin Williams, "Nigeria: A Political Economy," in Williams (ed), *Nigerian Economy and Society* (London: 1976), pp. 11–54.

16

International Security Issues

The most frightening effect of scientific and technological development has been the buildup of nuclear arsenals and the development of esoteric weapons of mass destruction. The race to destruction has continued despite the size of the existing military arsenals of the two superpowers, which, if employed in direct warfare, could create a nuclear winter that would engulf both the Northern and Southern Hemispheres. As I told assembled delegates to the 39th session of the UN General Assembly during the general debate, research has suggested that up to one-half of humanity would probably perish in a major nuclear conflict, while the other half would become secondary victims sooner or later.[1] We in Africa, who appear to be mere onlookers in the nuclear debate and irrelevant to the issues of strategic weapons deployment in Europe, would also find no hiding place. We would not be spared in the inevitable catastrophe, even though we had no part in it and repeatedly warned against the accumulation of these terrible weapons.[2]

Quite unmindful of warnings from non-nuclear states, including Nigeria and other African states (with the exception of South Africa), the superpowers and other major powers have engaged in a global arms race unprecedented in the sophistication of the weapons involved and the level of resources consumed. The arms race has indeed developed its own momentum, hardly related to legitimate security needs, while outpacing negotiations for its control. Rather than provide durable or credible security, the arms race has become a source of insecurity.

The very concept of deterrence—the pillar upon which nuclear weapons development has rested and the backbone of the security of the two global alliances—had been undergoing a credibility crisis. As soon as one side increased the accuracy and effectiveness of nuclear weapons, this triggered an alarm of perceived inferiority by the other. This was then used to justify the development of new systems in the never-ending circle of a nuclear arms race. This unstable strategic development had seriously undermined deterrence as a sure source of international security.

In any case, the possibility of waging an all-out nuclear war, with the resulting termination of all human life and present civilization, could hardly be contemplated except by the insane. Variants of the deterrence idea "could hardly be comforting to those who live inside and outside the nuclear umbrella. There is something bankrupt about security thinking which assumes the death of millions of people."[3] This fact probably underpinned the declaration made by President Reagan and General Secretary Gorbachev at the November 1985 summit in Geneva, that "a nuclear war cannot be won and must never be fought."

It is of course true that we have not yet witnessed a nuclear war, but the same cannot be said for the race in conventional weapons. Indeed, conventional weapons are closely related to nuclear weapons in the military doctrines and planning in both NATO and the Warsaw Pact. NATO would feel compelled to rely on nuclear weapons as long as it felt inferior to the Warsaw Pact in terms of conventional weapons. And once the Soviet Union attained rough parity with the USA in the nuclear arena, the race in conventional weapons became wide open.

Conventional weapons have been deadly. There have been more than 150 local wars fought with them since World War II, resulting in more deaths and casualties than in the last global war. The proliferation of conventional weapons and their ready availability for cash or ideological solidarity (or both) have inflamed domestic conflicts and regional tensions in the Third World.[4]

Outer space was not going to be spared militarization and an arms race involving the superpowers. President Reagan's Strategic Defense Initiative or "Star Wars," insofar as it appeared as seeking superiority on one side, would almost surely lead to the other side building up its own capability in outer space or increasing its military capability on earth. We shall return to the SDI and its opponents later.

Meanwhile, each new weapon or new attempt to alter the perceived strategic balance has been at the root of superpower fear and competition. This in turn inflamed their political relationships and also poisoned the general international political climate. Hence, widespread insecurity was generated among the nations of the world.

If one accepts the proposition that the global arms race has been more a source of insecurity than of real and lasting security, the question is how to reverse the present trend. Four suggestions are offered here which reflect Nigerian and African thinking or perspectives on issues of security, disarmament, and development in an *interrelated* manner. First, there would have to be a change in the strategy of military planning as it relates to the role of nuclear weapons in global security. At the commemoration of the 30th anniversary of the Asian-African Conference, in Bandung, 24–25 April 1985, members of the Non-Aligned Movement welcomed the commencement of negotiations between the United States and the Soviet Union, which were later held at summit levels, on the complex set of questions concerning space and nuclear arms, and further expressed the hope that the negotiations would yield positive results in a rethinking of the role of nuclear weapons in global security.[5]

Arms control negotiations must be based on a recognition that use of nuclear weapons would lead to far greater destruction than any conceivable contribution to the defense and security of the superpowers, their military allies, and the world as a whole. As an alternative, the West could strengthen its conventional forces at modest cost, a proposition close to the British Labour party's position. There is also Gorbachev's vision of a nuclear-free world, which may not be technologically feasible, because once a nation or terrorist group possesses a single nuclear warhead, the race for rearmament would likely begin again. There is President Reagan's Strategic Defense Initiative (SDI)—an impenetrable shield to protect the United States against missile attack, thus allowing the discarding of nuclear weapons. This is unlikely to be achieved in the near future. That may be why some experts advocated other missions for the SDI system (e.g., defense of missile sites or the partial protection of the population, or SDI-2). Whereas SDI-1 would substitute defensive for offensive weapons, SDI-2 would maintain offensive forces and add the defensive system to them, the rationale being that a leaky umbrella may offer no protection in a downpour but could prove useful in a drizzle.[6]

Although SDI-2 would collapse under a full Soviet first-strike, it could cope adequately with a second Soviet strike when the depleted forces that survived a U.S. first-strike would be fired in retaliation.

The main snag to such thinking is that the Soviets would respond with a large offensive buildup of their own. Any attempt to strengthen deterrence by adding strategic defenses to strategic offensive forces would control the arms race, *not* promote arms control.[7]

If it is acknowledged that nuclear warheads have no military use except to deter an opponent's use of them, then what may be needed for military strategic and planning purposes and would promote arms control is to work for a state of *mutual deterrence* at the *lowest levels* consistent with stability. The objective would be to restrict each side to a small number of warheads, something quite feasible with current verification technology. We would then have a totally different nuclear strategy of mutual security with vastly smaller forces—less than 1,000 warheads each instead of the present 50,000[8]

For us in Africa, any system that could lower the risk would be welcome.

After all, Africa is part of the world system and the continent is probably the weakest in military terms and the most vulnerable to nuclear disaster. We are greatly dependent on other regions of the world for dealing even with natural disasters, such as drought, flood, and desertification.[9]

Progress toward global disarmament would help promote regional disarmament efforts. Superpower restraint could have positive effects, not only on the African region but the Third World as a whole. Africa was the first continent to adopt a regional position on the issue of nuclear nonproliferation. The French nuclear test in the Sahara in 1960 provoked a national reaction in Nigeria and a breach of diplomatic relations with France, but also a United Nations resolution cosponsored by 14 African states in 1961, aimed at prohibiting any nuclear tests in Africa.[10]

The Organization of African Unity, at its 1964 summit, adopted a Declaration of Denuclearization of Africa, in which all states were called upon not to test, manufacture, or store nuclear weapons on the African continent. The concept of a nuclear-free zone was later developed in Latin America in 1967.[11] In addition, Africa was the first region, in an international treaty, under UN auspices, to agree not to manufacture or acquire control of nuclear weapons. South Africa has not followed these positive steps and thus poses a serious security dilemma to other African states. We shall return to this point later.

Should the superpowers and their allies adopt a new strategic and military doctrine focused on mutual security with vastly smaller forces, consistent with stability, enormous financial and other resources could be released to meet other government responsibilities, principally the welfare of all peoples. It is significant to note that in 1984, over $850 billion was spent for military purposes, while economic and social expenditure was only a small proportion of that.

The second major suggestion being advanced here for strengthening international security is related to looking deeper into the causes of international tensions and how to reduce them. There would be less need to increase national armaments if we had a more effective collective security system.[12] Collective action could also help lower the temperature of international tension.

The Cold War, between East and West has had a direct impact on raising international tension. The main theater of the Cold War was Europe but the ideological struggle to win influence spread to other regions. Military assistance has been one of the instruments in the struggle to win or hold allies. And military assistance has not been limited to conventional weapons; there may be up to ten countries in the Third World on the threshold of nuclear capability, resulting from active collaboration with the nuclear-weapons states. Israel and South Africa are in this group, and they may well have acquired nuclear weapons already.

The arms race, whether conventional or nuclear, has exacerbated disputes at the regional and ultimately global levels. There is no real alternative but to return to the Charter of the United Nations and strengthen the global system for collective security, with primacy given to the peaceful settlement of disputes. All members need to renew their commitment to collectively deter aggression and create an atmosphere conducive to friendly relations among them. Fidelity to Article I of the Charter, which provides for respect for the right of self-determination, the sovereign equality of states, and human rights and cooperation in solving international economic, social, and cultural problems, would promote the kind of international relations whereby tension among states would be reduced.

Concomitantly, Article 26 of the Charter entrusts the Security Council with the task of formulating plans for regulating armaments, "in order to promote the establishment and maintenance of international peace and security with the least diversion for armaments of the world's human and economic resources."[13] This should be implemented without further delay.

The third main recommendation is to emphasize the link between disarmament and development. This takes two major forms. First, there are threats to international peace and security which are non-military in nature. The present international economic order is both unjust and inequitable. The North-South dialogue aimed at addressing the situation is stalemated, thus covering up the serious clash of interests between the global "haves" and the "have nots," and capable of developing into a serious threat to international peace and security.[14] While the North constitutes less than one-third of the world's population, it disposes of more than 70 percent of the world's wealth. Official and unofficial assistance are on the decline, just as commodity prices for the produce of most Third World countries have been sharply declining. The debt burden on these countries retards the levels of investment necessary for economic stimulation. Such indebtedness was estimated in 1985 at about $850 billion (an amount roughly equal to the annual global expenditure on the arms race). Africa's share of this debt burden was about $170 billion, which although relatively small, is high compared to Africa's level of industrial output and foreign-exchange earnings from non-commodity exports. Still, most African countries had to spend 50 percent or more of their annual income on debt service, an intolerable situation that encouraged domestic turmoil and violence, worsened by external intervention. International financial institutions pressed upon the debtor nations a program of austerity measures which if accepted tended to bring domestic discontent and internal instability. If rejected, the Third World country involved might find its credit lines frozen and be deprived of some essential imports.

Another dimension of this problem concerns the competitive relationship between the arms race and development. As the final document of the United Nations First Special Session on Disarmament established in paragraph 16, "in a world of finite resources, there was a close relationship between expenditure and armaments and economic and social development."[15] The final documents and several resolutions passed by consensus at subsequent regular sessions of the General Assembly recommended that resources released as a result of disarmament measures should be utilized to improve economic and social conditions, particularly in the LDCs. In more concrete terms, the proposal was made to create an International Disarmament Fund for Development, based on the idea of a disarmament dividend.

The military has also tended to make disproportionate use of non-renewable resources. In the case of aluminum, copper, nickel, and platinum, for example, the estimated global consumption for military purposes was greater than the demand for these materials for all purposes in Africa, Latin America, and Asia combined.[16] Global expenditures on military research and development, in 1980 for example, represented approximately one-quarter of global expenditures on all research and development.[17] If the focus of research, science, technology, and the consumption of non-renewable resources were changed toward solving economic problems, not only in the Third World but in industrialized countries as well, this would lead to a healthier, more prosperous world.

The fourth and final major approach toward the strengthening of international peace and security is the need to widen the scope of those involved in the conversation on arms control. The preponderance of power between the two superpowers does not confer a monopoly of wisdom; indeed, the retreat from multilateralism in arms control and other related international issues could promote only short-term national interests. Bilateral detente cannot fully address, let alone resolve, major international issues. The exclusion of African issues from serious discussions of global security is unfortunate, not only for Africa but for the rest of the world.

A number of issues of special concern to Africa also impinge on global security. In addition to the link between disarmament and development; between development and enhanced internal stability and national security; and between the global arms race and regional arms races there is the security dilemma posed by South Africa. It is only proper, therefore, that this chapter should conclude by discussing this issue.

South Africa is not the only security problem facing us in the African continent. We have our intercommunal tension, civil wars, and other domestic disturbances, which often attract and are made worse by external intervention. Moreover, we have border disputes caused in large part by colonially imposed boundaries. Ideological differences often complicate border disputes. There is also the wasteful diversion of scarce resources toward the acquisition of armaments which we do not manufacture within the African continent.

All this admitted, however, South Africa constitutes the most dangerous threat to regional security in Africa and a possible threat to world peace. The regime keeps down its own people by violence and employs violence to keep its neighboring countries in a state of perpetual siege, aimed at destabilizing them and overthrowing their legitimate governments.[18] A monster with many ugly faces and dangerous tentacles, apartheid is racist at home, colonialist in Namibia, occupationist in Angola, destabilizing in Mozambique, and bullying in Botswana, Zambia, and Zimbabwe.

Worse still, for the security of the Southern African sub-region and Africa as a whole, the apartheid regime complicates security problems by its vast military establishment. According to the London-based Institute of Strategic Studies, since 1969 South Africa has spent more money on arms importation and acquisition than all other African countries put together.[19] The capital city of every independent African country is believed to be within the range of South Africa's air force. Western countries, especially France, Italy, Britain, and Israel, assist South Africa to manufacture small arms and some aircraft.[20] This is in contrast with the situation of almost all other African countries, which are totally dependent on the importation of arms from outside the continent.

Above all, South Africa is believed to possess nuclear weapons capability,[21] whereas most independent African states have signed the nuclear non-proliferation treaty. This raises some serious questions: What is to be done by Africans in the threat of nuclear war initiated by South Africa, or at least nuclear blackmail by the racist regime? Can the West be relied upon to check the very country whose nuclear capability it helped to build? Should African countries singly or collectively develop their own nuclear capability? At what costs to domestic social and economic programs? And what would be the impact on the global arms race were the Eastern bloc countries to be invited and agreed to help build black Africa's own nuclear weapons? Only an end to apartheid can remove this threat to peace and security.

It has become clear that international security cannot be usefully discussed in terms of conventional or nuclear weapons alone. There are demonstrable relationships between security and defense strategies on the one hand and disarmament, arms control, development, and the threats posed by South Africa to African and global peace and security on the other. Nigeria and other African and Third World nations have the duty to continue to stress those broader interrelationships at appropriate international conferences and fora.

NOTES

1. Speech at UN General Assembly, 39th session, New York, October 1984.
2. Ibid.
3. See Olu Adeniji, "The Concept of Disarmament in African Context," in pamphlet *Conference on Security, Disarmament and Development in Africa: Meeting of Experts* (Lome, Togo: United Nations, August 11–12, 1985, Lome, Togo). I am greatly indebted to Ambassador Adeniji, Director-General, International Organizations Directorate, Ministry of External Affairs, Lagos, for the data in this chapter and for a better understanding of disarmament issues as a whole.
4. Ibid.
5. Commemoration of 30th Anniversary of Asian-African Conference, Bandung, "Final Declaration" (Rev III/24–10–1985), p. 3. A promising effort was apparently made at the later Reykjavik meeting between President Reagan and General Secretary Gorbachev in October 1986, when they discussed the following guiding principles and objectives:

   (a) 50 percent reduction in strategic missile warheads, bombers, and missile launchers over a five-year period, and the total elimination of all ballistic missiles over a 10-year period.
   (b) Global limit of 100 warheads each, of intermediate-range missiles.
   (c) Proposals for a phased accord on nuclear weapons tests, starting with the issue of verification of existing treaties and working toward reduction of tests. Unfortunately, negotiations broke down on the Strategic Defense Initiative (SDI), which President Reagan was unwilling to give up and which the Soviet Union appeared to consider a real threat. Perhaps a way out could be a new strategic concept or military planning about nuclear weapons based not on unilateral advantage but on mutual security at minimum cost.

   On this possibility see former United States Secretary of Defense Robert S. McNamara, "Towards Nuclear Sanity: a Plan for Minimal Deterrence," *International Herald Tribune*, 24–25 January 1987, p. 4.
6. Ibid.
7. Ibid.
8. Ibid.
9. Adeniji, "Concept of Disarmament."
10. Ibid.
11. Ibid.
12. Ibid.
13. Ibid.
14. Ibid.
15. Lundbo, "The Relationship between Disarmament and Development," pp. 77–88.
16. Ibid.
17. Ibid.
18. The economic damage caused by South African raids into Angola and Mozambique alone was estimated at over $14 billion.
19. Adeniji, "Concept of Disarmament."

20. Ibid. South Africa produces French armored cars under license as well as Mirage fighters and Italian CMB326 fighters powered by British Rolls Royce engines which are assembled in South Africa.
21. In 1961, South Africa bought an atomic reactor—the SAFARI I—from the United States, which was supplemented by SAFARI II in 1968. West Germany helped South Africa to develop a pilot uranium enrichment plant in Valindaba in 1971. Five years later, France signed a contract to build two power reactors in South Africa. Meanwhile, South Africa refused to sign the Nuclear Non-Proliferation Treaty and failed to fully submit her nuclear programs to the International Atomic Energy Agency's safeguards. An alarm by the Soviet Union prevented South Africa from testing an atomic weapon in the Kalahari desert in 1977, but she went ahead in September 1979 to conduct a nuclear test in the Atlantic Ocean, which was picked up by an American satellite. These facts are given by Adeniji, "Concept of Disarmament," p. 39.

PART 6

Conclusions

17

Evaluation of the Buhari Administration's Foreign Policy

The Buhari; administration's foreign-policy achievements and disappointments must be discussed in the context of public perceptions of the goals being sought. We may begin with a consideration of some specific issues and move to the general orientation of the country's foreign policy.

Two major achievements were the Quadripartite Agreements and chairmanship of ECOWAS, both achieved notwithstanding the decision to close our country's land borders. The Quadripartite Agreements, involving Nigeria and her three neighboring countries to the west, was the first pact "of its kind between the leaders of the four countries." According to the *National Concord* newspaper, the "summit [hosted by Nigeria in Lagos] was impressively short on ceremony but long on serious business. And by the time it drew to a close the popular verdict was that something good had probably begun." The paper went on to say that "the issues most directly addressed by the Summit, namely border security, criminal investigation cooperation and extradition, mutual assistance on customs, trade and immigration were most timely if not in fact overdue." In addition to giving due credit to General Buhari for the success of the summit, the paper concluded that "the glaring success of the Summit attests to the correctness of the Buhari Administration's foreign policy with its emphasis on regional peace, stability and development."[1]

The second major achievement occurred in July 1985, when General Buhari was elected chairman of ECOWAS. This was the post which, for reasons of domestic schedules, he had declined to accept when it was first offered at the ECOWAS summit in December of the previous year. Some observers speculated that the leaders of the francophone members of ECOWAS deliberately chose General Buhari as chairman in order to induce his government to reopen its land borders and to dissuade Nigeria from pursuing actions which contradicted the spirit of the community. Nonetheless, the assumption of the chairmanship of ECOWAS was significant because it fell in line with our country's continued commitment to the community.

Aside from these two achievements, the Buhari administration had some success with other aspects of our foreign affairs. On Chad, our policies were, on the whole, correct and positive. Except for some impatience for concrete results, the informed public generally felt that Nigeria had gone as far as she could without having to commit troops. We tried to operate as "honest brokers." Despite his initial personal reluctance, General Buhari did receive Hussein Habre in Abuja, Nigeria, as the head of state of Chad. Our head of state discouraged Libya and some other OAU members which had wanted to challenge the legitimacy of Habre's rule in Chad and the credentials of his country's delegation to the 20th and 21st summit meetings of the organization in Addis Ababa.

Perhaps Nigeria was the only country in sub-Saharan Africa which could have dealt frankly with and obtained respect from both France and Libya on the Chadian issue. That was why, as noted earlier, both countries felt confident enough to ask the Buhari administration to provide facilities in Kano for Franco-Libyan liaison groups to monitor and control the process of withdrawal of their troops from Chad. The withdrawal of all non-Chadian troops from that wartorn country remained a key element of the Buhari administration, but we were not as successful in bringing about political reconciliation despite our bilateral as well as multilateral efforts.

At the continental level, the Buhari administration scored a victory in its efforts to play a leading role in African affairs by recognizing SADR. The successful move to turn the tide of OAU membership in favor of SADR was welcomed almost unanimously by the Nigerian informed public.[2] Recalling the remark attributed to Bismarck that "in foreign policy, courage and success do not merely stand in a casual relationship, they are identical," a serving Nigerian diplomat observed that our decision on Western Sahara illustrated the enduring truth of the Iron Chancellor's words.[3] Several other letters, telegrams, and personal representations were received from lecturers and staff of higher educational institutions as well as other organizations in Nigeria, congratulating the government for the decision to recognize SADR and aid her admission to the OAU.[4]

Nigeria's participation in the work of the historic 20th summit of the OAU at Addis Ababa was considered very positive and was generally well received at home. "Nigeria led several initiatives during [that] Summit for which it is credited with the huge success of the meeting," commented the *National Concord*;" it shows that this Administration could articulate a credible stand on African policy issues and give the necessary leadership."[5] The administration's decision to honor its pledge made at the summit to contribute $5 million to Africa's famine problems was also applauded. "In spite of our own economic crunch at home," one newspaper boldly declared, "it is well that the pledge did not end up a mere sentiment of intention. That is a way to an invigorated foreign policy."[6]

On Southern Africa, the *Guardian* observed that under the Buhari administration, "our country's leadership on issues affecting Apartheid in South Africa or independence in Namibia remained unchallenged and positively in tune with the world in general and Africa in particular."[7] We gave all possible diplomatic support and moral encouragement to the liberation movements in Southern Africa. The administration worked tirelessly and in close consultations with the frontline states, the OAU, the Non-Aligned Movement, the Commonwealth, and the United Nations, as well with other countries in the pursuit of anti-apartheid objectives.

Nonetheless the administration should probably have allocated more financial resources than it did in support of the liberation struggle. It is true that Nigeria was herself experiencing severe economic and financial difficulties, but greater expenditures and more logistical assistance to the freedom fighters could easily have been justified on the understanding that the security of the sub-region is inextricably tied to an enlightened view of our own longterm national security. This could have been done by re-launching and significantly increasing private and governmental contributions to the Nigerian Fund for South African Relief, which probably should have been renamed the Fund for the Liberation of Southern Africa.

Despite its vigorous and sustained efforts, the Buhari administration failed to persuade the Reagan administration to change its flawed policies of constructive engagement with the regime in South Africa and linkage of the independence of Namibia to the Cuban withdrawal from Angola. Our persistent criticisms of the Reagan administration's policies nevertheless found strong echoes in Congress and on several college campuses. The Reverend Leon H. Sullivan, author of the famous Sullivan Code of Conduct for American and other multinational corporations operating in South Africa, came out in favor of such companies' ceasing all business in the racist country. Although Congress passed legislation, overriding President Reagan's veto, which imposed selective sanctions against South Africa, the Buhari administration's goal of seeking comprehensive and mandatory sanctions against the racist remained valid.

The greater regret was that the Reagan administration maintained its policy of constructive engagement, after Secretary of State Shultz's own Advisory Committee on Southern Africa concluded in its report of 29 January 1987, that the policy was a failure. The committee recommended a stronger role for the United States in order to promote "good faith" negotiations between white and black leaders in South Africa.

With regards to dealing with Western Europe, the Buhari administration's policies toward France and Germany were positive and mutually rewarding, especially with the added potential of counter-trade agreements with both countries. However, the West German response to our economic difficulties was not as understanding as the French. On political matters we also made greater headway over Southern Africa with the French than with the West Germans. Still, the administration did not bring our political and economic relations with these two countries into a satisfactory alignment. Perhaps 20 months in office was not adequate for the administration to achieve such a realignment, especially during a period when Nigeria's own economy was in a poor state.

The worst bilateral relations between Nigeria and a major power that was also a leading trading partner were with Britain. As indicated in an earlier chapter, the Dikko affair merely exacerbated the underlying tensions in the generally unequal relations between Britain and Nigeria. In handling the diplomatic aftermath, the administration was far less aggressive than was demanded by nationalist sentiments in Nigeria. For example, a leading Nigerian expert in international relations argued that "Nigeria should remind Britain that by allowing Umaru Dikko to carry to carry out within her territory acts injurious to Nigerian interests, she has committed a breach of international law."[8] Others called for a total breach of diplomatic relations. Cooler heads prevailed, however, and the administration worked to normalize relations, a process not completed until after the overthrow of the administration. It would be difficult for any truly nationalist government in Nigeria to avoid coming into conflict with Britain over the kind of economic and political postures and advantages which British governments may assume toward our country.

Concerning the Middle East, the balance of public opinion agreed with our attitude toward the Palestinian people and support for the peace process. There was a strong pro-Israel lobby in Nigeria, but its pressures were not strong enough to effect a change in policy under the Buhari administration. Israel's connections with South Africa were well known and reinforced the collective decision made at the OAU to sever diplomatic relations with Israel. That decision had not changed. Nigeria, which had always considered the OAU as the strongest institutional instrument for her Africa-centered foreign policy, would find it difficult to break ranks and consider resumption of diplomatic relations with Israel.

There were, as noted earlier, responsible citizens who argued for the reestablishment of some official ties with Israel. Even they, however, would not oppose our country's support for the principle of self-determination for the Palestinian people.[9] The arrogance of Israeli power and that country's seeming insensitivity in dealing with her Arab neighbors had increased worldwide sympathy for the Palestinian cause. Nigeria continued to denounce the Israeli occupation of Arab lands, the annexation of the Golan Heights, the establishment of Jewish settlements on the West Bank, and the invasion and occupation of southern Lebanon. The limits of Nigeria's economic and military power might not have permitted us to do more, but our national conscience and commitment to self determination did not allow us to do less.

Regarding disarmament and arms control, Nigeria's impact was very limited, which is hardly surprising, because these issues were becoming the exclusive preserve of the superpowers and their military allies. As a faithful and long-serving member of the United Nations Disarmament Conference in Geneva, we strongly expressed our views on the dangers of the global arms race and the universality of the catastrophe that may result from accident, miscalculation, or the exercise of first- or second-strike options in any nuclear exchanges. We joined likeminded states to pursue the idea of linking disarmament and international development, and we constantly highlighted the special problem which South Africa posed for African continental security in particular and world peace in general.

The potential benefits for our country arising from closer ties with the Soviet Union, the Eastern bloc, Asian countries, and Australia and New Zealand were immense. Their political support for Nigeria's positions on Southern Africa and international, economic, and security issues was relatively easy to come by. However, it would require a major shift of our national focus to realize the full benefits of technology transfer, technical assistance, and an expanded volume of trade with these countries. One key instrument for promoting greater trade relations could be counter-trade arrangements. Unfortunately, a combination of factors slowed down movement toward the East during the Buhari administration. These included the sheer force of habit in Nigeria's trade and economic dealing with the West, the financial and other advantages and conveniences of our country's business and administrative elites, and the cancellation of the official trips planned for the Chief of Staff (Supreme Headquarters), Major-General Tunde Idiagbon.

In addition to the specific policy issues discussed in this chapter, the Buhari administration took significant initiatives aimed at improving and diversifying the process of making foreign policy. Mention has been made of our efforts to improve upon, expand, and institutionalize the training of all levels of External Affairs officers. The seminar organized for all the heads of our diplomatic missions abroad was part of the training and briefing process. Designed to stimulate the intellectual capacity of the participants, the seminar also gave diplomats the opportunity to make critical analyses of our foreign policy endeavors and exchange views with ministers and senior government officials from the home ministries. Several national newspapers wrote favorable editorials on the seminar, which was scheduled for about two weeks at the National Institute for Policy and Strategic Studies (NIPS) in Kuru, Jos, Plateau State of Nigeria.

For example, *National Concord* , while urging the diplomats to put more life into their assignments abroad, commended the idea of the seminar.[10] *New Nigerian* also endorsed the seminar's work and recommended to the participants "not only to question the relevance of the Commonwealth but to urge that we (Nigeria) get out of it."[11] *Sunday Herald* considered the seminar as timely and its duration good. The paper concluded that "the Ministry of External Affairs has done this country proud on a number of occasions since the present Administration came into power in December, 1983 . . . (and) if other government agencies should proceed the way our External Affairs Ministry has been going in recent times, this country's problems would be greatly minimised."[12] A very thoughtful article also appeared in the *Guardian* in which useful suggestions were made for the diplomats assembled in Kuru to ponder over.[13]

Another initiative concerned the efforts to democratize the sources of input into the making of foreign policy. We invited outside experts and other individuals from universities, national institutes, and the labor and business sectors to examine critical issues and make recommendations to the government. This departure from the norm was initially resisted by the bureaucracy, but as the involvement of non-governmental groups and individuals became more sustained and their recommendations yielded positive results, officials of the Ministry of External Affairs began to tolerate if not accept the opening up to outside participation. This initiative was close to my heart, and it was personally satisfying that we executed it while meeting with informed public approval.[14]

Mention should also be made here that the Buhari administration had the most successful Hajj operation in the recent history of the federal government's involvement in the arrangements for the annual Muslim pilgrimage. Beginning with the 1984 Hajj, our administration took the courageous step of limiting the total number of official pilgrims to 20,000, from the more than 100,000 of some past years. The new ceiling enabled the Nigerian Pilgrims Board and our consulate in Jeddah to cope with the arrangements for the transportation, housing, and medical and general welfare of the pilgrims. The administration's domestic "War Against Indiscipline" was extended to cover the behavior of the pilgrims before departure and throughout their stay in the Holy Land. As a result, trafficking in drugs and currency, prostitution, and other gross acts of indiscipline, which used to characterize the behavior of many Nigerian pilgrims, were greatly reduced. King Fahd of Saudi Arabia wrote a letter to General Buhari, commending the orderly behavior of the Nigerians.

In the report of the official delegation to Saudi Arabia for the 1984 Hajj, we recommended, among other things, that the total number of official pilgrims should remain at not more than 20,000, and that preference should continue to be given to those performing the pilgrimage for the first time. More intensive screening should be made to ensure that pregnant women, the very old, and the infirm were barred from going to Hajj. The so-called international pilgrims—Nigerians who got to the Hajj via international airline companies, outside the jurisdiction of our Pilgrims board—should be discouraged, since they often complicated the problems handled by the Nigerian authorities in the Holy Land. These and other recommendations made by the official delegation were aimed at consolidating the gains made in ensuring a hitch-free Hajj.[15] In accepting the recommendations, the Federal Military Government commended the Ministry of External Affairs and the Nigerian Pilgrims Board for the conduct of the 1984 Hajj. One would hope that Hajj operations could be completely self-financing and the role of federal and state governments in the operations would be reduced to the barest minimum consistent with the responsibility for the protection of the security and the promotion of the welfare of all Nigerians going abroad.

In general, the Buhari administration decided that the defense of Nigeria's national security and the welfare of her citizens would be the axes around which foreign policy would revolve. We then projected the country's national interests along the lines of concentric circles of policy priorities, an orientation of foreign policy that was conceptually sound and consistent with the recognition of reduced national financial resources and power. Unfortunately, the decisions to close our land borders and to expell illegal aliens from Nigeria were out of tune with the declared policy of concentric circles, which gave priority to relations with our neighbors. However much these decisions may have served our short-term national interests, the length of time during which the borders remained closed and the mass nature of the expulsion exercise did hurt Nigeria's long-term national interests, especially our commitments to ECOWAS and to African unity. We need to bring policy practice into alignment with the concept of concentric circles.

Indeed, after almost a year of operating its general foreign policy concept, the administration received widespread commendation from informed public opinion. In its editorial "The New Realism in Foreign Policy," *National Concord* praised the efforts to "re-define foreign spheres where we are in a position to exert any real influence; where we stand best to realise our national interests; a policy in which Nigeria would play the role of a sub-continental power and where our immediate neighbors would rightly be our priority."[16] The paper concluded that "there is wisdom in the new approach we have adopted in our foreign policy. There is little point in deceiving ourselves that we can play the policeman in Africa. We cannot. And it would be ridiculous to believe otherwise, because while ours may in fact be the most populous state on the continent, we seem to lack the economic status necessary for effective diplomacy on a continental basis." Indeed, Nigeria's ability to pursue continent-wide issues such as liberation, support for self-determination, and economic development would be enhanced by consolidating the leadership we offer to our immediate neighbors and, in fact, the entire West African sub-region.

In a feature article in *Weekly Democrat*, "A High Mark in Foreign Policy," Oscar Ede, a highly regarded analyst of foreign affairs, observed that "one does not need a microscope to see that 1984 was a success year for our foreign policy."[17] That this was made possible against the background of a weak economic base must be credited to the quality of the administration's foreign policy machinery. Ede also commended the idea of "concentric circles."

Africa Now magazine published a major piece on the Buhari administration's policies and praised the government for pursuing "a bolder foreign policy" which attempted to "recapture the image of the Mohammed-Obasanjo era."[18] Some of the credit was attributed to "two experienced exponents of Nigeria's foreign policy formulation, the Foreign Minister himself, and retired Major-General Joseph Garba . . . who has now come back as Nigeria's Permanent Representative at the United Nations." Personal letters were also received from some influential Nigerians expressing warm approbation of the general thrust of the administration's foreign policy.[19]

Punch gave a retrospective evaluation of the performance of the administration's Cabinet in 1984 and the general input of intellectuals. The newspaper argued that the administration could have achieved more if it used more progressive minds, but acknowledged the intellectual outputs from two federal ministries including External Affairs.[20] According to the paper, "in the theatre of external affairs, some of the clout we gained during the clear sighted era of Murtala Mohammed (May his soul rest in peace) and which we lost in the fog of the last civilian government is being gradually restored. The federal government richly deserves the accolades but we must also concede to the Minister of External Affairs his Ministry's building of a sound theoretical foundation for Nigeria's foreign policy." In conclusion, the newspaper said that, as a result of the administration's foreign policy endeavors, "OAU is gradually coming alive, SADR is recognised and some tough rhetorics have of late emanated from Dodan Barracks against nations inclined to thwart our efforts in the international forum." *New Nigerian* gave

General Buhari its "Man of the Year" award for 1984, a decision based on a nationwide opinion sample concerning the administration's achievements. Foreign policy was one of the key areas for which the administration was considered to be worthy of commendation.

In his own end-of-the-year assessment, Professor Gabriel Olunsaya, Director-General of the Nigerian Institute of International Affairs, identified a number of bold decisions, such as Chad, Western Sahara, ECOWAS, Namibia, and the OAU, and concluded that "an impartial assessment must return a positive verdict."[21] The achievements were there "for everyone to see—these include its dynamism, its independence of action, its commitment to the protection of Nigerians and Nigeria's interests in any part of the world, its commitment to the strengthening of the OAU and ECOWAS and to the dismantling of the Apartheid regime in South Africa and the eradication of colonialism in Namibia." The Director-General also praised the conceptual framework of the foreign policy and argued that although Africa had remained the centerpiece of Nigeria's foreign policy, under the concentric circles focus our national goals would be pursued from the particular to the general, from the immediate to the remote.

Two senior research fellows of the Nigerian Institute of International Affairs gave separate interviews in which each agreed that, after one year, Nigeria's foreign policy had developed a distinctive focus. The new sense of direction had earned great respect for the federal government in the eyes of the Nigerian public.[22] The publisher of the *Guardian*, Alex Ibru, accompanied by Yemi Ogunbiyi, a senior executive of the newspaper company, and on one occasion Sully Abu, the paper's Eastern and Southern African correspondent, made official visits to Burkina Faso, Tanzania, Libya, Israel, and Egypt and published their reports on how these countries and their leaders perceived Nigeria. In all five countries they found that Nigeria was held in very high regard and that great importance was attached to its foreign policy. The Buhari administration was urged to continue its bold foreign policy, because such vigorous involvement was expected from Nigeria.

Newswatch magazine devoted a special issue and cover story to what it called the administration's "activist" foreign policy.[23] In a detailed story, the influential magazine analyzed the dimensions of Nigeria's foreign policy and concluded that the government had "returned sparkle to Nigeria's international relations, bringing back the good old days of Murtala-Obasanjo's activist foreign policy."

Nonetheless, as 1985 progressed and the full effects of the administration's efforts to revamp the economy and instill public accountability and national discipline began to be felt, public alienation grew. There were reports of a widening split among senior members of the Supreme Military Council and rumors about an impending military coup. Under such conditions, public interest in foreign-policy issues diminished and the administration's achievements were consigned to the back stage.[24]

The Buhari administration was overthrown on 27 August 1985. Major-General Ibrahim Badamasi Babangida succeeded as Commander-in-Chief and President, Federal Republic of Nigeria. During his first broadcast to the nation, President Babangida gave reasons for the change of government and added foreign policy to the areas of public issues in which his predecessor was believed by the military to have failed the nation.[25]

It should be pointed out here that the Buhari administration tackled two main and interrelated challenges in foreign policy. First was the urgent need to define and defend our country's national interests: the reality of diminished national financial resources had not dampened public expectations of great successes in foreign policy. The second was how to employ resources and the position of our country within Africa to establish new realities. The main goal of the administration's foreign policy was to project Nigeria's national interests externally, while attempting, in a creative and positive manner, to address Africa's problems on a new scale of priorities. Considering the circumstances under which the policymakers were operating, these two challenges were met successfully and with general public approval. History will judge this understandably personal evaluation.

NOTES

1. Editorial, "The Summit of Solidarity," *National Concord*, 15 December 1984, p. 2.
2. See for example, Oscar Ede's thoughful article, "Reshaping Foreign, Defence Policies," *Weekly Democrat*, 2 December 1984.
3. Letter [name of diplomat withheld] to author dated 29 November 1984.
4. Notable among them were from Alaba Ogunsanwo, Professor of International Relations, University of Lagos (letter dated 20 November 1984), and Akanbi Sanni, chairman, Nigerian Peace Comittee.
5. *National Concord*, 23 February 1985, p. 2.
6. Ibid.; see Editorial, "$5 Million for African Famine."
7. "From Kuru to the World," in the *Guardian*, 7 August 1985, p. 9.
8. Professor Osita Eze, "The Legal Implications of the Umaru Dikko Affair" (School of Legal Studies, Imo State University, Aba Campus, 1984).
9. On its return from official visits to Egypt and Israel in March 1985, the Guardian Newspapers delegations, led by Alex Ibru, publisher, and including Dr. Yemi Ogunbiyi, Controller of the Directorate, made public its findings and gave some recommendations along these lines.
10. "Task Before Our Diplomats," *National Concord*, 6 August 1985, p. 2.
11. "Foreign Policy Review," *New Nigerian*, 7 August 1985, front page editorial.
12. Editorial, *Sunday Herald*, 28 July 1985, p. 3.
13. "From Kuru to the World," The *Guardian*, 7 August 1985, p. 9.
14. See *Africa Now*, October 1984, p. 63.

15. For more details, see *Report of the Official Delegation to Saudi Arabia for the 1984 Hajj* (Lagos: Federal Government Press, 1984).
16. *National Concord*, 10 December 1984, p. 2.
17. *Weekly Democrat*, 6 January 1985, p. 7.
18. *Africa Now*, October 1984, p. 63.
19. Among these were from Prince Ado Ibrahim, a prominent businessman, dated 3 January 1985, and Alhaji Nuhu Bamali, Magajin Garin Zazzau (Zaria), who served as Minister of State for Foreign Affairs (from October 1960 to November 1965), and later became the substantive Foreign Minister before the demise of the First Republic, who wrote on 8 April 1985.
20. See editorials in *Punch*: (i) "1984 in Retrospect: Moribund Intelligentsia" (14 December 1984) and (ii) "How the Cabinet Performed" (17 December 1984).
21. *Daily Times*, 31 December 1984, p. 9.
22. Dr. George Obiozor and Dr. Bassey Eyo Ate gave the interviews, which were reported in *New Nigerian*, 14 January 1985, p. 7.
23. *Newswatch*, 4 March 1985, pp. 11–31.
24. See my further observations on this point in Appendix 4 (ii).
25. See "Why We Struck," special edition, *Newswatch*, 9 September 1985, pp. 18–19.

18

Foreign Policy at a Crossroads: Some Reflections

Disagreements over foreign policy often center as much upon conflicting ideas or concepts as on concrete interests. Other important variables are the wider international system and a nation's total capability, and the proportion of national resources made available to the pursuit of external relations. The value of ideas and conceptualization lies principally in the direction to which the sum total of external relations may point. In Nigeria, we are still debating a nationally acceptable ideology and a set of higher national principles to govern the behavior of the leadership as well as the general population. Therefore, we need to put more efforts into developing a clearer conception of the thrust of our country's foreign policy.

The concept of Africa as a centerpiece of our country's foreign policy has been discussed earlier. Suffice it to say here that no government in Nigeria can ignore the reality of the African continent as the primary environment for the conduct of external relations. Similarly, no wise government can avoid reformulating or refining such an African-centered foreign policy to make it reflect the economic means available for projecting it. Nigerians fully appreciate the notion that charity must begin at home and in areas and issues closer to home. We have also shown earlier in this study that Nigeria's capacity to influence events becomes greater as the issues move from global to continental and sub-regional concerns.

The other ideas, concepts, and organizational structures to be discussed here are: the absence of a solid "national consensus" in foreign policy, the apparent separation of political from trade and economic issues in the conduct of our external relations, the bureaucracy and the policy-making process, and the idea of a dynamic foreign policy.[1] Although these ideas and tendencies have been deeply embedded in official as well as non-governmental thinking on our foreign policy since independence, they have become increasingly irrelevant if not positively harmful to Nigeria's needs in the late 1980s. By attempting here to show the poverty of these ideas, perhaps more focused and useful concepts and institutional arrangements may emerge.

Absence of a Solid Consensus

Although the vigor, attention, and level of resources committed to foreign policy have varied from one administration to another, all post-independence governments have sought a national consensus behind their foreign policy. No government has ever felt confident enough to ignore non-governmental criticisms of foreign policy; on the contrary, almost all governments have sought, or appeared to seek, to accommodate such critical views. Governments have tended to pursue a coalition strategy, and have avoided antagonizing major groups, whether regional, ethnic, religious, or ideological. Although the idea of establishing an all-party coalition government at the federal level has not been fully realized, it has never been really abandoned. Sir Abukakar Tafawa Balewa opted for it in the first period of his appointment as Prime Minister (from 1957 to 1959). In fact, the idea of an all-party government remained the personal desire of the late Prime Minister up to and beyond the federal parliamentary election of 1964, even when it was very clear that the coalition government (NPC and NCNC) over which he presided was collapsing. In the early days of the Second Republic, the idea of an all-party coalition was revived by former President Shagari. The demise of the NPN-NPP accord did not completely seal Shagari's hope for such an all-embracing coalition. In the political debate ordered by President Babangida, several influential Nigerians, inside and outside the government, advocated the establishment of a no-party or all-party government.

The idea of building a solid national consensus behind a country's foreign policy is intellectually sound. It suggests the seriousness with which other world nations take one's foreign policy positions, and would produce positions more durable and more externally respected than those which change whenever a party assumes office. However, the manner in which almost all post-independence federal governments have attempted to build a consensus is another matter. For the most part, they have tried to borrow the rhetoric of radical or dissenting groups, while essentially pursuing conservative policies. This is not an enduring or serious way of building national consensus, which is perhaps why a consensus on major foreign policy issues has remained elusive, except on apartheid, decolonization, and nonalignment. After a quarter of a century of independence, Nigeria had to organize a national conference to determine the direction of her foreign policy. Unfortunately, the All-Nigerian Conference on Foreign Policy, which took place in Kuru-Jos between 6 and 13 April 1986, resulted in more acrimony and divisions.

A solid and enduring national consensus on foreign policy will continue to elude Nigeria, largely because of the asymmetry between the pursuit of essentially conservative economic and political policies at home and the articulation of radical rhetoric for policies abroad. This situation has been compounded by the tendency to project domestic ethnic, religious, and class antagonisms on outside situations. As long as our country's economic structure and external trade remain largely capitalist and pro-West, Nigeria will continue to find it difficult to pursue truly nonaligned and anti-imperialist policies abroad. This reality has to be properly understood by analysts of Nigeria's foreign policy.

Another serious reality may be related to the relatively loose group which has consistently exercised a powerful influence on all governments since independence, and which has been mainly responsible for ensuring more continuity than change in our country's domestic and foreign-policy orientations. While those who are installed in public offices through "elections" or military coups may change from time to time, those groups that have exercised real power in Nigeria have not really changed. The alliance of the bureaucratic, military, and business elites has ensured that changes in regimes have produced little change in policy. As pointed out earlier, however, this is not to argue that it does not matter which government is formally in power. There will always be a margin of influence or room for maneuverability in advancing the national interests, especially in dealing with the outside world. Nonetheless, only a true change of government will lead to a sustainable change in foreign policy.

De-Coupling Foreign Policy and Foreign Economic and Trade Relations

Just as there is a distinction between being in office and being in power, there has been a clear difference between exercising primacy over foreign-policy formulation on the one hand and occupying the position of command and control over a broad range of a country's external relations on the other. Although the Ministry of External Affairs has often fought for and earned primacy in the formulation of foreign policy, it has never become the point of political or institutional coordination of all external relations. One major casualty has been the decoupling of foreign policy (essentially a political activity) from international trade and general economic relations.

In the United States and the Soviet Union, for example, the White House and relevant organs of the Central Committee or Politburo of the Communist party perform the role of authoritative focal point, to coordinate the broad range of external relations. In Britain, relevant Cabinet committees serve similar coordinating functions. Unfortunately for Nigeria, the growth in our external relations and responsibilites since independence has not been matched by an adequate and institutionalized point of overall command and control.

During the Buhari administration, there were some inter-ministerial committees and meetings. The committees were often convened to prepare for important state visits or joint commissions scheduled to take place in Nigeria or abroad. Such inter-ministerial committees were also constituted to deal with specific crises, such as the Dikko affair and Anglo-Nigerian relations, and problems which developed in Nigerian-United States relations over Southern Africa, as well as bilateral trade and economic issues between the two countries. We also had the relatively more permanent inter-ministerial task force on Chad, whose mandate was later extended to include our relations with Cameroon. Nonetheless, these inter-ministerial committees were ad hoc in nature, operated mainly at the level of officials, and hardly enjoyed the participation of more than one minister at a time. There was, of course, the National Defense and Security Council, presided over by the head of the federal government himself, which dealt authoritatively with broad foreign-policy issues. However, it hardly considered matters relating to joint commissions and international trade and wider economic relations. The council was not the kind of permanent but flexible machinery for supervising and coordinating the gamut of our external relations which has been badly needed and almost always missing.

A new and permanent inter-ministerial council should be established as an effective link between our general foreign-policy concerns and our external trade and international economic interests. The absence of such a council has been adversely affecting out country's performance and credibility in dealing with other countries with better organized or coordinated systems. Such a council would also be able to offer guidance for our missions abroad in the areas of trade and general economic activities. We may then be able to evaluate particular embassies abroad and the selection and performance of the heads of our diplomatic missions. The proposed council could be under the formal chairmanship of the president, but for greater effectiveness and flexibility, it should be chaired operationally by the foreign minister.

This leads directly to the related issue of the position of the Minister of External Affairs within the government. The growth and complexity of Nigeria's external relations will continue to require the foreign minister to either have prior and adequate knowledge of the subject matter under his portfolio or sound intellect to give leadership to the foreign service bureaucracy. We have drawn attention repeatedly to the high quality which our informed public has often expected from the foreign minister and the government. A typical example can be seen in Appendix 4 (i). Henry Kissinger was probably right when, in his celebrated memoirs, *The White*

House Years, he pointed out that few men ever grow in public office. According to Kissinger, holding public office may teach a man how to make important decisions but not what decisions to make. To be able to make the right decisions and perform well in office, a public man has to draw mainly on his previous educational and other qualifications, as well as relevant practical experience.

Another crucial ingredient in the success of a foreign minister is that he hold a suitably high political position within the administration. Leaving aside the personality issue, the foreign minister has to be regarded as a senior cabinet member, who should therefore sit on the highest policy councils of state. The fact that, as foreign minister, Professor Ishaya Audu was not a member of the NPN (the ruling party), let alone its inner policy caucus, during President Shagari's administration, was a serious handicap in his conduct of foreign policy. It was also impossible for the Ministry of External Affairs to become an authoritative point of inter-ministerial coordination for external relations, in their security, political, trade, and economic dimensions, when the foreign minister was not a member of the Supreme Military Council and Armed Forces Ruling Council, as happened under the Buhari and Babangida administrations.

The Bureaucracy and Foreign Policy

The Ministry of External Affairs has become a huge bureaucracy. As mentioned earlier, the Nigerian diplomatic service grew out of the first Prime Minister's office in 1957 into an organization with a staff of over four thousand and 92 overseas embassies by 1981. Although the number of overseas missions was reduced to 86, in response to the nation's declining economic fortunes, during the Buhari administration, the Ministry of External Affairs has remained probably the biggest single bureaucracy in the entire federal administration. Another unique feature of the External Affairs Ministry is that its staff contains more top management grade levels than all the home ministries put together.

The ministry's policy objectives are imprecise. They include the safeguarding of the security, independence, and territorial integrity of Nigeria; the promotion of the economic and social well-being of our citizens; the promotion of African unity and intra-African cooperation, and contributions toward the enhancement of world peace and security. These broad objectives are to be translated into specific national interests and a program of actions aimed at a constantly changing external environment that is not under our control.

These variables necessitate a diplomatic service which is highly professional and embraces properly motivated men and women. One of the principal tasks of the political leadership of this unique ministry is to manage the bureaucracy and sharpen it as a dominant voice in the making of foreign policy. The highest priority must therefore be assigned to enhancing the professionalism of the foreign service. Although the major civil service reforms of the 1970s highlighted the need for continuous training and specialization, the reality was different and the "cult of the generalist" has persisted. The intellectual laziness in the civil service, inherited from Britain, has been retained, long after the British have moved toward high-level training, retraining, and greater specialization in their own civil and diplomatic services. Having disbanded its own specialized corps of interpreters, international lawyers, and oil diplomats, the Ministry of External Affairs has seemed to hold the view that any officer may be assigned to any diplomatic task. The assignment or reassignment of officers both at headquarters and overseas missions is generally made with little reference to special skills or background. Once an officer is assigned to a particular desk, he may remain there until his tour is completed.

The first step toward a regime of greater specialization would be to utilize more effectively the special skills and talents already existing within the bureaucracy. A more conscious effort is needed to raise the intellectual output of officers through training and retraining. The ministry could emulate the Nigerian Army and other military establishments, which consistently pursue the continuous training of their officer corps. Although new efforts were made in the training of External Affairs officers during the tenure of the Buhari administration, the program adopted in 1985 needs to be expanded to include all categories of staff and a greater degree of specialization.

Specialization and training cannot be overemphasized. The functional responsibilities and the global location of our embassies require that recruitment, training, and specialization be accorded special consideration. The principle of maintaning a "federal character" for foreign-service officers need not sacrifice merit, talent utilization, and efficiency. Throughout the world, recruitment into the foreign service is highly competitive. If only the best is considered good enough in other countries' foreign services, only the best should be good enough for ours. Talent is fairly spread throughout our country, and with increasing numbers of young people interested in joining the foreign service from all states of the federation, the challenge is to recruit the best.

A carefully tailored program of training should be instituted, designed to meet the needs of the service as well as the individual officers, and be made operational at all levels and ranks. It is unfortunate that some officers who have attained the highest grade level since their initial entry into the service, in the late 1950s and early 1960s, have undertaken no further training.

The second reason for encouraging greater specialization has to do with any future rationalization of the multiplicity of attaches currently posted by the home ministries to serve in our overseas missions. Financial constraints and cost-effectiveness considerations may move the government to eliminate the need for the departments of immigration and customs and the ministries of education, trade, and information to send separate attaches to our embassies, when their tasks could be more cheaply performed by External Affairs officers. Should this happen, External Affairs would have to step in and take over the tasks previously performed by the attaches. To be prepared for this, the ministry's program of specialization and continuous training has to be pursued with conviction and vigor.

Third, an active training and specialization program would be good not only for the ministry but for the general morale of officers. The opening up of new opportunities, new vistas, and new skills would induce a feeling of relevance in those who take advantage of them. The officers who acquire the additional training and new areas of specialization would be encouraged to give their best when in the service and to contribute positively to the nation, following early or formal retirement, in such institutions as the university, press, banking, and finance, and the like.

The morale of the officers is related to their efficiency and must therefore be taken seriously by the political head of the ministry. A successful foreign minister is, in large part, one who identifies with the hopes, aspirations, and welfare of this staff. He needs to be at the forefront of the search for the solutions to problems such as the housing, transportation, and general welfare needs of the officers—especially those returning from overseas postings, who tend to be more severely affected. The minister must fight and be seen to fight for the legitimate promotion prospects and career expectations of deserving officers, especially over the sensitive political decisions on the ratio of career to non-career appointees as heads of overseas missions or ambassadors. It would be totally unrealistic to expect excellence in the output of foreign service officers if the minister was perceived as lukewarm toward their welfare and career advancement.

Perhaps the most crucial factor is an adequate level of funding. Unfortunately, the growth in Nigeria's external activities and responsibilities has not been matched, especially in recent times, by corresponding budgetary allocations. On the contrary, the financial resources available to the Ministry of External Affairs have been on the decline. For example, in 1982, the total budgetary allocation (including contributions to international organizations, agencies, and bilateral external aid) was N133,018,450, or 2.89 percent of the national budget. By 1985, the figure had declined to N92,079,190, or 1.52 percent. The costs of operating the ministry's overseas missions alone increased during this period by percentages ranging from 20 to 40 (due largely to inflation).

There are, however, several countries in Africa with lesser external responsibilities, fewer external missions, and much smaller consular problems, which allocate higher proportions of their natural budget to their foreign service. Such countries include Senegal (6 percent), Benin Republic (3.94 percent), Ivory Coast (3.3 percent) and Zaire (3 percent). The figures in brackets are for 1985. The Nigerian government, therefore, has to consider raising the proportion of the national budget allocated to the foreign service, otherwise, we would be setting large national goals and objectives abroad while blunting the very instrument with which to implement them. Nigeria cannot play a leadership role in Africa and an activist one in world affairs by words alone. To paraphrase an American expression, we have to put our resources where our mouth is.

Finally, there is the need to de-bureaucratize the ministry and enhance the intellectual quality of its output and contributions. In addition to the exposure of foreign-service officers to centers of intellectual activity through programs of training and specialization, the ministry could be further opened up to inputs from the informed public and interest groups and organizations. For example, senior officials in the ministry should be encouraged to represent their minister more often and deliver lectures on foreign policy in the universities, military institutions, national research institutes, and selected public fora. The give and take which usually follows such public lectures would be useful to both sides.

The initiative taken in 1984 whereby a committee of outside experts and leaders of some interest groups met informally with senior officials of the ministry to discuss sensitive and substantive policy issues should now be formalized. Furthermore, the idea of preparing an annual foreign policy agenda for the federal government, whereby the ministry recommends the priorities of programs, travel, and resource allocations for a particular year, should be institutionalized. The agenda should, in fact, be made part of a new four-year strategy of foreign policy.

The preparations of short- and medium-term, and eventually long-range projections of our external relations, along with indications of the level of resources needed for their implementation and policies to interact meaningfully with outside groups would invigorate the ministry, and help it think more creatively about the ends, means, and appropriate strategies of policy, rather than to react to issues or events in the usual predictable and bureaucratic manner.

The Bogey of "Dynamic" Foreign Policy

The bogey of "dynamic" foreign policy has haunted successive administrations in Nigeria since independence. As a new political vocabulary for evaluating our country's external relations, it emerged during the first comprehensive parliamentary debate on foreign policy, on 4 September

1961. Foreign Minister Jaja Wachuku introduced a motion in the Federal Parliament seeking the house's reaffirmation of the government's foreign policy, which was declared by the Prime Minister and approved by the house on 20 August 1960. In the same motion, Wachuku requested Parliament to give approval to the federal government's interpretations and conduct of foreign policy and also to congratulate the administration for its achievements in the international field.[2] However, the then shadow Foreign Minister and Acting Leader of the Opposition, Chief Anthony Enahoro, moved an amendment to the Foreign Minister's motion, to the effect that the administration's foreign policy, as declared earlier by the Prime Minister, lacked "dynamism." Chief Enahoro further urged the house to express its regrets that the federal government's interpretation and conduct of foreign policy were out of step with progressive opinion in Africa.[3]

Foreign Minister Wachuku appeared to have walked straight into the conceptual trap organized by the parliamentary opposition. He reviewed the activities of the federal government in the foreign-policy area since independence and, as expected, gave the administration high marks for its performance. He recalled the visible role which Nigeria had played in the reconciliation process during the Congo crisis, as well as the federal government's uncompromising postures over Algerian independence, French aggression against Tunisia in Bizerta, the decolonization of Angola, Mozambique, and South West Africa (Namibia), apartheid in South Africa, the French test of atomic weapons in the Sahara, and African unity. He then concluded his defense with the rhetorical statement, "If that is not dynamic, I do not know what it is."

Having succeeded in getting the Foreign Minister to apply the standard of dynamism in evaluating his own government's performance in foreign policy, Chief Enahoro then concluded that the record was a failure. He maintained that it was the radical elements in Nigeria who represented the true voice and temper of the generality of the people. Such radicals, in Chief Enahoro's view, regarded the foreign policy of the government as lacking inspiration and dynamism.[4]

In that atmosphere, the issue was not whether the positions of the federal government served the national interest, but how "dynamic" those positions were in relation to "progressive opinion in Africa." This tendency to avoid critical evaluations of the national interest outlived the Balewa regime and the First Republic. For instance, General Gowon's foreign policy, especially during the last few years of his administration, was characterized by several foreign-policy analysts as lacking dynamism. However, the successor regime of General Murtala Mohammed was clearly seen by them as dynamic. General Olusegun Obasanjo's administration shared the appellation of dynamism, attached to Murtala somewhat grudgingly at first but more warmly later. That was after Obasanjo's own government nationalized British Petroleum's assets in Nigeria in order to force Prime Minister Thatcher's hands on the issue of the decolonization of Zimbabwe under the leadership of Robert Mugabe, rather than her preferred option of giving independence to that territory through the puppet leader, Bishop Muzorewa.

In a similar vein, President Shagari's regime was generally regarded as lacking dynamic foreign-policy postures. On taking over power from that government, General Buhari felt that his administration owed the nation a "dynamic" but, in view of our country's economic condition, "realistic" foreign policy. The Buhari administration's handling of the Dikko affair, its retaliatory diplomacy in dealing with the British government, the recognition of SADR and its seating as the 51st member of the OAU, and the initiatives which led to the rejuvenation of the continental organization were generally hailed by the informed public as evidence of a dynamic foreign policy. However, in his first address to the nation on taking over as the new head of state, President Babangida criticized his predecessor's foreign policy for lacking enough dynamism.

Nonetheless, the more creditable standard for evaluating a maturing nation's foreign policy should not be dynamism or the lack of it. What the informed public in Nigeria could more usefully demand from successive governments are clearer definitions of the national interest and effective strategies for externally projecting it. After all, it may be conceptually possible for a government to pursue what appears to be a dynamic foreign policy but one which undermines true and lasting national interests. The public would be right to question foreign policies pursued for the sake of novelty that needlessly upset existing bilateral and multilateral relations. No important foreign-policy action is cost-free. Therefore, our nation should not be made to pay high costs for gimmickry which may outweigh real benefits in the long run. Dynamism or motion must not be substituted for substance.

In conclusion, Nigeria's policymakers need to transcend previous efforts aimed at building a national consensus behind a foreign policy that was, at best, the pursuit of the least common denominator and, at worse, rather dishonest in the sense that commitments did not match rhetoric. Our country surely deserves a better-defined and more actively pursued interest that would be more truly representative and broadly national. If the Buhari administration succeeded in making contributions to the process of achieving a clearer definition and more vigorous defense of our country's national interests, its foreign policy endeavors will not have been in vain.

NOTES

1. A version of this reflection appeared in the first issue of the house journal of the National Institute for Policy and Strategic Studies (NIPSS), 1986.
2. See Hansard: *Federal Parliamentary Debates* (Lagos: Government Printing Press, 4 September 1961), pp. 2782–83.
3. Ibid., p. 2805.
4. Ibid., p. 2808.

19. Postscript

As this book was going to press, the Organization of African Unity (OAU) was entering the silver jubilee year of its existence. The Nigerian government decided to convene a three-day National Seminar to Commemorate the 25th Anniversary of the pan-African organization. It was a great personal honor and privilege for me to be appointed chairman for the entire session of the seminar And, in a real sense, history was made in Lagos on 27 April 1988 when the seminar opened at the headquarters of the Ministry of External Affairs with the attendance of all but one of the living former Foreign Ministers of Nigeria. The participation of the present Foreign Minister, Major-General Ike Nwachukwu, and the former chief planners and spokesmen of Nigeria's foreign policy symbolizes the measure of continuity in our external relations since independence in 1960.

The seminar also demonstrated that a common concern to all post-independence governments in Nigeria has been the primacy of Africa in our country's foreign policy endeavors. From the late Prime Minister Tafawa Balewa to General Ibrahim Babangida, each administration has accepted the reality that the African continent is the primary environment for the conduct of Nigeria's foreign policy. Of course, the levels of concrete commitments and the vigor with which African continental issues were articulated and pursued by successive governments in Nigeria have depended largely on the combination of the often rapidly changing domestic and external political and economic environments under which they operated, as well as on the different personalities at the helm of national affairs. Nonetheless, the destiny of our country has been held by all the administrations to be inextricably linked to that of the African continent.

Appropriately, therefore, the Commemorative Seminar on the OAU Silver Jubilee recommended that Nigeria should continue the leadership role which she has been playing since the inception of the organization. And to sustain such a role, Nigerian leaders were urged to creatively and effectively utilize the country's relative demographic, economic, and diplomatic weight in Africa. After all, when Nigeria took unequivocal and strong leadership positions on critical African issues (such as the establishment of the OAU itself; the admission of MPLA's Angola to the Organization, adoption of an economic focus and agenda for Africa in 1980 and 1985, and the final admission of SADR to the OAU) the problems were resolved in ways that enhanced African Unity and also promoted our national interests. That positive track-record should be sustained and even improved upon whenever our country's financial resources permit.

The seminar also recommended that Nigeria should take the lead in promoting more "people-to-people" contacts within the African continent. It is unfortunate but real that our various peoples know and deal far more with the peoples of the former colonial metropolis than with their own brothers and sisters in Africa. This unsatisfactory situation needs to be changed. In addition to intra-African sporting contacts, where some progress has been made, there is a need to promote intra-African tourism, the exchange of scholars and other professionals. These are some of the concrete ways in which the OAU can move from being an organization of governments toward one which actively promotes the unity of African peoples.

The time has also come to create a new institutional arrangement within the OAU to effectively coordinate intra-African economic affairs as well as Africa's external economic relations. Unless this is done, documents such as the Lagos Plan of Action, the Final Act of Lagos (1980), and the more recent African Priority Program for Economic Recovery (1985–1990), as well as OAU summits resolutions on economic matters, cannot be implemented beyond the national level. There will also be little or no political direction for the OAU Special Fund for Drought, Famine and Desertification, which was established in 1985. And an effectively coordinated and African-centered program for dealing with the refugee problem our continent will continue to elude us.

The absence of a peace and security council or commission in the OAU continues to be an embarrassment to Africa. The present regime of ad-hoc, cumbersome, and ultimately ineffective responses to intra-African conflicts and security problems in our continent continues. This creates a vacuum which extra-African powers do not hesitate to fill. Africa needs to revive the moribund OAU machinery for mediation, conciliation, and arbitration, and establish institutional capability to organize and direct peace-keeping and even peace enforcement operations which may be required from time to time.

The seminar confirmed the continuing validity of the pan-African vision on our continent and the "Afro-centric" focus of Nigeria's own foreign policy. These conclusions should, however, not blind us to the realities of the international economic system, which works to our great disadvantage. Nigeria and other African states must continue to make determined efforts at the national, sub-regional, African continental, and global levels to seek a more just and equitable international order in general and a less dependent relationship with our former colonial masters in particular. Hence, the pursuit of Nigeria's foreign policy in the context of concentric circles of national interests within a global interdependence perspective commends itself for further thought and action.

The task of accurately defining the parameters of Nigeria's national interest and how to project it within available resources will continue to be a challenging one. That is why the opportunity provided for the continuing dialogue between foreign policy theoreticians and the former and present practitioners of diplomacy during the seminar on the OAU was a good and necessary one. We do not need a purely "academic" foreign policy any more than we need a purely "bureaucratic" one. A truly national foreign policy, in which the best talents of Nigerians with interest and expertise on the subject can be utilized, will continue to be needed. One clear advantage of such cooperative interaction of relevant talents would be the rejection of grandiose and ultimately futile posturings in foreign policy, whereby Nigeria is urged to behave like a global actor and put her diplomatic cart before the horse of a sound domestic economic and technological base.

One final word on the recent administrative *cum* political changes in Nigeria, which would have enormous impact on the relationship between the minister as political head and what used to be the permanent secretary position as the head of the civil servants in a ministry. In his 1988 annual budget speech, President Babangida announced that the post of the permanent secretary would be abolished. In later elaborations of the changes, a director-general was appointed for each ministry to replace the previous holder of the post of permanent secretary. The tenure in office of the new director-general would end with the administration that appointed him or her unless reappointed by a succeeding administration. The minister would be the chief executive in each ministry and would be responsible for financial matters as well as the appointment, promotion, and discipline of staff. The full implications of this new arrangement in a country like Nigeria, where more and not less accountability is needed from political appointed heads of ministries, are yet to be seen. Meanwhile, the hope is that the past antagonisms and ill-defined and colonially inherited relationships between the minister and permanent secretary, which often caused policy paralysis, may now be laid to rest. If this proves to be the case, the nation will be the ultimate beneficiary.

Appendices

APPENDIX 1

TRENDS IN NIGERIAN FOREIGN POLICY

Short Address by Dr. Ibrahim Gambari
Minister of External Affairs
Princeton University, New Jersey
10 October 1984

In an increasingly interdependent world, a member of the international community invariably has to constantly review its positions on issues vital to it and to the rest of the comity of nations. The constant reappraisal takes place against the background of a country's principles, interest, resources and capability in relation to and interaction with the interests, views, resources and capabilities of other members of the international system. Nigeria has been an independent nation now for twenty-four years. In this almost a quarter of a century, so much water has, as it were, passed under the bridge. The international situation has not been static and we have inevitably been part of the dynamic processes of the system.

Principles and interests guiding and forming the bedrock of foreign policy essentially remain basic and fundamental and therefore to that extent Nigeria's foreign policy remains constant and committed to the cherished principles and interests which successive Nigerian administrations have proclaimed. On this score, therefore, Africa, of which we are a part, remains the centrepiece or cornerstone of our foreign policy. We remain and shall continue to remain concerned with specific and general issues affecting the economic and social welfare, independence and territorial integrity of members of the international community located on the African continent and its surrounding islands. We remain committed to the principles of sovereign equality of states regardless of size, population and resources. At the same time we renew our total commitment to the principle of non-interference in the internal affairs of other states and non-violation of their territorial integrity and political independence. We have never believed and we do not now believe that the wealth or military strength of a country entitles it to intervene or interfere in any manner in the internal affairs of other sovereign states. This is a principle cherished by both the United Nations and the Organization of African Unity. In this direction Nigeria's foreign policy has not changed and no change is presently contemplated.

Successive administrations in Nigeria have reiterated their total opposition to the inhuman system of *apartheid*—that heinous institutionalisation of racism which has been condemned by all civilised nations as a crime against humanity. More than this, Nigeria has always been in the forefront of the struggle to eradicate this crime. The present Federal Government of Nigeria is unshakably and unequivocally committed to the international effort to liquidate the system of *apartheid* and end the tyranny of the majority by the minority of the people of that unfortunate part of Africa. Apart from the material resources which we devote and will continue to allocate to the prosecution of this just struggle, we have demonstrated our continued commitment to the cause by recently sponsoring an international seminar on the legal aspects of the *apartheid* regime. This seminar, which we co-sponsored with the United Nations Special Committee Against Apartheid, produced specific recommendations which the United Nations Organisation must find ways to implement.

In the same manner, we shall continue to support the just struggle of the Namibian people under the leadership of SWAPO—a struggle also officially supported by the United Nations, the OAU, the Non-Aligned Movement and progressive and freedom loving people all over the world. The South African racist regime, in continuing to illegally occupy the territory of Namibia in clear violation of Security Council resolution 435 of 1978, poses a great challenge to all African states and all humanity. SWAPO has offered on a number of occasions to hold serious discussions with the racist regime but this has always been rebuffed by the Pretoria authorities. We, on our part, shall continue to provide all the assistance within our resources to the forces of SWAPO who are in the forefront of the just struggle against racists. It is the policy of the present Federal Government of Nigeria to continue to provide multidimensional support to SWAPO, the ANC and the PAC all of whom are combatants in the just war against the inhuman racist system of *apartheid*. In effect, therefore, we shall continue with our policy of supporting anti-colonial and anti-racist efforts in Africa.

Ladies and gentlemen, a country's foreign policy revolves around its national interests. Nigeria is not and cannot be an exception to this. While Africa remains the centrepiece of our foreign policy, we cannot but operate within a series of concentric circles which now effectively guides our behaviour on the African and world scene. The innermost of the circles of national interests involves Nigeria's security—territorial integrity and political independence—and that of the neighbours of Nigeria. This is of paramount importance to us since without securing this primary security zone, we cannot be sure of our base. The second circle involves our relations with the ECOWAS sub-region where we intend to take more active interest in developments of social, economic and political nature. Nigeria is not a global power, therefore, and our commitments, pre-occupations and expenditure of resources must be made to reflect our capabilities and interests. It is for this reason that our primary focus is on the West African sub-region, since any event occurring in this area has an impact directly on Nigeria's interests.

We are ready to continue to promote the good neighbourly relations with our sister states in the region, without, however, compromising on any issue of vital national interest to us nor hesitating in affirmatively protecting such interests. We will continue to give as much assistance as is compatible with our limited resources but we shall no longer play the role of 'the big for nothing brother' of any other state. The third circle of national interests involves supporting self-determination and dealing with larger African issues. We have already mentioned the question of anti-colonialism. Suffice it to say here that on all other African issues, the measures we take will be determined by what meaningful, effective contribution we can make to the solution of the problems involved. We shall of course participate in international efforts designed to find solutions to the multifarious problems confronting the continent, as we have done so far.

The last circle of interests involves our relations with organisations, institutions and states outside of the African continent. This is not to say that we do not regard this level of relationships as important. We are quite aware of our limited resources and cannot but let this reflect in our postures and behaviour. A lot we will have to achieve in collaboration with others in the non-aligned movement, the Group of 77, the Commonwealth of Nations and the United Nations. We are alarmed at the seemingly uncontrolled and uncontrollable arms race between the big powers but we know that, as a country, Nigeria can only appeal to those concerned to let reason and good judgement prevail. While we will all suffer from the effects of a nuclear war, the final decision to plunge the world into that kind of holocaust can only presently be taken by the superpowers themselves.

We are greatly disturbed by a situation whereby over $700 billion is spent on the arms race at a time when large segments of the world's population, including several million Africans, are unable to enjoy the basic necessities of life. Yet, the arms race and the deployment of intermediate range nuclear weapons in Europe create greater insecurity rather than enhance global security or even the security of the superpowers and their allies. There is a dangerous parallel between the present international situation and the 1930s—a period which the late Harold Lasswell characterised as one of personal insecurity resulting from the world politics of the time. In a recent book, William Slurer described that decade as the nightmare years. We do not need any more nightmares!

The international economic system is also in a bad state of disrepair. The Bretton Woods system, constructed for the immediate post-World War II world, is becoming increasingly irrelevant to the needs of the majority of the present members of the international community. The present structure of the international economy and the response to the serious debt and deteriorating economic problems of the Third World by the industrialised countries do not inspire the necessary confidence which is essential to the preservation of interdependence in today's world. A drastic change of attitude, response and structure of the international economic interaction is necessary and cannot be postponed any longer.

Finally, ladies and gentlemen, I wish to say to this distinguished gathering that as a country, we are realists. And this is more so considering our present economic situation, which we, however, regard as a temporary set-back. Nonetheless, our realism in international relations will never mean the abandonment of fundamental principles such as self-determination, elimination of apartheid, promotion of African unity and pursuit of a safer world and a more just international economic system. On these we shall never cease to talk and we shall insist on being heard.

APPENDIX 2

THE QUADRIPARTITE AGREEMENTS (SIGNED IN LAGOS, 10 DECEMBER 1984)

1 (i) *Extradition Treaty between the Peoples' Republic of Benin, the Republic of Ghana, the Federal Republic of Nigeria and the Republic of Togo.*

PREAMBLE

THE GOVERNMENT OF THE PEOPLES' REPUBLIC OF BENIN,

THE GOVERNMENT OF THE REPUBLIC OF GHANA,

THE GOVERNMENT OF THE FEDERAL REPUBLIC OF NIGERIA,

THE GOVERNMENT OF THE REPUBLIC OF TOGO.

HEREINAFTER referred to as "the Contracting Parties";

ANXIOUS to preserve peace and security among their States;

DESIROUS of maintaining and fostering the firm relations of friendship and fruitful cooperation which unite their peoples;

PROMPTED by their common desire to work in peace, security, solidarity and harmony for the economic, social and cultural development of their countries;

DESIROUS of strengthening further legal cooperation; and

DESIROUS of fighting against crime in all its forms by facilitating the apprehension and trial of fugitive offenders from the territory of any of the Contracting Parties to the territory of each other;

HAVE agreed as follows:

ARTICLE 1

GENERAL PROVISIONS

The Contracting Parties undertake to extradite to each other on the basis of reciprocity, in accordance with the rules and conditions stated in this Treaty, those persons who being accused or convicted of any of the crimes or offences referred to in Article 2, committed within the jurisdiction of one party shall be found in the territory of the other party.

ARTICLE 2

RETURNABLE OFFENCES

(1) Extradition shall be granted in respect of persons accused of crimes or offences punishable by the laws of the Contracting Parties by at least two (2) years' imprisonment.

(2) Extradition shall also be granted for participation in any of the aforesaid crimes or offences provided that such participation be punishable by the laws of the Contracting Parties.

(3) Extradition shall also be granted in respect of persons who have been convicted by the requesting state for extradition offences whether they have served part of their sentence or not.

Article 3

Time Limit

Extradition shall be refused if the time limit for the action or sentence has expired under the legislation of the requesting or requested state at the time of receipt of the application from the requesting state.

Article 4

Political Offences

Extradition shall not be granted for crimes or offences of a political nature or if it is proved that the requisition for his surrender has been made with a view to trying or punishing him for a crime or offence of a political nature or if the request is to persecute or punish him on account of his race, religion or political opinion.

Article 5

Specialty Rule

The individual who shall have been surrendered may neither be tried, judged nor detained to serve a term for any offences nor shall be extradited except in the following cases:

(1) If having had the liberty to do so, the extradited person did not leave the territory of the state to which he has been surrendered within thirty (30) days following his final release, or if he returned to that state after leaving it;

(2) If the state which delivered him agrees, a request shall be made to this effect, accompanied by the documents stipulated in Article 7.

Article 6

Law Governing Extradition Proceedings

The Extradition of the fugitive criminals under provisions of the Treaty shall be carried out in the requested state in conformity with the laws of the requested state.

Article 7

Extradition Procedure

(1) The request for extradition shall be communicated through diplomatic channels. It shall be accompanied by the original or certified copy of a judgement of conviction or warrant of arrest or any other order having the same effect and issued in the form prescribed by the requesting state.

(2) The legal description of the offences for which extradition is requested, the time and place of their commission as well as the relevant laws under which the offences fall shall be stated as precisely as possible, the description of the person claimed as well as any information which can help determine his identity and nationality.

(3) In case of urgency, on the request of the competent authorities of the requesting

state a provisional arrest shall be made pending the formal request for extradition and the documents mentioned in paragraph 1 of this Article.

(4) The request for provisional arrest shall be transmitted to the competent authorities of the requested state either directly by letter or telegram or by any other means in writing. At the same time such a request shall be confirmed through diplomatic channels.

(5) It shall mention the existence of the documents listed in paragraph 1 of this Article and that it is intended to send a request for extradition. It shall state the offence for which extradition is requested, the time and place of its commission as well as very precise description of the person claimed. The requesting authority shall be informed without delay of the result of its request.

(6) Provisional arrest shall be terminated if within a period of forty (40) days after the arrest the authorities of the requested party have not received the documents mentioned in paragraph 1 of this Article. The termination of provisional arrest shall not preclude a new arrest if the request for extradition is received later.

(7) If supplementary information is required to ensure that the condition required under this Article have been fulfilled, the requested state shall, where the commission seems liable to be corrected, inform the requesting state through diplomatic channels.

This information shall be provided within a period of forty (40) days. This period begins from the date of the receipt of the request for supplementary information. After this period the requested state shall provisionally release the offender. The release does not preclude his rearrest if the supplementary information is received later.

Article 8

Communication of Decision

The requested state shall communicate its decision on the extradition request to the requesting state through diplomatic channels.

Article 9

Multiple Requests

If extradition is requested concurrently by more than one state, either for the same offence or for different offences the requested party shall make its decision having regard to all the circumstances and especially the relative seriousness of the case, the place of the commission of the offences, the relative dates of the requests and the possibility of subsequent extradition to another state.

Article 10

Transit Through Another State

Extradition involving transit through the territory of one of the Contracting Parties of an individual delivered to another party shall be granted on application by the requesting state. This application shall be supported by the relevant extradition documents.

ARTICLE 11

CONSENT FOR RETURN

(1) If the offender, where the law of the requested country permits, consents or voluntarily and with understanding asks to be extradicted, the competent judicial authority shall examine his case and decide whether he should be detained or released on bail pending his extradition.

(2) The requested state may subsequently order his extradition within fifteen (15) days starting from the date of his committal.

(3) In that case the provisions of Article 5 shall be applicable to the offender unless waived by him.

ARTICLE 12

PROPERTY OF EXTRADITED PERSONS

(1) When extradition is granted all the articles connected with the offence or which can serve as exhibits found on the person sought at the time of his arrest or which shall be discovered later shall, at the request of the requesting state be seized and returned to the authorities of that state.

(2) The articles may still be returned even if the extradition does not take place because that person has escaped or is dead.

(3) If, however, the said articles belong to a third party, they must be returned to the requested state as soon as possible and without any charges, after legal proceedings in the requesting state. The authorities of the requested state may keep the seized articles temporarily if they deem it necessary for legal proceedings.

(4) The requested state may also transit them while reserving the option of asking for them to be returned for the same reasons, if they undertake to send them back as soon as possible.

ARTICLE 13

EXTRADITION EXPENSES

The requested party shall bear expenses incurred by reason of the extradition except cost of land, sea and air transport to and from the requesting state.

ARTICLE 14

TRANSFER OF CONVICTED PRISONERS FOR EXECUTION OF SENTENCES

(1) Any national of one of the Contracting Parties, sentenced to a term of imprisonment may, at the request of his country and with written consent of the convicted person, be surrendered to the authorities of the State of which he is a national to serve his sentence. The transfer charges shall be borne by the requesting state. The release of such a person from prison before his term has ended may only be effected with the consent of the Contracting Party which convicted him.

(2) Only the state which passed sentence has power to grant a pardon or amnesty.

ARTICLE 15
FINAL PROVISIONS

(1) A Contracting Party may submit proposals for the amendments or revision of this Treaty.

(2) Any Contracting Party may withdraw from this Treaty.

(3) Notice of withdrawal shall be communicated through diplomatic channels at least six (6) months in advance to the depository state which shall inform the other Contracting Parties.

(4) This Treaty shall enter into force provisionally upon the signature by Heads of State and Government.

(5) It shall be ratified by the Contracting Parties in accordance with their respective constitutional procedures.

(6) The instruments of ratification shall be forwarded to the Government of the Republic of Togo which shall inform all signatory States when it receives each instrument.

(7) The present Treaty shall enter into force definitively after the last instrument of ratification is deposited.

1 (ii) *Criminal Investigation Co-operation Agreement between the Peoples' Republic of Benin, the Republic of Ghana, the Federal Republic of Nigeria and the Republic of Togo*

THE GOVERNMENT OF THE PEOPLES' REPUBLIC OF BENIN,
THE GOVERNMENT OF THE REPUBLIC OF GHANA,
THE GOVERNMENT OF THE FEDERAL REPUBLIC OF NIGERIA,
THE GOVERNMENT OF THE REPUBLIC OF TOGO.

HEREINAFTER called "the Contracting Parties";

CONSIDERING the need to fight against the upsurge of crime which poses a serious threat to security, peace and stability and hampers the development of the sub-region;

CONSIDERING that the fight against crime is worldwide, constantly requiring very rapid action and consequently, the movement of security agents from one country to the other;

CONSIDERING that within the framework of the International Criminal Police Organization (INTERPOL) a form of co-operation already exists between the security agencies of the Contracting Parties;

CONSIDERING the need to adapt this cooperation to the realities of the Contracting Parties by making more flexible the regulations applicable in this area;

PREOCCUPIED with the promotion of very close cooperation between the security agencies of their respective countries with a view to ensuring adequate protection of life and property;

HAVE agreed as follows:

General Provisions

Article 1

A Criminal Investigation Co-operation Agreement is hereby established between the Contracting Parties.

Article 2

The competent security agencies of the Contracting Parties shall assist in searching for pesons involved in ordinary law crimes in the territory of any of the Parties.

Article 3

The National Central Bureau (INTERPOL) shall be the coordinating bodies between the security agencies of the Contracting Parties.

Article 4

The Heads of the National Central Bureau assisted by appropriate officials of INTERPOL of the Contracting Parties shall meet at least once a year to appraise the level of cooperation among them.

Missions Abroad

Article 5

The officials of the Contracting Parties so empowered by their national legislations shall be competent to carry out criminal investigation operations abroad.

Article 6

(1) The movement of police officials of the four states outside the frontiers of their countries shall be planned and organized through the National Central Bureau.

(2) To this end, the requesting National Central Bureau shall first forward to the requested National Central Bureau a request in line with the conditions and norms stipulated by the International Criminal Police Organization (INTERPOL).

(3) However, in emergency cases, a letter of introduction addressed to the Head of the National Central Bureau of the requested State prepared in line with the same conditions and norms as the request and duly certified by the Head of the National Central Bureau of the requesting country shall suffice to enlist the assistance of the requested country.

Article 7

The Heads of the National Central Bureau (INTERPOL) shall contact the competent Authorities of their countries in order to facilitate the accomplishment of the mission being undertaken by the foreign officials.

Article 8

The police officials of the host country shall carry out investigations on the subject on the arrival in the host country of police officials from the requesting country.

However, on authorization by the Heads of the National Central Bureau, the police officials of contracting states may be associated with the execution of various investigative operations.

ARTICLE 9

(1) Culprits arrested may be handed over to the delegation of the requesting National Central Bureau (INTERPOL).

(2) Any other culprits wanted by the competent authorities of the visiting country who shall be found in the process may be placed under provisional arrest pending the accomplishment within a maximum period of 30 days for the formalities prescribed by this Agreement before being handed over to the requesting National Central Bureau (INTERPOL).

(3) The provisions of this article shall be without prejudice to the national legislation and existing Agreements between the Contracting Parties.

ARTICLE 10

(1) To facilitate investigations, the officials on missions may be accompanied by any person necessary for the investigation.

(2) At the request of the officials on missions any such persons may be placed in the custody of the security agencies of the host country during the entire period of the mission. They shall be handed over at the end of the mission, even if they are nationals of the host country.

ARTICLE 11

The National Central Bureau of the four states shall assist each other in the proper application of the provisions of this agreement.

EXCHANGE OF INFORMATION

ARTICLE 12

The contracting states shall exchange regularly amongst themselves information likely to facilitate the search for and arrest of criminals. Such information shall include:

(a) Movement and activities of criminals;
(b) New devices employed by criminals in the commission of crimes;
(c) Arrest of a national by any of the Contracting States.

SEIZURE

ARTICLE 13

All articles relating to the offence found and seized in the host country shall be kept and handed over to the visiting country, without prejudice to the right of third parties.

FINAL PROVISIONS

ARTICLE 14

(1) This Agreement shall come into force on the date on which the last instrument of ratification shall be deposited.

(2) Any Contracting Party may withdraw from this Agreement by giving notice of such withdrawal through Diplomatic channels at least six (6) months in advance to the depository state which shall inform the other Contracting Parties.

ARTICLE 15

(1) This Agreement shall be ratified by the signatory States in line with their respective constitutional procedures.

(2) The instruments of ratifications shall be forwarded to the Government of the Republic of Togo which shall notify all signatory states as and when it shall receive each instrument.

1 (iii) *Agreement on Mutual Administrative Assistance in Matters Relating to Customs, Trade and Immigration between the Republics of Benin, Ghana, Nigeria and Togo*

PREAMBLE

THE GOVERNMENT OF THE PEOPLES' REPUBLIC OF BENIN,
THE GOVERNMENT OF THE REPUBLIC OF GHANA,
THE GOVERNMENT OF THE FEDERAL REPUBLIC OF NIGERIA,
THE GOVERNMENT OF THE REPUBLIC OF TOGO.

HEREINAFTER referred to as "the Contracting Parties";

CONSCIOUS that offences against Customs Laws are prejudicial to the economic, fiscal and commercial interests of their respective countries;

CONVINCED that action against these offences can be made more effective by cooperation between their respective Competent Authorities;

ANXIOUS to reinforce on the basis of complete equality between parties in the mutual interest of their peoples, close and continuing cooperation in the spirit of solidarity which unites the four states within the framework of the Economic Community of West African States (ECOWAS);

HAVE agreed as follows:

CHAPTER I: DEFINITION AND SCOPE

ARTICLE 1

For this purpose of this agreement:

a) The term "Customs Legislation" means all statutory or regulatory provisions applicable by the Customs Authorities of the Contracting Parties on the importation, exportation, transit or circulation of goods, capital or means of payment whether involving the collection of duties or taxes or the enforcement of prohibitions, restrictions or exchange control regulations as well as those relating to security.

b) The term "Customs Offences" means any breach or attempted breach of Customs Laws.

c) The term "Competent Administration" means any national Customs Department or other National Authority appointed to assist the administration of the Customs Laws.

d) The term "Trade Offences" means infringement of the rules in the Territories of the Contracting Parties governing importation and exportation of goods including false documentations used in the import and export trade.

e) The term "Foreign Exchange Offences" means any offences connected with the financial legislation regarding declaration of currencies either without conforming with written procedure or requisite formalities or without being in possession of requisite authorization or satisfying laid down conditions stipulated in this authorization.

Article 2

The Competent Authorities of the Contracting Parties shall afford each other mutual assistance on terms set out in this agreement for the prevention, and investigation of Customs, Trade Immigration and Foreign Exchange Offences.

Chapter II: Provision Concerning Certain Goods

Article 3

(1) The Customs Authorities of the Contracting Parties shall annually communicate to each other lists of goods, the exportation and importation of which are prohibited or restricted in their respective countries.

(2) The Customs Authorities of the Contracting Parties shall not permit the exportation of goods, the importation of which is prohibited or restricted in the country of destination by any of the Contracting Parties without evidence that the importer has obtained proper license to import.

(3) The provisions of paragraph 2 above are applicable to goods in transit.

Chapter III: Trafficking in Arms and Ammunition

Article 4

The Contracting Parties shall not permit the exportation or the transit of arms and ammunition into the territory of another Contracting Party without prior permission from the Competent Authority of the country of destination.

Article 5

Any person in possession of arms on the territory of one of the Contracting Parties has to declare them as soon as he enters the territory and conform to the laws in force in the country.

Chapter IV: Trafficking of Drugs, Narcotics and Psychotropic Substances

Article 6

The Contracting Parties shall not permit the exportation, or the transit of drugs, narcotics and psychotropic substances into the country of the Contracting Parties without prior permission from the competent authority of the country of destination.

Article 7

With the help of the Competent Services like INTERPOL, the authorities of each

Contracting Party shall communicate for useful purpose any information to each other on the nature of drugs or substances seized and the identity of traffickers.

Chapter V: CURRENCY TRAFFICKING

ARTICLE 8

The Customs Authorities of the Contracting Parties shall take every necessary step to arrest the wave of illegal trafficking of currency between the territories of the Contracting Parties. All such currencies transported shall be subject to declaration at the point of entry.

ARTICLE 9

Payments between two or more of the Contracting Parties shall be made in the currencies acceptable to the parties or through the West African clearing house and in conformity with the Foreign Exchange Regulations in force in each member country.

ARTICLE 10

The possession of currency is subject to the exchange control regulations in force in the territory of each of the Contracting Parties.

Chapter VI: BORDER TRADE

ARTICLE 11

(1) The Customs Authorities of the Contracting Parties shall take all necessary measures to ensure that goods exported and imported through their common borders pass through the approved Customs routes and in conformity with their respective Customs Regulations.

(2) The Customs Authorities of the Contracting Parties shall as soon as this agreement comes into force and when changes occur communicate to each other a list of their respective Customs Offices situated along the Common Borders as well as approved routes including details of the powers and the opening hours of these Customs Offices.

(3) The Customs Authorities of the Contracting Parties shall endeavor as much as possible to coordinate the powers and the working hours of the officers at the corresponding Customs offices.

ARTICLE 12

In order to promote relations of good neighborliness among the border populations of their respective states, the Customs authorities shall show tolerance towards the movement of goods across borders devoid of any commercial character and meant for personal consumption of the said populations.

ARTICLE 13

The movement of goods referred to in Article 12 which shall be properly valued is exempted from Customs formalities.

Chapter VII: FREE MOVEMENT OF PERSONS AND GOODS

ARTICLE 14

(1) The Contracting Parties shall as far as possible facilitate the free movement of persons and goods in the promotion of normal trade among their States.

(2) When the need arises to repatriate an illegal immigrant whether he is involved or not in illegal activities, the Contracting Parties shall do everything possible to alleviate the sufferings of the affected persons.

In the event of expulsion, the safety of such person and that of their families shall be guaranteed and their personal effects safeguarded and returned to them.

The Government of the affected persons shall be informed of the measures taken against them.

When the need arises and after due consideration, the Contracting Parties shall do everything possible to help immigrants regularize their stay.

(3) The Contracting Parties shall undertake to educate their citizens on the need to conform with entry requirements into the territories of member States.

Chapter VIII: SURVEILLANCE ON PERSONS AND GOODS AND MEANS OF TRANSPORT

ARTICLE 15

The Competent Administration of each of the Contracting Parties shall maintain special surveillance on the means of transport and the movement of goods along the common border with a view to detecting and stopping goods known to be subject of illicit traffic.

ARTICLE 16

The Competent Administration of one of the Contracting Parties shall at the express request of any of the other Contracting Parties, maintain special surveillance over:

a) The movements, particularly the entry into and exit from its territory, of particular persons suspected by the requesting party, to be habitually engaged in activities contrary to the Customs Laws of the requesting party;

b) Movement of particular goods stated by the requesting party to be the subject of illicit traffic towards its territory;

c) Particular places of the requested party where stock of goods have been built up and in respect of which the requesting party furnishes reasons for suspecting that the goods are earmarked for illicit importation into the territory of the requesting party;

d) Any particular vehicle, ship, aircraft or other means of transport suspected of being used to commit Customs Offences in the territory of the requesting party.

Chapter IX: COMMUNICATION AND INFORMATION

ARTICLE 17

The Customs Authority of one of the Contracting Parties shall proprio motu communicate to the Customs Authority of any of the Contracting Parties any available information regarding:

a) Any operation in the territory of one Contracting Party which is suspected will give rise or has given rise to Customs Offences in the territory of any of the Parties;
b) Persons, vehicles, ships, aircraft and other means of transport suspected to be engaged or used in committing Customs Offences in the territory of the other Contracting Parties;
c) New means or methods of committing Customs Offences;
d) Goods known to be subject of illicit traffic.

Article 18

On express request, the Customs Authority of one of the Contracting Parties shall communicate to the Customs Authority of the requesting Contracting Part, as promptly as possible any available information:

a) Contained in Customs documents relating to movement of goods between their two countries, which is suspected to be in breach of the Customs Law of the requesting Party;
b) Enabling false declarations to be detected, especially with regard to dutiable goods;
c) Concerning certificates of origin, invoices or other documents known to be relevant to the illegal importation or exportation of goods.

Article 19

(1) On express request, the Customs Authority of one of the Contracting Parties shall communicate to the Customs Authorities of the requesting Contracting Party, where appropriate in the form of an official document, information concerning any of the following matters:

a) The authenticity of any official document produced in support of a goods Declaration made to the Customs Authority of the requesting party;
b) The proof that the goods which have benefitted from a favorable regime from the country as a result of their destination to another country will be consumed in the country of destination;
c) Whether goods imported into the territory of the requesting party have been lawfully exported from the territory of one of the Contracting Parties;
d) Whether goods exported from the territory of the requesting party have been lawfully imported into the territory of any of the Contracting Parties.

(2) The Customs Authorities of the Contracting Parties may by the issue of a special document, make special provisions for the control of goods which are known to be subject of illicit traffic. Such special document issued by the Customs Authority of the country of exportation shall be surrendered to the Customs Authority of the country of importation in order to certify that the goods are lawfully imported.

Chapter X: Investigation and Notification

Article 20

At the express request of the Custom Authority of one of the Contracting Parties, the Customs Authority of the requested Contracting Party shall, within the limits of its competence and in accordance with its legislation:

a) make enquiries and obtain evidence concerning any Customs Offences under investigation in the territory of the requesting party;

b) take statements from any person connected or suspected to be connected with those offences; or from any witnesses willing to give evidence in the matter and transmit the result of such enquiries to the requesting Contracting Party.

Article 21

The Customs Authorities of the Contracting Parties shall take measures to ensure that the services which are specially or mainly charged with the investigation and repression of smuggling maintain direct and personal contacts among each other with a view to exchanging information. In this way they can prevent or discover violations of customs regulations in their respective countries.

The information thus provided could be produced as proof in the minutes, reports and evidence as well as during procedures and trials in the courts and tribunals.

Article 22

At the request of the Customs Authorities of one of the Contracting Parties, the Customs Authority of the requested Contracting Party shall in accordance with the laws in force in its territory take all necessary measures to communicate:

- The names of persons connected with Customs Offences;
- Any action or decision taken by the Administrative authorities;
- It shall also inform the Customs Authority of the requesting party of all measures it may have taken in connection with the offence.

Chapter XI: Action of Customs Authorities of One of the Contracting Parties in the Territory of a Contracting Party

Article 23

(1) Where in the investigation of any Customs Offence it is necessary to obtain proof of the facts alleged against some named persons, officials specifically appointed by one of the Contracting Parties may on written request by that Contracting Party and after being duly authorized by the requesting Contracting Party, inspect relevant books, registers and documents and extract any information or particulars relating to the offence.

(2) The officials designated under paragraph 1 above may make copies from the books, registers and documents referred to in that paragraph.

(3) In the application of this Article, all possible assistance and cooperation shall be given to the authorities of the requesting party to facilitate their investigation.

Article 24

Upon the request of the Competent Authority of one of the Contracting Parties, the Customs Authority of the requested Contracting Party may authorize its officials to appear as witnesses before a court or tribunal in the territory of the requesting party, in any proceedings relating to Customs Offence.

Chapter XII: Final Provisions

Article 25

(1) Any communication received, or information obtained under this Agreement shall be treated as confidential in the sense that it shall be used only for the purpose of prevention, investigation and repression of Customs Offences.

(2) Any communication received, or information obtained under this Agreement may be used during proceedings and prosecutions before administration or judicial authorities, of one of the Contracting Parties, unless the Customs Authorities of the Contracting Parties have made specific reservations to the contrary.

Article 26

The requested Contracting Party shall not be required to give the assistance provided for by this Agreement if it considers that such assistance is likely to prejudice its sovereignty or security.

Article 27

Within the framework of this Agreement, representatives of the Customs Authorities of the Contracting Parties shall meet at least once a year in the territory of one of the Contracting Parties.

Article 28

The implementation of the provisions of this Agreement shall be without prejudice to any existing Agreement between the Contracting Parties.

Article 29

The Agreement shall come into force on the date on which the last instrument of ratification is deposited. Any of the Contracting Parties may withdraw from this Agreement.

Notification of withdrawal shall be by diplomatic channels at least six months in advance to the depository state which shall inform the other Contracting Parties about such withdrawal.

Article 30

This Agreement shall be ratified by the signatory States in line with their respective constitutional procedures.

The instrument of ratification shall be forwarded to the Government of the Republic of Togo which shall notify all signatory states as and when it shall receive each instrument.

DONE at Lagos this 10th day of December 1984, in two original versions, in French and English, both texts being equally authentic.

....

H.E General Mathieu KEREKOU
President of the Republic of Benin.

....

H.E. Flt. Lt. Jerry John RAWLINGS
Head of State and Chairman of the
Provisional Defence Council.

....

H.E. Major-General Muhammadu BUHARI
Head of the Federal Military Government,
Commander-in-Chief of the Armed Forces
of the Federal Republic of Nigeria.

....

H.E. General Gnassingbe EYADEMA
President of the Republic of Togo.

APPENDIX 3

SPEECH OF I.A. GAMBARI ON THE OCCASION OF THE CONFERMENT OF HONORARY PROFESSORSHIP AT CHUNGSAN UNIVERSITY, GUANGZHOU, PEOPLE'S REPUBLIC OF CHINA, 7 MAY 1985

Mr. President, Deans, and Faculty Members of Chungsan University, Distinguished Guests.

I wish to thank the Board of the Chungsan University and the Faculty of Humanities for their generous gesture in awarding me an honorary professorship in the Faculty of Humanities and thereby inaugurating my personal association with this great University, founded by and named after an illustrious son of China, Dr. Sun Yatsen, the leader of the 1911 Peasant Revolution and the first provisional President of Nationalist China. That revolution led by him was the precursor of the great Chinese proletariat revolution that ushered in modern China. The conferment of this honorary professorship on me is a unique scholarly privilege. It is also a great honor to my country and a clear demonstration of the friendship between the government and people of China and Nigeria.

The last twenty years have seen a flowering of the relations between China and Africa, and, in spite of the many changes that have taken place in international politics, the Chinese and African peoples have remained steadfast in their friendship. Both the African and Chinese peoples cherish their warm and profound friendship, which derives from common experiences of colonialism and oppression, foreign exploitation and degradation. However, parts of Africa are still plagued by the evils of racism and apartheid and, while some nations have continued to pay lip service to the rectification of these evils and have sought full-time to pursue an unworkable policy of "constructive engagement" toward South Africa, China has remained faithful to her commitments and continues to support the African peoples and the African liberation movements in the struggle to rid the world of racism, colonialism, and apartheid in Southern Africa.

The excellent relations between Nigeria and China, which partake of these wider relations in Africa, have equally been based on the affinities of interests between our two countries. Both Nigeria and China are developing countries which belong to the Third World, and they share certain basic ideals and understanding. Apart from their common abhorrence of colonialism, racism, and apartheid, both our two countries uphold the principles of respect for the sovereign independence and territorial integrity of all states, peaceful resolution of all disputes, and non-interference in the internal affairs of other countries. Unfortunately, there are, in many parts of the world, wanton violations of these principles which have resulted in military intervention and occupation in many others.

The infractions of these basic principles of international conduct that we both uphold distract attention from more fundamental and urgent problems that confront mankind. There is, in the first place, the question of disarmament. The arms race would appear to have taken a turn for the worst. Men have not only overmilitarized our territorial environment, they have already begun the militarization of outer space through new and huge expenditure of resources, in order to further an illusion of a capability to erect a complete nuclear umbrella against ballistic and other missiles that carry nuclear weapons. There is no doubt that resources devoted to armament, which by the latest calculation represent more than 95 percent of official development assistance (O.D.A.) are a waste and contribute nothing to human general welfare, and indirectly, to that extent, add to human misery and impoverization.

There is another unfortunate aspect to the ongoing race to build more technologically advanced and budget-bursting armaments or their antidotes. The great movement which was started toward the middle seventies toward a New International Economic Order through a North/South Dialogue seemed to have been stalled. In the meantime, the problems that a New International Economic Order was supposed to solve have worsened due to higher debt-servicing costs, heavier debt burden, and a widespread regime of protectionism. No area of the world has been more hardhit than the African continent, where economic problems have been aggravated by a long-drawn drought and a recession much deeper in its impact than at any other time since the end of the Second World War. These developments have taken place at a time, at a higher rate, and at a more sustained level in United States of America. But this expansion has had no effect on the African economies. Indeed the expansion is at the expense of these commodities produced by African countries. The consequent collapse in the export earnings of African countries have worsened by a decline in the real value of Official Development Assistance (O.D.A.) and stagnation in private capital flows.

The international trade and financial institutions have been unable to cope with these negative developments in Africa and other similarly placed developing countries, because the institutions have been starved of additional resources, and, where they have offered help, the terms and conditions are so onerous as to set in motion severe internal political convulsions and instability. The persistent call for a reform of these institutions, to enable them meet the challenges of our times have, been opposed by some of those who originally planned these institutions to meet their own interests at a different epoch. There is, therefore, an urgent need to restart the stalled North/South dialogue for a new International Economic Order, especially an urgent reform of the international monetary system, and to address those issues that hamper a broad-based expansion of world trade and growth of the world economy, especially the economies of the developing countries, so that all mankind may benefit from the bounties of nature. We also believe very strongly that South-South dialogue is an essential instrument to promote economic cooperation among developing countries and to reduce their dependence on traditional state patterns. A first step in this direction has been the growing number of economic groupings among developing countries, especially at the regional or sub-regional levels. ASEAN and ECOWAS, though having different structures, are prime examples of this.

The conferment of this honorary professorship is both a scholarly occasion and a political act. Permit me, therefore, to say a few words on what I believe to be the proper role of a scholar in government. In order to be relevant, a scholar must appreciate and share with the supreme leadership of a nation the constraints, difficulties, and limitations of national resources whenever important political decisions are being made. However, the scholar-in-government must always look beyond the present and struggle to inspire and encourage those who exercise supreme political power, to transcend present difficulties and move the nation in the direction not only of physical and economic growth, but also human and intellectual development of their people.

Great leaders of nations are long remembered not for the increase they bring to the gross national product or the resulting increase in the per capita income, but for the national pride, national consciousness, and sense of national purpose and direction which they provide. Material progress without emotional national fulfillment and moral as well as intellectual upliftment of the people cannot long endure. It seems to me that the scholar in government has a role not only to perform the duties under his assigned portfolio, but to try to act as an outlet for the moral conscience of the people. He should also act as a balancer between the desirable and the possible, between the theory and practice of good government. I sincerely look forward to developing this idea further with my fellow scholars when, at the end of my present stewardship as a government minister, I shall return here to perform my duties as an honorary professor of this great university.

Once more, I wish to thank you, Mr. President and the authorities of Chungsan University, for this great honor bestowed upon me and my country. Indeed, I consider the award as a possible means of forging a link with Nigerian universities, and my hope is that this will lead to an exchange program—of students and faculty members—between your great university and some of our own universities in Nigeria. Thank you.

APPENDIX 4

AN EMBLEMATIC EXCHANGE OF LETTERS WITH AN ACADEMIC COLLEAGUE

4 (i) "Letter to Gambari" in the Guardian *(Lagos), 11 November 1984*

I have always wanted to send out an open piece like this to you but one way or the other, I did not come around to it until now. The situation has been compounded by the fact that, this is not a piece which I would want you to read in an aircraft, or in a Nigerian Embassy somewhere in Europe. Rather, I would want this piece to meet you at your desk, or in the deep recesses of your home. I am sure that from the foregoing, you can easily discern the implicit point I am making: You are usually on the move; but more about that later.

In a sense, you currently have a unique place in the scheme of things. To date, Nigeria has never had it so good in terms of having an External Affairs minister who combines the theoretical underpinnings of foreign policy with the empirical practice of the diplomatic craft. In this respect, personalities like Jaja Nwachukwu, Joseph Garba, and Ishaya Audu come readily to mind. At the risk of being contradicted, none of these men as far as I know had your range of theoretical exposure in foreign policy.

Indeed, long before you occupied your present post, I got acquainted with an article of yours in International Affairs (Columbia University), and in the said piece, you acquitted yourself honorably on the domestic constraints which beset Nigeria's foreign policy. Since then you have had a book published on around the same theme.

It is against this backdrop that one expects much more from you in the formulation and implementation of Nigeria's foreign policy. I am aware that you have your own problems—problems that border on the aberrant nature of our current political climate. But this can hardly be an excuse for the schizophrenia which increasingly constitutes the dominant theme in Nigeria's foreign policy.

The well-known gamut called Anglo-Nigeria relations is a case in point. Some time ago, when rightish Thatcher granted an audience to her counterpart in Pretoria, you reacted by saying that Nigeria would shortly review her links with the Commonwealth—an organization that has rightly been described as the loosest international organization in the global system.

You were probably not aware of it, but this declaratory statement of intent as regards Nigeria and the Commonwealth, went down very well with many people who felt that our umbilical links were long over-due for severance. But just immediately after, another voice, this time, our acting High Commissioner in Britain, assured (?) us that no such move was being contemplated. Evidently, you and I know that credibility is a necessary ingredient in this business of foreign policy. Consequently, when you say one thing and our High Commissioner says another thing over there, the country comes across as being rather schizophrenic in the pursuit of her interests in the comity of nations. But aside from this double-faced perception I believe that, more than ever, we need to engage in a cost-benefit analysis of our current links with the moribund body called the Commonwealth.

As a rallying point for ECOWAS, and since we often accuse many of our neighbors of being more French than France, don't you feel that the doctor should take the first step by healing himself?

On an equally related level, long before you assumed the mantle of office, you were of the view that Africa as the centerpiece of our foreign policy was too farflung as a manageable policy thrust. Rather, you argued that the hub of our diplomacy should really revolve around the sub-region, i.e., ECOWAS. Undoubtedly, you have a point there. And one was hoping to see this novel emphasis in the conduct of our foreign policy. But till date and from the available evidence, one is inclined to feel that West Africa happens to be just another item on our foreign policy agenda.

Indeed, I went as far as checking up the files so as to know the exact nature of your travels since you assumed office. And findings reveal that apart from a four-nation meeting in Lome, in which you and others represented Nigeria, the locus of your travels is firmly located in the Western world—particularly France and Germany. To be sure, the entire globe should be our theater of operation, but then this writer believes that Nigeria has come a long way from the days when Balewa contended that "we shall never forget our western friends". And moreover, it is not asking too much that you live up to your verbal commitment.

Again, as regards Akinjide's present opulent preoccupation at the United Nations, you and Nigeria's number-2 man have left the public wondering about what the stance of the government is. Earlier on, you were quoted as saying that the government was aware of the gentleman's whereabouts, pointing out that there was unnecessary furor over the whole issue. But on the other hand, the Chief of Staff, Tunde Idiagbon, had cause to point out in a recent interview that the Federal Government is quite displeased about the appointment. Evidently, a certain level of vagueness exists here.

Incidentally, it is this element of vagueness which best describes our current foreign policy thrusts. Indeed, some 10 months after your assumption of office, one is inclined to feel that definite directions ought to have been charted out now. And this is why one would urge you to be conscious of your place in history. For at the end of it all, you would not want chroniclers to see you as just another humdrum administrator but as a scholar-diplomat who, when the occasion called, dared to fulfill dreams for his country. And of course, even within the short range you are being critically watched by peers like Aluko, Akinyemi, Sam Oyovbaire, Elaigwu, and the rest of them.

Even then the bottom line question is this: Would your acclaimed hero Chou-En Lai play things this way? So while you are mulling over that question, let me say bye, and here's hoping that you had a nice time at New York.

Your compatriot,

(Signed)
Kayode Soremekun,
International Relations Department,
University of Ife,
Ile-Ife

4 (ii) *Reply of I.A. Gambari*

It is about one year ago this month when your piece "Letter to Gambari" appeared in the *Guardian*. Although my attention was drawn to it at that time, it is only now that I am able to send you a response. I am sure you will understand.

First of all, I thank you for reminding me that given my "range of theoretical exposure in foreign policy" I was better placed than all my predecessors to combine theory with practice in our country's diplomacy. Actually, I was aware of this, and that is why I spearheaded the effort to have a conceptual framework of our foreign policy which was a departure from the vague idea of "Africa as centerpiece of our foreign policy." In addition, I tried to bridge the gap between professional diplomats and the academic community by establishing the Informal Consultative Committee on Foreign Policy, which involved academicians, research officers, and later trade union and business groups in foreign policy discussions, especially prior to Nigeria's participation in important international conferences.

History will, of course, be a judge of our administration's endeavor in foreign policy. But I do take it that if one had been a real flop at the ministry, it would not have been easy to appoint, as my successor, someone of almost identical academic and professional background as myself.

Now, to the substance of your letter. You pointed out quite rightly that I have always indicated, in my academic writings, that there are important domestic constraints which beset Nigeria's foreign policy. My practical experience in government confirmed my academic views on this linkage. As the domestic political climate deteriorated, the true achievements of the Buhari administration's foreign policy were not given appropriate recognition. I was appalled, for instance, that Nigeria's role in the July 1985 OAU summit in Addis Ababa, which focused on economic matters and elected a substantive Secretary-General, was at the time given short shrift by the media and informed opinion on such matters. Still, it must be clear to all except those who prefer self-delusion that we cannot now pursue a "dynamic" foreign policy in the face of continuing economic dependency on the West and political instability at home. Unless, of course, we are content to substitute appearance and motion for the substance of defining and defending vital national interests.

It might interest you to know that I am engaged in the process of writing a book which would try to put the record straight on the Buhari administration's foreign policy since independence. Any point of view which you may want me to consider in my proposed book will be greatly appreciated.

On the issue of Nigeria's continued membership of the Commonwealth, which you touched upon in your piece. You should not put too much premium on the apparent contradiction between my public statement and that of the Ag. High Commissioner in London at that time. Policy was being made in Lagos. And we were indeed reviewing our membership of the Commonwealth, but a final decision was not reached before the termination of our term in office. Had we gone to the Bahamas (I was to lead the Nigerian delegation) and faced the kind of obstinacy displayed by Thatcher, we would have then known what to do about the Commonwealth.

Finally, I wish to comment on your point about my pattern of travels while minister and our declared policy orientation, with ECOWAS and Africa as inner core of our concentric circles idea. Except for travels on bilateral issues to France, Germany, China, New Zealand, and Australia, all other travel, including New York, Washington, India, and Indonesia, concerned African continental issues, especially Namibia, and South Africa's policy of apartheid and its destabilization policy toward neighboring countries in that sub-region.

In that connection, you are no doubt aware that I was elected chairman of the OAU Liberation Committee at the meeting in Arusha. My boss was also elected chairman of the ECOWAS at about the same time. Of course, we also achieved the unprecedented feat of getting agreement involving Nigeria and our three western neighbors, aimed at cooperation on security, immigration, customs, and police matters and concerns. The current difficulties facing my successor in convening a successful meeting of Foreign Ministers of these countries on the same issues, proves the point I am trying to make. In any case, as you are aware, in our foreign relations, it was not a question of choosing between ECOWAS, Africa, and the rest of the world, but rather a question of priorities. Believe me, we did spend far more time and efforts on issues relating to our neighbors and Africa than all other matters combined during the Buhari regime.

In conclusion, you did touch on a sensitive issue when you urged me "to be conscious of [my] place in history." Honestly, a new Minister of External Affairs of an important country like Nigeria soon finds himself immersed in an endless stream of events, visits, and visitors, while battling to get on top of the ministry's bureaucracy and retain for the ministry the primary role for the formulation and implementation of foreign policy within the government as a whole. Yet he is the head of state's principal adviser and spokesman on foreign policy. It is like walking through a minefield, and one considers oneself lucky to escape any fatal explosion. While it is a great honor and privilege to serve in that high office, a truly committed and hardworking Foreign Minister would feel a sense of relief to let someone else try and see! In that wise, one's place in history is a consideration which recedes into the far background, while one is engaged in the pressing, practical duties as External Affairs Minister.

This reminds me of an interview which the British television personality David Frost had with Israeli General Moshe Dayan before he died. The general was asked how he would like to be remembered after his death. Dayan replied, "I do not care. [Not to care] is what I would be dead for." As for me, I *do* care about how my stewardship as Foreign Minister is going to be remembered by posterity, but now that I am out of office, that is outside my control.

Permit me to stop here, while remaining yours sincerely,

(Signed)
Ibrahim A. Gambari
Ahmadu Bello University,
Zaria
November 27, 1985

Index